Catholic School Leadership

This is a critical juncture in history for Catholic schools. The Church has changed; the world has changed. How can those who prepare Catholic school leaders ensure that they are ready to lead with the unique mission and vision and history required to be professional educational leaders as well as educational ministers?

Catholic School Leadership addresses many of the challenges facing those who prepare faith leaders and education leaders for the Catholic schools of the future. The well-known editors and contributors to this volume have written about their personal experiences with Catholic schools; the educational foundations of Catholic schools; teacher preparation and development; Catholic school leadership; dealing with parents and families; and the challenges of technology for Catholic schools.

The contributions emphasize the perspectives of both scholars and practitioners within Catholic education and will interest anyone who has experienced time in a Catholic school as a student, teacher, or administrator, as well as those interested in what is happening within Catholic schools today.

Thomas C. Hunt is currently professor in the School of Education at the University of Dayton. Until recently he was professor of foundations of education at Virginia Polytechnic Institute. Over the last 17 years he has authored or edited nine books on religion and education. He presently serves as co-editor of *Catholic Education: A Journal of Inquiry and Practice*, and as editor of the *Private School Monitor*.

Thomas E. Oldenski, SM is an assistant professor in the School of Education at the University of Dayton. He has been a teacher, counselor, and principal of Catholic secondary schools in the United States, Nigeria, and Ireland for 21 years. He is a member of the Society of Mary (Marianists).

Theodore J. Wallace is director of the Dare to Dream Foundation and of the PACE Scholarship Program in Dayton, Ohio. He has served as director of the Center for Catholic Education at the University of Dayton and as president and principal of Catholic high schools in Sandusky and Dayton, Ohio.

Catholic School Leadership

An Invitation to Lead

**Edited by Thomas C. Hunt,
Thomas E. Oldenski, SM,
and Theodore J. Wallace**

London and New York

First published 2000
by Falmer Press
11 New Fetter Lane, London EC4P 4EE

Simultaneously published in the USA and Canada
by Garland Inc.,
19 Union Square West, New York, NY 10003

Falmer Press is an imprint of the Taylor & Francis Group

© 2000 Thomas C. Hunt, Thomas E. Oldenski, and Theodore J.
Wallace

Typeset in Times by Routledge
Printed and bound in Great Britain by Biddles Ltd,
Guildford and King's Lynn

British Library Cataloguing in Publication Data
A catalogue record for this book is available from the British Library

Library of Congress Cataloging-in-Publication Data
Catholic school leadership: an invitation to lead / edited by
Thomas C. Hunt, Thomas E. Oldenski, and Theodore J. Wallace.
p.   cm.
Includes bibliographical references and index.
alk. paper
1. Catholic schools–United States–Administration. 2. School
management and organization–United States. 3. Educational
leadership–United States. I. Hunt, Thomas C. II. Oldenski, Thomas E.
III. Wallace, Theodore J.
LC501. C3484   1999   99–28041
371.071'2'73–dc21   CIP

ISBN 0–750–70853–0 (pbk)
ISBN 0–750–70854–9 (hbk)

We, the editors, have a twofold dedication.

First, we would like to dedicate this book to all those who have ministered in Catholic schools in this nation.

We have a special dedication to Joseph F. Rogus. Joe, a beloved husband, father, teacher, colleague, and friend died of cancer this past fall. Joe was a committed advocate of Catholic schools, in his life and scholarship. REQUIESCAT IN PACE!

Contents

Contents

Illustrations

Foreword

Catholic schools have been part of the educational scene in the United States since the beginning of the democracy. For much of that history, until the 1960s, the majority of teachers and administrators in those Catholic schools were religious sisters, priests, and brothers. These members of religious congregations were educated to their roles as teachers and educational ministers in a variety of ways. All received in depth religious formation, education in theology, scripture, liturgy, prayer, etc. All took part in communal prayer, regular retreats, liturgy, and theological updates. Most were educated, over a long period of time, in colleges and universities to prepare them for their roles as quality teachers in excellent Catholic schools – all of them learned to teach from master teachers, members of their own religious congregations, who mentored them on a daily basis. Thousands of master teachers were developed through this religious community method of mentoring. At the same time school administrators worked their way up through the system, often becoming principals by appointment of a religious superior and learning the role on the job. Again, mentors were present to help with supervision of personnel, budgets, facilities, and program development. All of these teachers and principals of Catholic schools understood that as Catholic school teachers and administrators they were professional educators, but even more so, they were educational ministers who were called to share in the teaching ministry Jesus left to his church.

In the 1950s, the national Sister Formation process began to professionalize the educational preparation of religious sisters for their roles as teachers and principals. More sisters than ever were professionally prepared for their roles before entering the classroom or principal's office. Religious congregations of priests and brothers did likewise. All their young members were well educated before they entered into ministry.

Since the 1960s and Vatican II Catholic schools in the United States have gone through major changes. The Church has changed; the world has changed. Catholic schools continue to play an important role as quality educational institutions and as part of the teaching mission and ministry of the Church – in many ways these Catholic schools seem more important now than ever. A major change in Catholic schools is that now the majority of teachers and principals are lay persons. They are prepared for their roles in schools of education. They are certified as teachers and administrators. Catholic schools are recognized nationally for their academic success and excellence.

Now the challenge for those who prepare the next generation of Catholic school leaders is to make sure that they are taught and formed with materials and processes which prepare them to lead Catholic schools. Leaders of Catholic schools must be prepared to lead schools with a unique mission and vision and history. Catholic schools must be quality academic institutions where students are challenged to use their talents and gifts to the best of their abilities. So Catholic school leaders must be prepared to be educational leaders, who are current in their understanding of educational standards and practice. A Catholic school leader must know how to form and shape a faculty into a Christian educational community.

The challenge for those who prepare Catholic school leaders for the future is to prepare those leaders as the very best professional educators possible. Most importantly, Catholic school leaders must be prepared and developed to lead a Christian educational community. They must understand that their role is more than that of professional educational leader. They must also be developed as educational ministers, persons called to *serve* as faith leaders of a Catholic school community.

The book you are about to encounter is a book which meets several of the challenges facing those who prepare faith leaders and education leaders for the Catholic schools of the next millennium. In this book topics needed to become a quality school leader are presented within a context of the uniqueness of the Catholic school. In addition, the unique history, mission, and vision of the Catholic school are explained. The role of the Catholic school in the educational ministry of the Catholic Church is introduced. Recognized experts and scholars, who have researched Catholic school administration and Catholic schools as ministry, present their areas of expertise in clear and challenging chapters.

This book will certainly prove to be of great assistance to those who prepare Catholic school leadership for the next century. This book will also serve as a source of reminder and update for all those who presently serve in roles of administrative leadership and ministry in Catholic elementary and secondary schools.

Many thanks to all the contributing authors for their depth of research, scholarship, and writing. A special thanks to the editors and publishers who recognized the need for such a book. How appropriate to prepare a text which is specifically focused on issues of educational leadership for Catholic schools. Enjoy and learn from this overdue book.

Elaine M. Schuster, Ph.D.
Superintendent of Schools
Archdiocese of Chicago

Acknowledgements

We, the editors, are appreciative of the support and cooperation of the contributing authors for this book.

We are also grateful to the members of our families and the University of Dayton community for their continual support to us during this undertaking.

We pray with thankfulness to God for the many years we have ministered as teachers and principals in Catholic schools and for those to whom we have ministered.

We also are thankful to Elizabeth Naughton and Cindy Giner for their indefatigable labors in assisting us with assembling and arranging the manuscript for publication.

Introduction

Catholic school leaders are faced with a vibrant invitation to lead in a new way. Catholic schools like the Catholic Church and contemporary society have experienced an array of changes since the time of the Council of Vatican II in the 1960s. These changes within Catholic schools created a whole new set of issues for Catholic school leadership. Many of these issues, such as the identity of Catholic schools and the contemporary scene of Catholic schools, are addressed by our esteemed colleagues in Catholic education in *The Contemporary Catholic School: Context, Identity and Diversity* (Falmer Press, 1996). In that book, an array of essays on Catholic education provided a perspective on central questions, which confront Catholic schools from both sides of the Atlantic. Many contributors to that volume call forth a new awareness of justice and diversity in Catholic schools, which continues to challenge both the research with Catholic schools as well as the practices within Catholic schools.

Our hope in putting together a collection of essays is to create another volume on these issues, which is our way of responding to an invitation to lead. Each of us has experienced Catholic schools as students, teachers, and principals. Now the challenge in our lives, like that of many of the contributors to this book, is to assist with the development of Catholic school leaders through either formal classes and programs, or staff development and in-service programs. This invitation to lead needs to include the voices of both the scholar and the practitioner as we confront the issues for Catholic school leadership for the present times and for the future. This volume will encourage further dialogue with the ideas developed and presented in *The Contemporary Catholic School*. We realize that this present volume emphasizes the perspectives of both scholars and practitioners within Catholic education. By collaborating more and more, both scholars and practitioners can benefit what happens in Catholic schools and, in turn, benefit the individual students in Catholic schools with their personal faith and academic development.

One of the major changes with Catholic schools is who do these Catholic schools serve, both in numbers and demographics? Subject to a catastrophic

1

decline from the enrollment high of 5,601,000 in 1964 to 2,475,439 in 1990–91 (a drop of approximately 57%), Catholic schools have experienced a remarkable renaissance in the last several years. Not only has this enrollment stabilized, and slightly increased, but the Catholic educational enterprise has also been revived in spirit. This regaining of a *raison d'être*, if you will, has been attested to in ways beyond positive enrollment figures. In 1994–95, there were 123,655 lay teachers and 2,769 full-time religious in Catholic schools. These numbers of lay educators are certain to continue to increase in future years. It is for them and their preparation as Catholic school leaders which is indispensable to the mission of Catholic schools that we hope that this book will serve as an invitation to lead.

Another issue for Catholic school leadership is the struggle to ponder and respond to the question, "Just how Catholic are Catholic schools?" How well versed are those who lead, teach, and work in Catholic schools in Church and Catholic school history, the documents, and scripture? Catholic school leaders need to be truly spiritual persons who are willing to participate and immerse themselves in Catholic education. The challenge for Catholic school leaders is to assure the transmission of Catholic culture and beliefs to ongoing generations of young people. And to also guarantee that Catholic schools will continue to be a means of transforming society from the perspective of peace, justice, and love in order to ameliorate the plight of the poor and victims of oppression and injustices.

We, as faith-filled persons, must respond to the invitation to lead Catholic schools at this critical juncture of history. The chapters of this book are a way to invite others to be informed about issues for Catholic school leadership and to help others to ponder on their response to take up this invitation to lead. The first four chapters present a sharing of personal experiences in Catholic schools. Brother Tom Oldenski shares his personal history within Catholic schools, presenting a challenge to keep this rich historical tradition a part of the heart of the Catholic community. Brother Tom Giardino presents his reflections on Catholic schools throughout the world from the perspective of his role as the Director of Education of his religious congregation, the Marianists. Tom Hunt develops an historical summary of Catholic schools in the United States. William Losito struggles with the question of what is a Catholic philosophy of education.

Chapters 5 and 6 continue the focus upon the educational foundations of Catholic schools. Charles Russo provides a current conversation on significant court cases and legal issues affecting Catholic schools. Michael Guerra presents what he considers are the key issues for the future of Catholic schools.

Teacher preparation and development is the focus of Chapters 7 through 13. Louise Moore focuses upon her experiences as a Catholic elementary school principal with staff development. William Radell reflects upon the challenges which he has experienced and continues to experience as a high school religion teacher. Gini Shimabukuro develops a schema for dealing with curriculum issues in Catholic schools. Karen Ristau and Margaret Reif highlight pre-service preparation of Catholic school teachers. Sister Mary Peter Traviss also offers her reflections upon the past, present, and future concerns for teacher preparation for Catholic schools. Joseph Rogus and Colleen Wildenhaus focus upon continual staff development of Catholic school teachers. Sister Angela Zukowski focuses upon the role of technology as a pedagogical mode and the challenges of technology for Catholic schools.

In Chapters 14 through 18, Catholic school leadership is the main concentration. T.J. Wallace presents the call of principals as faith leaders in Catholic schools. Father James Heft reflects on ancient and contemporary sources in relation to leadership in Catholic schools. Father Joseph O'Keefe focuses upon the situation and the challenges for leadership in urban Catholic schools.

The final two chapters are unique from each other and yet are concerned with realistic issues for Catholic school leaders. Father Michael Garanzini provides practical lessons for education leaders within Catholic schools on how to deal with parents and families, while Father Ron Nuzzi reflects upon Jesus as leader.

Hopefully, the chapters of this book represent a variety of issues for Catholic school leadership. In reading this book, you have read the words of a variety of persons who are immersed in Catholic schools, and hopefully their words will serve as an invitation to the reader to respond in faith to take up the invitation to lead within Catholic schools.

Tom Hunt
Brother Tom Oldenski
T.J. Wallace

Part I

Educational Foundations and the Future of Catholic Schools

1   Who Will Keep Our Hearts Burning Within Us?

Brother Thomas E. Oldenski, SM

The other day I had lunch with a graduate student from my Philosophy of Education course. This particular student has his bachelor's degree in history and political science and is presently completing his initial certification in social studies. He will begin his first year teaching at a coeducational Catholic high school in an inner city setting. As we were discussing some points of John Dewey's Pedagogical Creed, he pointed out what a life span John Dewey had from his birth in 1859 to his death in 1952. Just from the perspectives of wars, we identified that Dewey lived through the Civil War, the Spanish American War, World War I and II, and the Korean conflict. From the perspective of human development and innovation, Dewey's life saw the advent of the telephone, car, airplane, and other modern appliances and conveniences, as well as the development of a variety of hair and clothing styles, including the bathing suit. I was more moved in this conversation about the reality that each of our lives spans a period of human history which has its affects and effects upon us during the period of our own personal history. It is this insight that moves me to reflect upon and share some of my own history with Catholic schools.

There is no doubt that the history of Catholic schools and our involvement is likewise a time spanning experience within the development of our own faith and our immersion in Catholic schools. In one sense, our lives within Catholic schools intersect with the history of Catholic schools. Both of these histories are influenced by the social and cultural realities of what it means to be Catholic at any given time and how Catholics were part of the larger social and cultural reality of our country.

Concerning the development of the curriculum in schools, Patrick Slattery (1995) states that "the challenge for curriculum scholars in the 1990s is to examine critically their own story in the context of the history of curriculum development" (p. 38). I strongly feel that this challenge is the same for all of us who continue to be involved with Catholic schools, and even more so for educational leaders of Catholic schools. There is no doubt in my mind that Catholic educators need to examine and reflect upon their own schooling stories in relation to the development of curriculum. In addition, I believe that Catholic educators need to examine and reflect upon their stories within Catholic schools in order to value our own experiences and to continue to keep some aspects and practices of these experiences as part of Catholic schools today. Our personal histories within Catholic schools do indeed mirror the history of Catholic schools, and for most of us these include decades of transition and changes within Catholic schools. Developing this type of historical consciousness on the part of educational leaders and teachers in Catholic schools will lead to an affirmation and a recommitment to the purposes of Catholic schools. As the recent document of the Church on Catholic schools states:

> And so, now as in the past, the Catholic school must be able to speak for itself effectively and convincingly. It is not merely a question of adaptation, but of missionary thrust, the fundamental duty to evangelize, to go towards men and women wherever they are, so that they may receive the gift of salvation.
>
> (Congregation for Catholic Education 1997: 36)

Thus, I will share some of my personal history. As I share my reflections, I hope that you are moved to ponder and articulate your own personal history within Catholic schools. I assure you that you will experience a few moments of grace as I did while I pondered and wrote these reflections.

The beginnings of Catholic schools in the United States are traced to early missionary efforts which eventually led to the development of schools as we know them. Professor Hunt presents the historical development of Catholic schools with more events and details in his chapter of this book. However, my own Catholic school experience is not rooted in these early missionary efforts but more as the result of the Third Plenary Council and the wave of immigrants to the United States after World War I.

I grew up in a small river town along the Allegheny River, not far from Pittsburgh, Pennsylvania. This town developed as the result of immigrant waves after World War I and even during my own childhood in the 1950s. The population of this town was mostly Catholic and could boast of four Catholic parishes with four Catholic schools. These four parishes and schools were St. Joseph, St. John Cantius, Madonna of Jerusalem, and St. Mary's. These schools represented the practice that the Plenary Council advocated, namely, a Catholic school would be part of every Catholic parish. Religious congregations of women, which were identified with their own unique ethnic heritage, staffed each of these four schools. St. Joseph School was run and staffed by Mother Seton's Sisters of Charity; St. John Cantius by Felician Sisters; Madonna of Jerusalem by the Sisters of the Sorrowful Mother; and St. Mary's by the Sisters of Divine Providence. Most of the teachers in these schools were religious sisters. During my eight years at St. John Cantius, all of the teachers were Felician Sisters.

These schools also represented the ethnic make-up of the local community. Thus, St. Joseph's was the Irish parish; St. John Cantius was the Polish parish; Madonna of Jerusalem was the Italian parish; and St. Mary's was the German parish. These Catholic elementary schools were proud of their twofold task of making their students both Catholic and American, while being proud of their European traditions and roots in the Catholic faith. These schools were a living testimony to the Catholic faith which our grandparents or parents brought with them from the other side of the Atlantic.

All of my grandparents arrived from Poland after World War I. My maternal grandparents settled in my hometown and were members of St. John Cantius. My mother, her five sisters, and two brothers were raised in this same town and all were members of St. John Cantius parish. They all went to St. John Cantius School like myself and my brother and two sisters.

St. John Cantius parish included a medium-size building which housed the church on the second floor, and the lobby, library, and four classrooms on the first floor. The basement included the lavatories, maintenance and boiler rooms, a classroom, and an all-purpose room, which was utilized for showing movies to the whole school, other school gatherings as well as for the weekly Rosary Society Bingo, and the meetings of the Boy Scouts and other parish groups. This building which is now demolished would never have won any prizes for its architectural uniqueness. Besides this older building, the parish buildings also included the rectory and the convent.

I really don't remember my first day at St. John Cantius School, but I know how I got there. I probably know more so as the oral tradition handed down to me by my parents than actually remembering this event. When I was 4 going on 5, the parish priest announced that there were very few boys enrolled in next year's first grade. Thus, the plea came from the pulpit that if any family had younger boys and was willing to send them to school, they would be accepted and would move on in their schooling if they succeeded in the first grade. I am not sure if my mother wanted to get rid of me in the house since there were already two younger sisters to keep her busy, or if I was a gifted child able to skip kindergarten and begin my schooling with the first grade. Whatever was the actual reason, she and I walked the four blocks to St. John's one day while my older brother was already in the first grade to register me for the next school year. There we met Sister Geraldine who welcomed me with open arms and told me that I could begin the first grade in September. (As a tribute and a sign of gratitude to these individual Sisters, I have chosen to retain their names; many of these Sisters have experienced death and are now in the fullness of the Kingdom of God.) I guess I was excited with this news, but let's face it, what 4 year old, soon to be 5, would be excited about going to school?

So in September of 1953, I began my history of formal Catholic schooling. I was already a student of Catholic education, since at home we were taught how to pray and to know God, Jesus, and the Blessed Mother – both as individuals to be loved by and as individuals to fear if you were not a good boy. I probably began my Catholic schooling with having a bit of guilt already developed. During that first year, I shared both the same teacher and room as my older brother since St. John's had double grades in each room except for the seventh and eighth grades. At the end of the year I was promoted to the second grade so I must have been a successful student.

The second year was marked by two big changes. For the first time, I was in the classroom without my brother. This gave me a new sense of freedom without big brother watching. And Sister Seraphica, who had taught my mother in the first grade as well as many of my aunts and uncles, replaced the young Sister Geraldine. I don't know which was worse – having one's older brother in the same classroom or having the Sister who taught most of the adults in your extended family.

The years at St. John's went by quickly from my present perspective. My teachers included Sister Clarice for the third and fourth grades, Sister Alma for the fifth, sixth, and seventh grades, and Sister Ignatius for the eighth grade. Sacramental preparation and liturgical practices marked these years. Sister Clarice prepared me for my first confession, first communion, and confirmation. She did the same for my brother and one of my sisters. Each school day began with the 8:10 Mass, which usually was a sung requiem, with catafalt, candles, and incense. Certain months of the year were marked with devotions and these just seemed part of the school day, even though they took place on Wednesday and Friday evenings and Sunday afternoons. October was observed with Rosary devotions; Lent with the Stations of the Cross and the singing of Gorzkie Zale (Lamentations); May with Marian devotions including the annual May crowning; and June with devotions to the Sacred Heart. Each year all-day adoration of the Blessed Sacrament marked the observance of forty hours, the patronal feast of St. John Cantius, and the feast of Christ the King.

Educationally, my experiences at St. John's were excellent. The school was characterized by a firm and caring discipline, cooperation, and learning. A commitment and involvement in parish life were taken for granted as part of our school life. Current innovations and the contemporary language of education like looping, caring, cooperative learning, direct instruction, levels of questioning, Bloom's taxonomy, and critical thinking characterized the pedagogy employed by my Sister teachers. We were taught how to become loyal Polish Americans and loyal Catholics. My teachers employed individual and group learning each day. Seat work and Think and Do Books were part of the daily curriculum, as well as a focus on religion (including memorizing the Baltimore Catechism), arithmetic, and English with a heavy dose of diagramming. Art and music were reserved to Friday afternoons and all the other subjects seemed to take place after the 1:45 recess.

So a typical school day for eight years could be characterized in the following way. The morning schedule included Mass followed by time to eat breakfast after receiving communion. This breakfast involved utilizing your desk as a table, an old mayonnaise jar as a milk thermos, and usually a peanut butter and jelly sandwich from home. Religion including the recitation of a few catechism questions and answers took up the first hour of class time. The morning recess was at 10:00 and this was followed by math until lunchtime from 11:30 to 12:30. Most students lived nearby so there was no cafeteria in the school and we went home every day for lunch. The afternoon began with reciting a series of prayers (Our Father, Hail Mary, Glory Be, Apostles Creed, etc.), the pledge of allegiance, and singing a national song like "My Country 'tis of Thee." English, explaining diagrammed sentences, followed this opening ritual. In time, the English lessons expanded to writing more sentences, which eventually evolved into paragraphs, compositions, and essays. Then it was time for the afternoon recess, which was followed by various courses each day from the menu of science, history, geography, and civics.

The curriculum and the schooling practices of St. John's reflected the ideals and words of many of the Church documents which focus on Catholic education, even though most of these documents were written more recently than my Catholic elementary school days. For example, the academic atmosphere of St. John's indeed was a "place of integral formation by means of a systematic and critical assimilation of culture" (Congregation for Catholic Education 1977: 16). Daily life, year after year, at St. John's School was

> fundamentally a synthesis of culture and faith, and a synthesis of faith and life: the first is reached by integrating all the different aspects of human knowledge through the subjects taught, in the light of the Gospel; the second is the growth of the virtues characteristic of the Christian.
>
> (Congregation for Catholic Education 1977: 16–17)

St. John's curriculum and climate also mirrored many words from the Vatican II Declaration on Christian Education (1965), such as "the school develops with special care the intellectual faculties but also to form the ability to judge rightly, to hand on the cultural legacy of previous generations, to foster a sense of values, to prepare for professional life" (p. 10).

Eight years at St. John's taught me the value of Catholic schools as a believing community. My grade school education ended in June of 1961. There is no doubt in my mind that these religious women who were my teachers taught as Jesus did. They created a community spirit within the school, which was a key part of the parish community. We were taught our faith and how to defend and publicly witness to it. We were also taught how to care for others, including our family, the parish, and civic community, and those less fortunate than ourselves, even if it were by a class adoption of a "pagan baby." The atmosphere of the school from day to day depicted and made real the words of the American Bishops Document *To Teach As Jesus Did*:

> The educational mission of the Church is an integrated ministry embracing three interlocking dimensions: the message revealed by God (didache) which the Church proclaims; fellowship in the life of the Holy Spirit (koinonia); service to the Christian community and the entire human community (diakonia).
>
> (National Conference of Catholic Bishops 1972: 4)

St. John Cantius School characterized the reality that "community is at the heart of Christian education not simply as a concept to be taught but as a reality to be lived" (1972: 7).

Besides these aspects of my Catholic elementary education, I can recall those big events of history which occurred during my elementary school years. For example, I can recall the reality of the Cold War when the basement of the school also served as a Civil Defense Fallout Shelter with enough food and water for a significant number of people for a lengthy period of time. Amidst my thoughts, there are memories of Sputnik; the 100th anniversary of Our Lady of Lourdes; the death of Pius XII and the papacy of John XXIII; the Nixon–Kennedy debates and the election of John F. Kennedy, the first Catholic president; and the winning of the World Series by the Pittsburgh Pirates with manager Danny Murtagh and players such as Bill Mazeroski and Roberto Clemente.

The leap of transition to a Catholic high school was a challenge. I found myself quickly in a diocesan Catholic single-sex high school of 1,200 young men with a variety of ethnic backgrounds and with a faculty of lay teachers, religious priests, and Brothers of the Society of Mary (Marianists). The principal for all four years was a Marianist priest and most of my teachers were Marianist Brothers. All of my teachers during my junior year were Brothers.

I could no longer simply walk to and from school nor go home for lunch. The students of North Catholic High School from my neighborhood went by the city bus to and back from school. Our lives had two realities, the first one being what we did at school and the social life and activities associated with school; and the other one being our social life in the neighborhood with some friends who went to other high schools, either the public high school or the local Catholic high school at St. Mary's parish, which was coeducational but mostly for girls.

North Catholic High School's physical appearance was so enormous compared to the comfortable homey building of St. John's. The high school included many classrooms (three floors and a basement full of them), a gymnasium, an auditorium, a cafeteria, the chapel, and the Brothers' House.

The curriculum was a little freer than that of grade school, to the degree that you could have chosen which of the two courses of study you wanted – either college prep or general. My parents and I chose the college prep program that included two years of Latin, two years of a modern language (the choices being German or Spanish), four years of religion, science, English, math, and history. One of my new experiences was having a homeroom and a locker. This was also the first time that I had men as teachers with most of them being a religious Brother, and the first time I was taught by lay men. Daily Mass, confession, and communion services also were part of the routine of being in this school.

There were many extracurricular activities at my high school. I became a member of the Sodality and Stamp Club during my freshman year. Other activities over the four years also included being involved in the school play, Future Teachers of America, Student Council, and the National Honor Society. Through my involvement in these activities, I got to know many of the Brothers not just as teachers but as mentors. With them and other students, my high school gave me a real sense of belonging to the school community. My relationships with other students and the Brothers influenced my own sense of personal identity. It was through a series of personal interactions with many Brothers as teachers and adult friends that, during the winter of my senior year, I definitely decided to continue my relationship with the Marianists by entering this congregation a month after graduating from high school.

The history of my high school years was marked by a variety of events and movements. These included the space race and men orbiting around the earth; the Cuban crisis which resulted in long confessional lines; the assassination of President Kennedy; and Vatican II and the initiation of many liturgical changes, such as Mass in English without the Final Gospel, and the altar was now facing the people. The Beatles and changes in hairstyle also plagued the final years of my high school education.

My twelve years of Catholic education in elementary and high school mirror the Catholic school history of that time. Most of the teachers in Catholic schools were religious women or men with a few lay teachers. The salaries for these religious teachers were minimal and those for lay teachers were also low. Academic rigor and discipline characterized most Catholic schools. Catholic schools were supported mainly by parish subsidies. For example, my grade school tuition was $6.00 a year and my high school tuition was a total of $90.00. But most of these years truly gave life to the hopes and aspirations of Catholic education. They were indeed years of experiencing "a special atmosphere animated by the Gospel spirit of freedom and charity" (Declaration on Christian Education 1965: 12). My years of Catholic education were no doubt within schools distinct in their religious dimension. These years were characterized by "the educational climate, the personal development of each student, the relationship between culture and the Gospel, and the illumination of all knowledge in the light of faith" (Congregation for Catholic Education 1988: 3).

Shortly after my early years of being in Catholic schools, I found myself on the other side of the desk. In September 1969, I began my teaching career as a religion teacher at Catholic High School for Boys in Memphis, Tennessee. The local Marianist community there was considered a small community with eleven of us and all of us taught in the school except for one Brother who was the Assistant Superintendent of Catholic schools. The school was relatively small and for boys only. This was the last year of this school because it merged with two other schools to form Memphis Catholic High School, which was coeducational as well as integrated. I stayed on and taught for an additional year in Memphis. At this point in time, the religion curriculum changed from year to year, using a variety of resources including the popular songs of the day. In one sense, it was teaching religion utilizing Simon and Garfunkel, the Beatles, and the Jackson Five.

My beginning years as a teacher in Catholic schools still clearly demonstrated the strong role of religious in these schools. They also reflected the shift of Catholic high schools becoming coeducational as the result of declining enrollments in these schools as well as in religious congregations. The turmoil about what should be taught in the religion class was expressed in the ambivalence of what was to be the religion curriculum.

After two years in Memphis, I was transferred (as we used to say) to Dayton to complete my Bachelor's degree while teaching at Chaminade High School. A modular schedule, a curriculum of multiple electives and themes, and a free-floating atmosphere characterized this school during the early 1970s. There were no grades for religion and the religion class only met once or twice a week, with more time given to meet with the students individually. A pastoral focus dominated the religion curriculum as opposed to a knowledge-based curriculum. I didn't even possess a grade book during this one year there. There were still many Brothers on the faculty of this single-sex school. However, as a result of declining enrollment several faculty members were cut for the next school year, including several Brothers who were new to the scene.

Thus I moved on to Monsignor Hackett High School in Kalamazoo, Michigan. This school was in its second year of a merger with the local girls' Catholic High School, Monsignor O'Brien. So it was already coeducational with numerous problems still existing as the result of the merger. When I arrived, the faculty was around half lay teachers and the other half Marianists or Sisters of St. Joseph. Religion was taught as a team with some direct classroom electives. As my six years there went by, the religion curriculum became more stable and the faculty became more and more lay teachers. Tuition was on an increase to more realistically cover the increase of salary expenditures. An active retreat program evolved as an important component of the school's curriculum, both for the students and the teachers.

Spending two years at a minor seminary in Nigeria interrupted my involvement with Catholic schools in the States. Upon returning to the States I was back in Dayton, at Chaminade–Julienne High School, a co-educational school as the result of the merger of Chaminade High School (the Marianist boys high school) and Julienne High School (the Sisters of Notre Dame girls high school). The climate of the school was stable and personal. The religion curriculum was stable and remained so during the next four years there. Each year the number of religious on the faculty declined while enrollment remained stable, in spite of the rising cost of tuition. The administration consisted mostly of religious.

Again I interrupted my involvement with Catholic schools in the States by going to the Marianist school in Ireland as the headmaster. But after five years there, I again found myself back at Chaminade–Julienne High School. Now I was the only Brother in the religion department, which was mostly lay teachers, and this reflected the make-up of the faculty. The religion curriculum was the same as five years before but with different textbooks. The enrollment was growing and the principal was a lay man.

My years as a teacher in Catholic high schools reflect some of the changes which Catholic schools experienced in the post-Vatican II years. The reality of moving from single-sex schools to coeducational high schools, as the result of declining numbers of religious in schools, declining enrollments, increasing tuition to adjust to more just salaries for both lay teachers and religious. My involvement in Catholic high schools as a religion teacher reflects the turmoil of what it means to be Catholic and how we transmit our faith to young men and women. They reflect the "freedom" or uncertainty which characterized the years immediately after Vatican II. The issue of the Catholic identity of Catholic schools was definitely a part of this history.

These years within Catholic high schools were also marked with an enthusiasm for beginning and creating service projects and programs with social justice and community involvement becoming a part of the language of the curriculum. These years also witnessed a development of the pastoral aspects of dealing with young men and women as they develop their faith. Becoming a community of teachers and becoming a community characterized the process of numerous activities both within the school day and beyond. The personal and individual concern and interest, which I experienced as a student, also marked my life as a teacher towards my own students. Many other teachers, both lay and religious, shared this sentiment.

Catholic schools have changed a lot since Vatican II. Statistics provide one indication of these changes. Michael Guerra (1991) reported that "at their peak in 1965, 10,879 Catholic elementary schools served 4.5 million students, and 2,413 Catholic schools served 1.1 million students" (p. 5). More recently, Brigham (1995) pointed out that "in 1994-95, there were 8,293 Catholic schools; of these 6,979 were elementary, 76 were middle, and 1,238 were secondary" (p. 8). Even though the number of schools has continued to decrease, the number of students attending these schools recently has been on the increase. Still, the number of Catholic schools and students today remains far below that of the 1965 peak year.

In addition to the numbers of Catholic schools that existed or now exist, numerous other changes have occurred within these schools, changes that reflect the theological and ritual changes in the Catholic Church and thus affect the identity of the schools. For example, a sense of social consciousness and service learning now appears in the curriculum and climate of Catholic schools. The issue of the identity of Catholic schools is a crucial one as these schools continue to reflect on who they are and what is the basis for curriculum and policy decisions.

The history of Catholic schools over the recent decades is a messy one. It does not have in one sense the cultural climate of the way Catholic schools used to be. Today as well as my years as a teacher in Catholic high schools have taught me that we need to struggle with our identity, articulate, and proclaim it. The challenge for the leadership of Catholic schools is to assist the components of the Catholic school community in this process of formulating the identity of that specific Catholic school. Our personal histories can serve as a resource in these discussions and formulations. This challenge includes identifying what were the values behind the practices which we experienced in our own history of pre-Vatican II Catholic schools, and how we continue the best practices of this era and keep these values alive and present in the experiences of students in Catholic schools today and in the future.

By reflecting upon our personal histories, both individually and collectively, we gain insights into what helped us to develop our faith and our personality and competencies. By reflecting upon the history of a specific Catholic school, we gain insights into the history of Catholic schools as well as the tradition of how this Catholic school assisted numerous young men and women with their faith, personal and professional development. These histories of persons and institutions lead over and over again to a stance of affirmation of the role of Catholic schools within the history of the Catholic Church as well as the cultural history of the country.

Timothy Walch (1996) in his recent account of the history of the parish school identified five themes which emerged from this history. They are survival; immigration; variety of responses to the parish school movement; adaptability; and community. These themes characterize my history within Catholic schools and most likely will probably emerge in the personal history of others. The details of these themes change with time and location, but they offer Catholic schools the challenge to continue to be part of the reality of schools in our country.

Another important theme as I reflect upon my history and the history of Catholic schools is an Emmaus theme. Going to a Catholic school and reflecting upon our history within Catholic schools is like an Emmaus experience – it is like "talking with each other about all these things that had happened" (Luke 24: 14). Our years in a Catholic school, either as a student, teacher, or administrator, are a journey with each other along with Jesus.

And on this journey over and over again we meet Jesus; sometimes we recognize him and other times we do not. My own experiences attest to my meeting of Jesus in the persons of my teachers and my students. Our faith also assures us that we always meet him as we break bread together in celebrating the Eucharist. My reflections and many other memories as a student and teacher in Catholic schools cause my heart to burn within as I realize what a ministry Catholic schools have offered and continue to do so. The challenge for us as Catholic educators is to insure young men and women now in Catholic schools as well as the future generations of students that there will be those teachers and institutions, which will continue this Emmaus journey. We need to make sure that these schools and teachers will be the source for causing their hearts to burn within as they come to know and recognize the Lord Jesus. To me, this is the most important lesson that I have learned from my personal experiences and from the history of Catholic schools. Statistics and historical data cannot capture these experiences of numerous young men and women who have gone to a variety of Catholic schools at different times and have also experienced recognizing the Lord while their hearts burnt within them.

Thus, the challenge for educational leaders and teachers of Catholic schools is to become aware of their own histories – those memories of persons, events, and places – which caused their hearts to burn within them as moments of grace. But not only to stay at a level of romanticism about the past but also to make sure that as the history of Catholic schools continues to develop there will be those persons, namely, themselves. The document "The Catholic School on the Threshold of the Third Millennium" maintains that

> the personal relations between the teacher and the students, therefore, assume an enormous importance and are not limited simply to giving and taking. Moreover, we must remember that teachers and educators fulfill a specific Christian vocation and share an equally specific participation in the mission of the Church, to the extent that it depends chiefly on them whether the Catholic school achieves its purpose.
>
> (1997: 46–47)

Today the teachers and leaders of Catholic schools must accept the responsibility to help the hearts within their students to come to know the Lord as they break bread together and as they explain the things about Jesus in all the scriptures.

Brother Thomas E. Oldenski, SM

References

Brigham, Frederick H., Jr. (1995) *United States Catholic Elementary and Secondary Schools 1994–95*, Washington, DC: National Catholic Educational Association.

Congregation for Catholic Education (1977) *The Catholic School*, Boston: Daughters of St. Paul.

Congregation for Catholic Education (1988) *The Religious Dimension of Education in a Catholic School*, Boston: St. Paul's Books & Media.

Congregation for Catholic Education (1997) *The Catholic School on the Threshold of the Third Millennium*, Vatican City, Rome: Vatican Library.

Declaration on Christian Education (1965) Boston: St. Paul's Books & Media.

Guerra, Michael J. (1991) *Lighting New Fires: Catholic Schooling in America 25 Years after Vatican II*, Washington, DC: National Catholic Educational Association.

National Conference of Catholic Bishops (1972) *To Teach As Jesus Did*, Washington, DC: United States Catholic Conference.

Slattery, Patrick (1995) *Curriculum Development in the Postmodern Era*, New York: Garland.

Walch, Timothy (1996) *Parish School: American Catholic Parochial Education From Colonial Times to the Present*, New York: Crossroad.

2 An International Perspective on Catholic Schools

Thomas F. Giardino, SM

> In confronting the many challenges that the future holds in store, humankind sees in education an indispensable asset in its attempt to attain the ideals of peace, freedom and social justice.

This opening quotation from the recent "Report to UNESCO of the International Commission on Education for the Twenty-first Century"[1] reveals a perspective that Catholic school leadership worldwide shares with its colleagues in public or other private schools. Leaders, as leaders, have distinct levels of motivation, resources and skills, and shared aspirations that equip them to strive for these ideals. Educational leaders make this effort even while confronting the daily issues of academic excellence, scarce finances, and the legal labyrinths that develop in an atmosphere where increasing numbers of persons are seeking to act upon their desire to be more the agents of their own destiny – with education as a critical vehicle.

In this chapter I will share some of my experiences over the past seven years as International Director of Education for Catholic schools in the Marianist (Society of Mary) orbit of twenty-nine countries in Latin America, Africa, Europe, Asia, and North America. In the interactions, I encountered Catholic school leaders with the ideals previously mentioned. They combined these ideals with the commitment and competence to work at them in circumstances not always conducive to the challenge. In my role I have visited almost 135 schools (primary, secondary, university levels) and dialogued with principals, presidents, students, administrative teams and councils, parents, alumni, bishops, etc. What I have learned is that there is Good News for our planet. This Good News is united with the courage and witness of school leadership to enter the journey of the death and resurrection of Jesus Christ, the teacher of the Reign of God.

I will begin with a brief overview of some general issues that touch many of the educational institutions I have observed. Then I will comment upon issues and dynamics in the following geographical areas in which I have experience: Asia, specifically Japan and South Korea, and the subcontinent,

India; sub-Saharan Eastern, Central and Western Africa; Latin America; and Europe.

General Issues and Trends Affecting Education

Most educational leaders are aware of the major trends in our world today, so I will comment only on several selected issues or trends on the world stage and within the orbit that I have described, which I think have particular relevance for discernment and orientations for the future of education.

Globalization and Fragmentation

In a sense these two now-familiar phenomena can be understood as trend and counter trend. In some locales, fragmentation of social institutions is a reaction to the global tendencies present or perceived. As with all generalizations of this sort, both globalization and fragmentation tendencies vary by country and are unevenly felt within the same country and throughout the world. The globalizing tendencies are most easily seen as an emerging world (market) economy, in international advertising, and in the development of an information society, especially with the concentration of mass communications in the hands of a decreasing number of multinational companies. Moreover, whether I was in Bangalore, Bogotá, or Karonga, I heard strains of similar popular music and saw T-shirts with Michael Jordan's picture on them.[2] Television programs from Los Angeles often shape the vision of the good life in Abidjan. The yearning for participation in social and political decisions, usually in a democratic strain, is also a worldwide movement.

I notice the effects of the global market tendencies when I talk to students and parents and they see the dominant horizon for the future in terms of employment: either getting the most secure and high-paying job, or fear of getting no job at all. The economy is the idol. On the other hand, more students are interested in learning a foreign language and willing to spend part of their scholastic time in another country.[3] In responses to a question I ask each group of students I meet with, I found that generally they have no heroes nor much of a desire to act upon the world in altruistic ways.[4] The exceptions are notable, such as the two students in a Spanish Marianist school who thought that the "voluntary" service in which they were involved helping the poor ought to be required, since this was a Catholic school and service is integral to the faith. While such a requirement is normal these days in the United States, it is not so in most other countries, where they usually only hold religion classes once or twice a week and parents, students, and government would resist any more. Still, another student told me "I want to learn how to learn, and to learn to be a human being," when I asked him what he wanted from his time in school.

Fragmentation is revealed not only in families and communities. Ethnic, religious, and national identities are being reasserted in ways that continually threaten the common good even as the energy behind it is prompted by a certain vision of the benefit or preservation of some group's good.[5] "The reason my parents sent me to this school is that there are no foreigners here, so the education is better," remarked one student I met from a rather wealthy European country.

As transnational tendencies increase, so do the localizing tendencies. When the tension is creative, everybody benefits; however, it is all too clear that most cultures do not yet have a unified, coherent set of beliefs broad and strong enough to invite, sustain, and benefit from a rich diversity. Some groups have the insight and the language, but not, I believe, the virtues and skills to achieve the vision. Many young people that Catholic schools serve, in the face of this fragmentation, discontinuity in values, and the explosion of disconnected information, understandably seek stability and identity – or escape. These often lead them into sects or self-destructive behavior. National governments often respond to the localizing tendencies with exaggerated policies of security and self-determination. Such policies translate into racist policies as is evident in the difficulty in obtaining visas by some of our African, South American, and Asian Indian brothers attending educational training programs. Catholic school leaders and international religious institutes can make a prophetic stance in the face of such movements. However, there is a significant personal and collective price for such internationality.

The clash of these two movements of globalization and fragmentation often affects educators in educational institutions in adverse ways. Sometimes I notice much *activity* but not necessarily an *action orientation*. That is, there is an immense amount of analysis and diagnosis of educational–social problems, but often a paralysis of strategic action at critical points of change. In speaking with educators, I sensed that many feel more a *victim* than an *artisan* of their life – a culture of complaining reigned rather than one of creativity in faculty lounges. Furthermore, they often have a feeling of being disconnected. The information overload can undermine insight and paralyze the imagination that stimulates creative action for developing alternative futures.

The overarching educational trends that are found in most countries relate to: national educational reform movements; financing of education at the national and local levels; enhancing and assessing academic performance; developing environmental awareness; ethnic, language, and gender issues; expanding educational opportunity; and concerns regarding religion (e.g., fundamentalism) and social unrest (e.g., divorce, violence). Smaller families and proportionally fewer persons of working age to support educational costs are almost a universal reality. There is a movement toward lifelong education, viewing education as related to solidarity among peoples, and empowerment of individuals and groups toward participating in the decisions that affect their lives. The UNESCO "World Conference on Education for All" in Jomtien, Thailand, in 1990 was a major impetus for national and religious groups to collaborate at all levels of education.

Another trend that may be almost universal is the marked sense of low self-esteem among students. In almost every school I visited there are programs and dynamics developed to respond to this matter that worries educators and parents alike. In a similar vein, I found that teachers have a sense of low self-esteem and speak about it as diminished social status reflected in low pay and little recognition and affirmation for their efforts by administrators, parents, and students. The education apostolate is growing in the areas where the numbers of children are increasing:

> Nearly 7 out of 8 of the world's children under the age of 15 now live in developing countries. In sub-Saharan Africa nearly half the total population is under 15 years of age, compared to only one-fifth in North America, Europe and Japan.[6]

These are, of course, the areas in which the Church is increasing and there is a certain emphasis on primary school education to meet the growing numbers.

The World Declaration on Education for All, adopted at the Jomtien World Conference mentioned above, provides the background that many dioceses and religious congregations, North and South, are responding to in broadening the base of their education apostolate. The components involved in responding to the changing nature of the basic learning needs of children, youth, and adults are:[7]

* learning begins at birth (therefore the need to work with families);
* the main delivery system for the basic education of children outside the family is primary schooling (non-formal educational alternatives serve those with no access to formal schooling);
* the basic learning needs of youth and adults are diverse and should be met through a variety of delivery systems;
* all available instruments and channels of information, communications, and social action could be used to help convey essential knowledge and inform and educate people on social issues (to the traditional means are added electronic and mass media).

I have found a significant response to the insight that to transform a society, education for women and girls is a critical variable. Educators seem keen to structure programs and processes to promote the dignity and rights of women.[8]

In many countries that I visited, serious and extensive educational reform movements have been mandated by the national governments. These call for the expending of significant amounts of human and financial resources.

Sometimes governments are helping with financial aid, but mostly they are not, which is putting a significant burden on Catholic schools. In general, enlightened educators are responding positively to the reforms since they are aimed at a more interactive and student-centered education. The orientations affect curriculum, teaching methods, and most of all the mind set of the teacher.

In the context of the above trends, and the others not touched upon, I find one challenge for educational leaders is to understand educational policies, strategies, and day-to-day actions as related to the signs of the times and to the evangelical transformation called for especially in *Gaudium et Spes* and more recent ecclesial documents. This stimulates the question of motivation, which as I mentioned previously is a key factor in leadership. I would phrase it: "What would God's unconditional love look like for these particular people?" The specifics will differ and so will the response in various countries. This leads me to outline some responses that various countries are giving to this question.

South Korea and Japan

My emphasis in this section will be upon the impact that certain aspects of the larger culture have in placing demands upon schools, their educators, and students. Unlike most other countries, in neither of these countries is there a problem with the low status of teachers nor education. In fact, so much emphasis is put upon schooling that other problems arise.

For example, in South Korea I was surprised when talking to school leaders who told me that in the final years of high school, students come to school at 6:30 or 7:00 a.m. and return to their homes only about 10:00 p.m. While classes run from about 8:00 a.m. to 4:00 p.m., the rest of the time is spent in solitary study. The goal is to get into university – not just any university, but the most prestigious, which results in higher pay and status. One principal told me that when one of his students returned home early, he received a phone call from the parents saying: "What is wrong with your school, other kids don't get home till 10:00 p.m.?" Naturally this puts demands on administrators and teachers to be at the school with the resulting effect on their home life. Nevertheless, studies and degrees are so important in the culture that home life seems to take second place, at least from a Western perspective.

In recent seminars that I gave to school faculties in South Korea, I noted a serious concern about a real desire to educate the "whole person." However, the educators often felt overwhelmed and helpless in the face of the cultural forces. Nevertheless, I was greatly encouraged during a presentation I gave to the Catholic school principals of South Korea entitled "Catholic Education Responds to the Demands of Democracy in an Electronic Information and Entertainment Era." The determination of these Catholic school leaders to confront critical leverage points in the culture promises real hope for the future.

Japan finds itself in a similar situation regarding a tradition of high regard for learning. Salaries for teachers in Catholic schools might average $70,000, and students normally pay $340 per month for tuition in a 230 day school year – teachers theoretically work year-round with some vacation. The amount of government subsidy per student is about $1,900 per year. Education in Japan looks and feels rather rigid from a US perspective: at least 40–45 students per class with the teacher as the center of attention and lecture and memorization as the normal methodology. Students, however, respond very warmly to those principals who know their names and greet them at the beginning and the end of the day at the school gates as is the custom in some schools.

What seems clear to me is that there are cracks in the traditional Japanese culture that are reflected in such phenomena as the rise of students refusing to attend school, often related to the incidents of "bullying" – which are in turn often related to the rise of individual differences. I noticed that the young people were asking interesting questions about wanting to spend more time in the future with *their* sons than their fathers do with them presently. It seems to me in this case that the challenge for educators is to help students to understand the consequences of such desires (e.g., decreased upward mobility in their careers) and to help them build the interior strength to act on their desires.

I found it noteworthy that young Japanese boys (most Catholic schools are single sex) are quite aware of the rest of the world and have perceptive insights. They often asked me about the violence in the United States: "How is it that people in your country can have guns? They aren't allowed here." After I struggled to respond, I was greeted with indulgent smiles and, "Well your culture and country is so young, what can you expect?" Naturally, in a country where Catholics are only 0.03% of the population, most of the students in Catholic schools are Shintoist or Buddhist. Typically in a school of 1,500 there might be 25–50 Catholics with about 30% of the faculty Christian. This puts additional strain on school leaders. Historically the bishops asked "mission schools" to focus on "education" whereas "catechesis" would be the role of the parishes. Presently, there is the raising of some questions regarding this distinction as more schools try to implement some type of "campus ministry" activity at least for the Catholics, with invitations to all students.

India

We are relatively new in India and have focused on social ministries such as work with street children. However, recently we have assumed responsibility for a primary school and a vocational–professional school. Both are Hindimedium institutions, which means that the young Indian Brothers are the main educators and in charge of the administration. This reveals a situation with much energy and enthusiasm but not much experience. However, the results are gratifying. At the primary school, educators are constantly battling school absence as parents push students to work in a neighboring brick-making scheme, which assures money in the here-and-now, while employment after education is still a risk.

Similarly, a bishop asked us to establish a school for low-caste Christians (almost synonymous in that area) who found it difficult to find employment after high school, since most schooling simply prepares one for more schooling. We have begun a technical institute teaching stenography, typing, spoken English, and some computer skills. Perhaps one of the most important educative witnesses is that all castes are welcome. As the local parish priest told me when we witnessed some mumbling by locals to visitors warmly greeting outcasts: "The students know that when they enter this campus, caste doesn't count."[9]

Africa: Eastern, Central, Western

The areas are so vast that generalizations may not be as helpful as some anecdotal reporting to give a flavor of the issues and concerns. The countries involved are Kenya, Malawi, Zambia, Ivory Coast, the Congo, and Togo. It is also important to say that in each of these countries there is rapid educational and political change – mostly for the better – so that some of these data and interpretations might rapidly become dated.

In some African countries, such as Zambia and the Congo, the government is presently very much interested in negotiating with private agencies such as the diocesan Catholic Church or specific religious congregations to have them resume administration or to take over the administration of schools that had been nationalized.

The issue for the Church in several African countries, as some educators said to me, is who will form the "elite" that will eventually be running the country. Some Church educators say if it is not the Church somebody else will. Others recall that this was the mentality in the 1950s and 1960s and it didn't work then: mission schools formed minor bureaucrats or corrupt politicians as did all the other schools.

In most of the schools the teachers are pleased with the presence of the Church, through diocesan and religious congregation personnel, as the teachers note a seriousness regarding academics which they and the parents appreciate. In the pastoral realm, religion teachers are continually seeking to find or develop texts that are indigenous to their country/culture rather than import ones from Europe or North America. This is not an easy task.

I noted that a significant issue for teachers in their relationship with the school and its administrators is asking for help in getting relatives placed in the school. Because of the extended family system, this demand is some-times experienced as a burden for the teachers who then come into conflict with the administration over preferential treatment for placing relatives in the school. I recall vividly the sad face of one teacher who said she was looking for an opportunity to "flee her family" as she was the only one with a job and all the relatives expected her to pay for the many youngsters to enter school. Likewise personal safety and security along with securing housing are major concerns for many teachers and administrators.

In most of the countries I visited there has been a crisis of access to primary school. For example, a few years ago in Zambia, some primary schools were running three sessions per day with 80 to 100 per class with many students dropping out after grade 4. In a secondary school, one head-master told me that he spends almost 50% of his time raising funds.

In discussions with students, I observed that they were quite aware of the pressures that they feel to be like the images of Europeans or Americans that they see on television or in print advertisements. They look toward opportunities for education and leisure that they see other cultures experi-encing although they are often quite pessimistic (realistic?) as to their chances of achieving such opportunities.

In speaking with teachers about issues that are obstacles to their ministry, they reported that the families of students are so close or structured that sometimes students are not able to express themselves and develop their individuality at home. Therefore, they often come to school to act out their individuality, thus causing difficulty in teaching. Increasingly, though, students are coming from fragmented families, causing its own difficulties.

In some places in West Africa, there is a tendency for parents to have a bias in favor of expatriates in the schools, giving little trust to the indigenous administration. The local principals feel this is a kind of reverse discrimina-tion that hinders morale.

A major issue for education in these areas is that at first, second, or third level, the education is not an "education for life," but here, too, students seem to be prepared mostly for more schooling. Hence there is a need to make the curriculum more practical, though this does not necessarily mean simply job oriented. In both the Congo and Ivory Coast, we have conducted agricultural educational institutions that seek to provide opportunities for young men in the area to develop farm skills. This seems to be a particularly helpful response to the local cultures.

Latin America: Argentina, Chile, Colombia, Ecuador, Peru

In a recent assembly of the presidents and principals of the Marianist schools in these countries (August 1998), these educational leaders came to a consensus that the quality they most thought was needed for their ministry was faith. This seems to me to represent a realistic appraisal of both the great treasure that they bring to their vocation and the needed response to the contemporary challenges. Latin America has come through the difficult economic and political times of the 1980s to a certain emerging affluence and stable democracy (though this is quite uneven among the various countries and their 466,000,000 inhabitants on the continent). Now they face the globalization and fragmentation issues mentioned above, the challenges to a fragile democracy, and, for the Church, serious erosion from evangelical and fundamentalistic cults.[10] The schools are in the center of this whirlwind.

Private Catholic schools, usually under the sponsorship of religious institutes, have banded together into consortia in order to have a means to talk with the government regarding educational issues. These are independent of the Conferences of Bishops. Some educators feel that the bishops tend to be neutral in front of the government regarding advocating for questions of finances and other questions. (Not all bishops would agree!) One principal told me that after the Apostolic Nuncio in his country, the consortium was the most influential voice for Catholic education. The consortia are significant in providing ongoing formation for administrators and classroom teachers.

Educational reform in Chile is typical of the kind of major change that is going on in many Latin American countries.[11] Some years ago the government initiated a national reform movement that affected all dimensions of education. Whereas once the typical secondary curriculum included eleven or twelve subjects per week for students, there is an effort to reduce these to six or seven. However, what is having more of an impact is the change from a school day with at least two full shifts to one per day. In 1965 a previous reform required all schools to have two or sometimes three "school days" per day in each neighborhood in order to accommodate the number of children. The present reform reduces this to one *jornada completa*, with the school day running from approximately 8:00 a.m. to 4:00 p.m. (by the year 2002). Since previously most teachers were "taxi" teachers (i.e., teaching in at least two different schools per day), the new system is having a major impact on their lives and on family life. Though the government provides some subsidy for the schools, the principals have liberty to hire and fire teachers with just cause.

In Chile the government seems rather enlightened and after securing significant loans from an inter-American banking organization has aided private and public schools. The issue now is "quality." I heard from educators that as yet the quality is uneven to poor in many schools, particularly the public schools. In the face of a statistic that 80% of the nation's students in the fourth grade only have a "mechanical" reading ability, there is a major effort (borrowed from Canada and the United States) called *Programa de Lectura Silenciosa Sostenida* to develop better reading habits along with the attitude and interest for reading on one's own and for recreation.

Along with Chile, other Latin American schools (often at government insistence) are focusing on their *proyecto educativo*, or "mission/philosophy statement." For Catholic education this is stimulating the leadership and the teachers to look seriously at the signs of the times, the positive and negative *megatendencias* as they are called, and to clarify what the schools offer as an alternative to the dominant culture.[12] What I heard as a very important question at the above assembly was the witness of a "coherent" life. Students are looking for some adults who live by the words that they profess. A significant movement to enhance this dimension has been the "Teaching as Ministry" programs that some Catholic schools have implemented based on the "Colloquium" programs developed by the Jesuits. The Marianist schools in Peru are also concentrating on developing and clarifying their educational anthropology as a way continually to deepen the foundations for the reforms and the implementation of the project regarding the "Characteristics of Marianist Education." This latter project has helped our Latin American schools (and those on other continents) to focus many of the *proyectos educativos* and the formation of teachers with a common orientation for principles and pedagogy.

In most schools I observed a serious attempt to develop a sense of critical thinking. For some this has been stimulated by a recent history of military dictatorship. Likewise, there is a movement to learn how to work in teams. Several schools I visited had major campaigns that focused on *service to others* as the characteristic of the school. In Argentina, the Marianist schools have been concentrating on developing the ability and desire for silence or quiet. They recognize the fundamental necessity for this habit in the face of the impact of electronic and information technology. They program space and time for quiet into the school day.

I found in almost all the Latin America countries I visited a strong pressure from parents and sometimes among students for them to go to university no matter what the student's ability or desire. What students may need more are courses in vocational or technical areas, especially where employment is beginning to rise due to the development of the economy. Along with the courses, there is a need for more value to be put on these orientations from school leaders and teachers, in particular as they seek to appropriately educate parents regarding their children and the labor market. The ranks of unemployed university graduates grow daily!

A general issue faced by most Latin American countries is that the reform movements are often coming from a desire to give youth a better education in order to compete in the labor market, especially concerning technology. Educational leaders are pressured to make some tradeoffs that compromise the person and educational values *per se*. Schools are pressured to develop like small business – this is a common problem worldwide where the economy becomes the idol.

"We want the people of the world to know that there are young people here in our country who want to change the reality and the image of Colombia that is projected to the rest of the world." This was the message that I heard in several recent meetings with students in two different cities in Colombia. They are aware of how the world sees Colombia: a country of violence and drugs. The school leaders seek to respond to this desire (and their own) with a goal stated by the Marianist schools: for example, "To form new men and women who work for a new society."

This may seem simplistic but it is as real to them as yesterday's 11 o'clock news. This came home to *me* tragically and forcefully even as I was writing this chapter when I received news that one of our young Brothers – who was with me only two weeks before in the assembly I mentioned earlier – was murdered by a paramilitary group. He was on his way to serve in our ministry to the indigenous people in the forest–river area in the west of Colombia. This 25-year-old educator knew something of the risk he was taking, but believed that education in the faith was integral for full human development. These are the challenges that school leaders and their teachers face in undertaking educational ministries in a country with a fragile democracy and immense pressures from outside countries.

Europe: Austria, France, Germany, Ireland, Italy, Spain, Switzerland

The image of Europe that often persists among the population inside as well as outside Europe is that of "Christian countries." A deeper look raises serious questions about this image. A recent survey

> conducted among 7000 people in six countries [revealed] that the most familiar international symbol is the five interlocking rings of the Olympic movement (recognized by 92% of those interviewed), followed by the trademarks of Shell Oil and McDonald's (88%). Only 54% of those interviewed recognized the Christian cross.[13]

While the governments of most West European countries (except Italy!) subsidize private, Catholic education, what must educational leaders think and do in the face of the *meaning* of this education for parents and children?

There are no easy answers to another problem felt in analogous ways in the United States. The old method of assuring "Catholicity" by large numbers of vowed religious women and men no longer is possible. So, in Europe also, Catholic schools are concerned with the formation of committed and competent laity (who, of course, have always been present as teachers and staff) to assume the administration of schools where the diocese or a religious institute retains the sponsorship of the school. Changing the mentality for all parties has been the main struggle, from my observation. Vowed religious find it difficult to share responsibility with "outsiders" (language sometimes used), and lay principals are often too deferential to religious or priests regarding questions of professional competency or spiritual leadership of faculties. Likewise there is a reluctance by all to understand this issue as a responsibility of the *total* local church and not just of religious institutes who had basically assumed the responsibility of Catholic education. Few European dioceses even have anything like a Catholic schools office or superintendencies.

Lay leadership in Catholic schools where there are a few (usually older) religious is faced with women and men in the midst of personal and collective fears about identity. "If I am not teaching, who am I?" or "If this school closes, who are we?" is the sense I have noticed in some of these situations. Or, on the other hand, "We are the owners, who are *you* to ... ?" This takes great pastoral delicacy and diplomacy by lay administrators – without relinquishing a firm leadership that comes from an understanding of one's own call rooted in baptism and confirmation.[14]

In fact in my visits I have seen as much good happening as problems arising. In France there is a major effort on the part of the religious congregational leadership to act collaboratively with lay leadership in schools under their *tutelle* (sponsorship). Visiting teams made up of lay and religious; frequent seminars, workshops; associations of teachers working under the same educational charism, etc. – all respond to needs and requests for formation in the philosophy that drives the school. I also found a great desire by local school educators to learn about the larger, international network of which they are a part. I recently took part in a gathering in Vienna, Austria, of presidents and principals of Marianist schools in Europe as they confronted the needs of contemporary European youth in a secularized environment indicated above. They also sought to respond to the challenge of the emerging European reality stimulated by the free market, easy travel, and a single monetary currency. This is changing the possibilities of careers of students and educators.

Reform movements are also afoot in Europe. Spain has been in the midst of such a reform since laws passed in 1985 and 1990. As the effects on the pedagogy, curriculum, and the physical premises come into play each year, educational leaders have been faced with enormous challenges. Beginning with the latter, for example, the government required that primary classrooms have no more than twenty-five students per class and secondary classes no more than thirty. Since the norm had been around 40–45, this has called for new classroom space, as students remain together and teachers change rooms. The government, however, has not usually provided any financial support for Catholic schools for this matter. So a school faces the dilemma of reducing its enrollment or finding financial resources in an environment where fund raising from parents or alumni or business is not the custom.

The focus of the new pedagogy and curriculum is that the "student becomes more the agent of his or her education." Again, this forces a change of mentality on all involved since the magisterial or lecture method has been the accepted way of teaching for centuries – and with success. In a conversation with some university students in Italy regarding methods of education, as some were admiring the practical aspects of education in the United States, one of them reflected: "Yes, students in the USA know *how*, but we know *why*." The challenge for the administrators is to learn how to motivate the faculty to adapt their mentality and methods to complement their pedagogy in order to stimulate more discussion, library research (where there are often poor library facilities), work in small groups and teams, group projects, etc. In fact there are movements in this direction, even when there is pressure from parents simply for more classes in English (seen as resulting in better jobs) or acquiring of computer labs.[15] Perhaps one of the best developments in Europe is a decreased fascination with whatever happens on the US educational scene as necessarily good for them.

Conclusion

Catholic school leaders worldwide face the gift and task that is Catholic education with the humble and confident trust that the Holy Spirit accompanies them day after day. "In this way a community of learning becomes an experience of grace, where the teaching programme contributes to uniting into a harmonious whole the human and the divine, the Gospel and culture, faith and life."[16] My experience on the international scene is that this desire that "a community of learning becomes an experience of grace" characterizes the best of educational leadership as the nuances of culture, history, and language bring beauty and benefit to the common task.

Furthermore, a common request that I have heard from educators in the countries I have visited is to pass along the desire for solidarity in the mission to educators in other locales. My hope is that this chapter has contributed to the understanding and appreciation upon which solidarity is founded.

Notes

1 *Learning: the Treasure Within*, Report to UNESCO of the International Commission on Education for the Twenty-first Century, Jacques Delors, Chairman, et al. (Paris: UNESCO, 1996), p. 13.
2 There is a concurrent trend developing rapidly that emphasizes local music and localized advertising that takes something from the international trend and adapts and enriches it. This is a perennial process that is raising the consciousness of both the multinationals and the local entrepreneurs.
3 "In 1994 more that 100,000 students attended a European institution outside their own country through such programs," as "Erasmus," "Lingua," and "Socrates" (*Encyclopedia Britannica Book of the Year 1995*, p. 176).
4 An exception regarding heroes was in Tunis, where a class of Arabic youth told me that their hero was Saddam Hussein.
5 As one example, the cultural heterogeneity of the former Yugoslavia – "two alphabets, three major religions, four main languages, five principal nationalities, and six republics" – hindered its attempt to shape education to the newer forms

of political organization that were emerging before the Civil War (*Encyclopedia Britannica Book of the Year 1992*, p. 151).
6 *World Education Report 1991*, UNESCO, p. 23.
7 *World Education Report 1993*, UNESCO, p. 19.
8

> Pope John Paul II committed all of the over 300,000 social, caring and educational institutions of the Catholic Church to a concerted and priority strategy directed to girls and young women, and especially to the poorest, to ensure for them equality of status, welfare and opportunity.
> (Intervention by Mary Ann Glendon as head of the Vatican delegation to the Fourth World Conference on Women, 5 September 1995)

And "The main obstacles to faster progress in improving world literacy are economic conditions in the majority of countries which have low literacy rates, and social factors in most countries hindering the educational participation of women and girls" (*World Education Report 1991*, UNESCO, p. 26).
9 This incident was a concrete example of the best of the intentions in Catholic education: "From the first moment that a student sets foot in a Catholic school, he or she ought to have the impression of entering a new environment, one illumined by the light of faith and having its own unique characteristics" (*The Congregation for Catholic Education, The Religious Dimension of Education in a Catholic School*, 7 April 1988, No. 25).
10 One teacher related this incident: he asked his class how many of them were Christians. One student raised a hand. Upon questioning the others, they said, no, we are Catholics.
11 Ecuador would be an example of a country that has no real educational reform as there has been strong resistance by teachers' associations.
12 At the assembly mentioned above, in a presentation entitled "Educación, Jovenes y Megatendencias de la Globalización," by Dr. Giovan María Ferruzzi, the speaker identified the following as the major megatrends: the relation of information and communication; work and free time; consuming things and experiences; governmental and private initiatives regarding the great social problems. These occasion the following problems for generation X and Y youth: lack of social points of reference; lack of clarity of identity and role (e.g., gender); relevance of school and work; spirituality and intellectual manipulation; love and sexual freedom; drug, alcohol, cigarette abuse; violence and irresponsibility.
13 *Ecumenical News International*, No. 16, 15 August 1995, release 95–0312.
14 Religious themselves need to know that they have several challenges. One is to become aware of attitudes and actions that *de facto* exclude or discourage laity or dioceses from assuming or acting on their responsibility in this matter of education. The other is to avoid what I recall vividly from one meeting with a group of teachers where I heard from one, "Have you noticed here that the Brothers are the bosses and the burden of teaching is on the lay teachers?" – even while another said, "This is my home, my second home."
15 These types of pressures are reflected in many countries of the world. As stated in the "Report to UNESCO of the International Commission on Education for the Twenty-first Century,"

> Key [educational and political] decision-makers, on the other hand, are falling prey to a perplexity of a different kind, though of identical origin, at a time when nations-states' organizational structures are, as it were, subjected to upward pressures created by the imperatives of globalization

and to downward pressures generated by the demands of local communities.

(p. 48)

16 John Paul II, *Vita Consecrata*, Apostolic Exhortation on the Consecrated Life (25 March 1996), No. 96.

3   The History of Catholic Schools in the United States

An Overview

Thomas C. Hunt

The purpose of this chapter is to trace the story of Catholic schools in what is now the United States, focusing on major developments within the schools, the Catholic community, and on those events outside the Catholic world which had a major impact on the existence, nature, and operation of these schools.

A little known fact is that Catholic schools were established in Florida and Louisiana as early as the seventeenth century. Lay teachers, who were predominant, were joined by Franciscans, Jesuits, Capuchins, Carmelites, and Ursulines in the conduct of these schools. There were schools at all levels, with the lines between them often blurred. Sometimes they were racially integrated, as in New Orleans; there were also separate schools for free blacks, conducted by black religious orders, mainly in Louisiana.[1]

Missionary zeal was a major reason for the establishment of pre-Revolutionary Catholic schools, which were established in the Southwest under French or Spanish jurisdiction, and in what were to become the states of Connecticut, Illinois, Maine, Maryland, Michigan, New York, and Pennsylvania. Some of these schools were for boarders; some for day students. Schools were frequently segregated by gender, with some coeducational institutions.[2]

Conflicts with civil authorities sometimes occurred, especially in colonies under Protestant (English) rule. Buetow refers to the colonial and national periods as "Transplantation" and "Formative Foundations" respectively.[3] They ended with the onset of the nineteenth century, which was to witness the establishment of the common free school by Horace Mann and others, which posed a new series of challenges for Catholics and their schools in the United States.

The Advent of the Common (Free) School

John Carroll, the first American bishop, instructed Catholic parents in the Baltimore Diocese in 1792 on the importance of the lifelong benefits of a Catholic education, dedicated to the service of God and the welfare of the nation.[4] The Provincial Councils of Baltimore, held in 1829, 1833, and 1837, also made reference to the importance of Catholic education.[5] It was not until the fourth such Council, held in 1840, that the bishops referred to specific troubles Catholics were encountering in the public schools, troubles which related to the Protestant influence in the system, and in some practices, such as devotional Bible reading and curricular materials.[6] These problems arose due to the hostility which greeted rising Catholic immigration (the country was about 1% Catholic in 1800;[7] between 1821 and 1850 almost 2.5 million Europeans arrived in the United States, with more than 1.7 million, a considerable number of whom were Catholic, in the 1840s;[8] and over a million of these were Irish, with 780,719 arriving in the 1840s[9]). The conflicts were also due to the state-founded, state-regulated, Common (Free) School movement which was inaugurated under the leadership of Horace Mann in the late 1830s in Massachusetts, and subsequently in other northern states. The common school backers were united in their advocacy of free schools, supported by public taxation, public oriented and controlled, which would produce social harmony in the republic. All private schools, especially those under sectarian control, were viewed as divisive and as a threat to societal peace. Mann, for instance, denied that his schools were neither religious nor moral; he claimed they were not sectarian, but were both religious and moral, basing their claim to religiosity and morality on what was termed "common-core Christianity" and the reading of the King James version of the Bible, without note or comment ("Christianity has no other authoritative expounder"[10]).

The tensions which arose due to these two phenomena resulted in riots, burning of churches, and open warfare over school matters. In New York City the educational battles were part of what historian Diane Ravitch has termed a "great school war."[11] Turmoil existed in other areas as well, and spilled over into school matters. One result of the struggle was the establishment of a separate system of Catholic parish schools, founded to teach the Catholic faith "in its entirety."[12]

Though a number of Catholics, clerical and lay, felt that the Church's resources should be applied to social problems, the official Catholic policy, as enunciated in the organs of the Church, e.g., in the First Plenary Council of Baltimore, called for the establishment and support of Catholic schools for Catholic children.[13] German–American Catholic bishops, in particular, were outspoken in their conviction of the need for Catholic schools to preserve the faith and customs of their flocks.[14] Pastors were mandated under "pain of mortal sin" to found schools in their parishes;[15] parents were admonished about the "unwise system" of public schooling, which would produce a "generation of religious indifferentists," who would be dangerous to "religious principles."[16]

The Challenge of the Secular School

The Civil War era ushered in a new threat to Catholic youngsters, in the eyes of some Catholic leaders. No longer did the pan-Protestant school of Horace Mann pose a threat to the faith and morals of Catholic children. Mann's allegedly non-sectarian but religious, moral common school had been replaced by the secular school, which found its identity in patriotic American values, based on civic, natural virtue.

The ranks of Catholics in the nation were swelled by immigration in the third quarter of the nineteenth century, with a concomitant growth in school enrollment. *Sadliers* reported in 1875 that the Catholic population had grown to 5,761,242 with 1,444 parish schools.[17] As they grew in number, and faced with a sometimes hostile public school, efforts of Catholics to obtain tax money for their schools increased.[18] Fundamentally, Catholic policy-makers argued that education belonged by natural right to the parents. The civil state had the duty of assisting the parents to meet their God-given responsibility. Catholic parents were to fulfill their divinely imposed obligation by adhering to the teaching of the Church which called for attendance of their children at Catholic schools.

The Catholic campaign for public funds alarmed Americans, a number of whom may be classified as nativists. Arguing that the public schools were necessary for the survival of American democracy, they vigorously opposed the Catholic efforts. In 1875, speaking to the "Army of the Tennessee" in Des Moines, Iowa, President Ulysses S. Grant called on the veterans to "Encourage free schools, and resolve that not one dollar appropriated for their support shall be appropriated to the support of any sectarian school."[19] Shortly after Grant's speech, Congressman James G. Blaine of Maine introduced a bill that would have accomplished Grant's purpose. The bill passed the House, but failed in the Senate. Walch points out, however, that the "Blaine Amendment", as it was called, was enacted by twenty-nine states between 1877 and 1917.[20]

The nation's Catholic bishops gathered in Baltimore for the Second Plenary Council in 1866. Here they reaffirmed the pre-eminence of religious teaching in education and reminded Catholic parents of their duty to follow the Church's teaching in educational matters.[21] Throughout the 1860s and into the 1870s individual Catholic bishops lent their support to the Catholic school movement. Not all of the bishops joined in this crusade, however; nor were all of the laity heeding their bishops' mandates. Responding to a call from several American bishops, the Congregation of the Propagation of the Faith, the missionary arm of the Catholic Church based at the Vatican, issued a statement on the school question directed to the American hierarchy. Adjudging public schools as constituting the source of "evils of the greatest kind," the Propagation called on Catholic authorities to build Catholic schools, and on the laity to support, maintain, and have their children attend them.[22] It was left to the judgment of the bishop to decide when

the danger of perversion of the faith was sufficiently remote to permit attendance at public schools. Catholic parents were reminded of their solemn
charge to protect and strengthen the faith of their children, upon which
their eternal destiny depended.[23] The Congregation's statement was interpreted as a victory for those bishops who were advocates of Catholic
schools.[24] It is apparent, from the use by Catholic writers and speakers of
the terms "atheistic," "godless," and "secular," that Catholic opposition was
no longer directed at the schools' Protestant nature as it had been earlier in
the century.[25] Indeed, one Catholic writer called on the Protestants to join
with Catholics in opposition to the secular public school: "Fight, therefore,
Protestants, no longer us, but the public enemy."[26]

The Epochal Third Plenary Council of Baltimore

As Peter Guilday observed, the presence in and fate of the Catholic children
in public schools was the overriding concern of the American hierarchy as
the Council approached.[27] After considerable discussion and exhortation,
the bishops set forth two decrees which were to guide Catholic policy on
educational affairs in the United States for decades:

I. That near every church a parish school, where one does not yet
exist, is to be built and maintained in perpetuum within two years
of the promulgation of this council, unless the bishop should decide
that because of serious difficulties a delay may be granted.

IV. That all Catholic parents are bound to send their children to the parish
school, unless it is evident that a sufficient training in religion is given
either in their own homes, or in other Catholic schools; or when
because of a sufficient reason, approved by the bishop, with all due
precautions and safeguards, it is licit to send them to other schools.[28]

It is clear from the decrees that the decision as to the erection and/or
support of a Catholic school, to the delight of the conservatives, was in the
hands of the local bishop.[29]

The prominence of the school issue in the minds of Catholic leaders as
the conciliar era drew to a close was evident. Two assessments, written more
than eighty years apart, attest to the crucial role the schools were seen to
play in matters of faith. In 1883, a year before the Council, James Cardinal
Gibbons of Baltimore (the nation's sole cardinal at the time) wrote:

It may safely be asserted that the future status of Catholicity in the United
States is to be determined by the success or failure of our day-schools.[30]

In 1964, Mary Perkins Ryan, the New Hampshire housewife–critic of
contemporary Catholic schooling, penned:

in the midst of a predominantly Protestant society, hostile both to Catholicism as such and to the traditionally Catholic immigrant groups, the Church established a school system of her own and attempted to establish a parochial life which would keep Catholics away from harmful influences, enabling them to preserve their faith and some semblance of a Catholic pattern of life.[31]

The "Americanism" Question at the Turn of the Century

In the latter years of the nineteenth century, and on into the first few decades of the twentieth, "Americanism" or citizenship education, founded on natural moral premises, continued to serve as the ethical basis for public schooling. In this arrangement moral education was divorced from religious education (which belonged to home and church), and became a function of the citizenship-oriented public school system.[32] The trend in public education toward centralization, bureaucratization, and systematization was closely tied to immigration, urban development, and citizenship education.[33] Catholics were again especially numerous in the immigration figures, contributing to the increase of Catholic population in the United States from 6,143,22 in 1880 to 17,735,553 in 1920.[34]

Education, like marriage, was viewed in official Catholic teaching as a "mixed matter," i.e., one in which church, state, and family each had a role. In a series of encyclicals Pope Leo XIII set forth the teaching of the Church. He declared that the right to rule came from God, and that Catholics were bound to dissent from laws which were at variance with the law of God. Civil authorities were urged to work in "friendly agreement" with the Church.[35] Civil states were called on to worship God, to acknowledge the true faith of Christ, which was the Catholic religion, and to allow the Church full sway in those areas the Church considered to be its field – one of which was education.[36]

Papal encyclicals, conciliar decrees, pronouncements in Vatican documents, and canonical penalties notwithstanding, disagreement over the priority and function of Catholic schools remained. The motto "Every Catholic child in a Catholic school" was never close to fulfillment. For instance, in 1884 there were 6,613 Catholic parishes, 2,532 of which had schools. Three years later the number of parishes had increased slightly to 6,910, of which 2,697 had schools.[37] Despite the castigation of public schools as "godless,"[38] and the imposition of canonical penalties, such as denial of the sacraments, on parents who failed to heed the Church's directives on attendance, this ideal was to remain "distant" throughout this period.[39]

The laity were not alone in their opposition. Occasionally, priests joined them. For instance, Father Edward McGlynn of the New York Archdiocese spoke out on behalf of the public schools and appealed to the nation to "Show no favor to any rival system."[40] The nation's bishops were divided as well. Perhaps the struggle between the liberal John Ireland, Archbishop of St. Paul, and the conservatives Michael Corrigan of New York, Bernard McQuaid of Rochester (New York), and Frederick Katzer of Milwaukee most clearly outlines this high-level conflict.

The controversy over Catholic schools had been simmering for several decades within the Catholic Church in the United States when Ireland addressed the annual meeting of the National Education Association (NEA) in 1890. Fundamentally, Ireland granted the civil authority the right to make schooling compulsory, a right his opponents denied; called for cooperation between church and state in education for the good of the people; and praised the public school: "The free school of America – withered be the hand raised in its destruction." Ireland ended his controversial address with a call for a "Christian state school."[41]

Wisconsin's bishops, all German born, conservative, and ardent backers of Catholic schools, were livid. Katzer, their leader, was engaged at the time in a grim struggle with the state over the Bennett Law, which he and others claimed would destroy Catholic schools in the state.[42] They were joined by other prelates, most notably Corrigan and McQuaid. Complaints against Ireland were sent to the Vatican.[43] Ireland defended himself, and advanced the concept of a Christian school supported by the state, as was present in his "Faribault Plan."[44] (It should be noted here that this kind of cooperation was not new; it had been in existence in Massachusetts in an earlier part of the nineteenth century in the "Lowell Plan."[45])

The Pope had written another encyclical in 1889 in which he maintained that parents have "exclusive authority in the education of their children," and have been divinely commanded to exercise this responsibility by choosing schools which imbued their children with the principles of Christian morality, and "absolutely oppose their children frequenting schools where they are exposed to the fatal poison of impiety." Leo pointed to those Catholics as worthy of praise who "at the expense of much money and more zeal, have erected schools for the education of their children.[46] The conservative bishops relied on this papal teaching for support for their position.

The conflict was so bitter that the Pontiff sent his personal legate, Archbishop Francis Satolli, to end the strife. In May of 1892 the Vatican had ruled that cooperation with public schools, as called for in Ireland's plan, can be allowed ("tolerari potest"). Debate then centered on the meaning of "tolerari potest:" did it mean toleration, permission, or approval?[47] Satolli presented his Fourteen Propositions to the bishops in November of 1892. Basically, his proposals called for the support of Catholic schools and accepting attendance at public schools "with a safe conscience" if the danger of loss of faith was remote in the eyes of the local bishop.[48]

Still the controversy raged. The American Catholic world had been treated to a "pamphlet war" of sorts, with the Reverend Thomas Bouquillon arguing for the "liberal" position, and the Jesuit, Rene Holaind, espousing the "conservative" cause.[49] The public dissension was ended in May of 1893 when Pope Leo wrote to Cardinal Gibbons, at the latter's request, that Catholic schools were to be "most sedulously promoted," leaving to the local bishop's judgment "when it is lawful, and when it is unlawful to attend the public schools."[50]

Much of the drive for Catholic schools emanated from the desire to preserve ethnic heritage. The public school, used as an instrument to "Americanize" the immigrants' children, was often viewed as the enemy, not only of faith but of the entire culture and tradition of ethnic groups. Within the Church, Peter Cahensly spearheaded the movement known as Cahenslyism, which opposed the assimilation of Catholics into the mainstream of American life. Among its major tenets was the position that Catholic parishes and dioceses be established along lines of national origin, rather than by territory, each to be headed by pastors and bishops respectively of that nationality.[51]

The alleged heresy of "Americanism" provides a context for the tensions that existed over education within the Church and with its relations with the civil state at this time. Pope Leo had condemned the errors in an encyclical on "Americanism," which called on the Church to adapt itself to modern civilization, show indulgence to modern theories and methods, de-emphasize religious vows, and give greater scope for the action of the Holy Spirit on the individual soul.[52] The Pope specified that his denunciation did not apply to the American people; American Catholic liberal leaders, such as John Ireland, who had been recommending cooperation with this nation's institutions, immediately accepted the papal teaching, at the same time denying that they had ever espoused the condemned doctrines.[53]

The overwhelming percentage of American youth enrolled in school, public or parochial, at the turn of the century was in elementary schools. Public secondary education received impetus from several NEA committees at this time, most notably the Cardinal Principles Report in 1918. Pastors, the heads of parishes with their elementary schools, were not convinced of the need or desirability for Catholic high schools.[54] Thus, despite the activities of the recently formed Catholic Educational Association and its advisory board, only a few interparochial high schools, e.g., the Roman Catholic High School in Philadelphia, had been established.[55] For the most part, Catholic high school activity was conducted by religious orders. Meanwhile, the Catholic elementary school population grew from 405,234 in 1880 to 1,701,219 in 1920, in 2,246 and 5,852 schools respectively.[56]

The entry of the United States into World War I, with the War's aftermath, increased the hostility towards anything deemed "foreign," especially of German vintage. Measures were enacted to curb this foreign influence, and to insure patriotism. Some of these activities included legislation which was aimed at foreign languages. The keynote law, though, passed in Oregon, was directed at the very existence of private schools, alleging that the public schools were necessary for American citizenship. It took a decision of the United States Supreme Court in 1925, which overturned the law under the Fourteenth Amendment, to stem the tide of this life-threatening activity. The Court ruled that parents have the right to send their children to private and church-related schools, providing those schools offer secular as well as religious education. Further, the court reasoned that attendance at public schools was not necessary for citizenship, and declared that the "child is not the mere creature of the state."[57]

The 1920s to World War II – A Settled System

In the first decades of the twentieth century, Thomas Edward Shields of the Catholic University of America (CUA) had endeavored to apply the teachings of Progressive Education to Catholic schools. As part of this effort, Shields had authored several textbooks. He was not able to gain the support of conservative Catholic clerics and educators.[58] Shields was succeeded by his pupil, George Johnson, who gained the title of "bridge-builder" between Catholic organizations, such as the bishops' National Catholic Welfare Council (NCWC), the National Catholic Educational Association (NCEA), and the Education Department of CUA, as well as with secular agencies such as the US Office of Education, the NEA, and the American Council on Education. It was Johnson who spearheaded Catholic participation in professional educational activities at the national level.[59]

The emphasis on professionalism, witnessed by arguments over issues such as school accreditation and teacher certification, affected Catholic schools and their personnel. Walch describes the debates within the Church as to how and by whom the Sister–teachers were to be educated. Ultimately, a compromise was reached which left the basic role in training to the respective religious orders.[60] (It would not be appropriate to pass by the contributions these religious women made to Catholic education over the years. Often living in poverty, they not only made immense contributions, but were also indispensable in making Catholic schools a living reality.)

The world was witnessing other events which influenced Catholic schools. Amidst a rising sea of totalitarianism, Pope Pius XI issued his famous encyclical, "The Christian Education of Youth," on the last day of 1929. In this letter the Pontiff reiterated Catholic teaching that there are three societies which have rights in education: the family, the Church, and the state. Parents have the basic duty in educating their children, which must be carried out in consort with the teaching of the Church. The state must respect this God-given arrangement. The Pope declared that there can "be no true education which is not wholly directed to man's last end," that there can be "no ideally perfect education which is not Christian education," that the goal of education is to "form Christ Himself in those regenerated by baptism," so that the true Christian will result, a person who "thinks, judges and acts constantly and consistently in accordance with right reason illumined by the supernatural light of the example and teaching of Christ."[61] Pius XI concluded his letter with the familiar exhortation that "Catholic education in a Catholic school for all Catholic youth" was the ideal to be sought.[62]

This period witnessed a growth in secondary schools, especially those of a diocesan or central nature, and the creation of school boards for these extra-parochial schools. Questions arose in curricular affairs, such as the proper place of vocational education in these schools, and the extent of the Church's responsibility to serve youth who were in terminal, not college preparatory, secondary programs. Meanwhile, Catholic schools reported a steady rise in enrollment. In 1936, for example, Catholic sources reported 1,945 secondary schools with an enrollment of 284,736 and 7,929 elementary schools with a total of 2,102,889 students.[63]

The Post-war Years

Writing in 1959, Neil G. McCluskey penned that "since the times of Archbishop Hughes of New York and the controversial 1840s, the Catholic position on education has remained substantially the same."[64] His assessment was correct. Catholic schools were crowded; recently established suburban parishes were hard pressed to meet the demands of parishioners for Catholic schools. Non-public-school enrollment increased 118% between 1940 and 1959, compared with a 36% gain in the public sector.[65]

The demand far outstripped the supply, resulting in a number of challenges for Catholic educational leaders. For example, which students should be admitted and which denied? on what criteria? Should elementary or secondary schools receive primary emphasis? on what grounds? How should funding and control for interparochial schools be set up? operate? How would the growing number of lay teachers affect the mission of Catholic schools? their financial stability? What part should the laity have in the governance of these schools? How should the laity operate in conjunction with the pastor and/or religious order in operating the school? How can the schools, with their escalating costs, be supported? Should government assistance be sought? If so, how and what kind?

There were curricular issues as well. Between 1945 and 1955 Catholic educators faced a more diverse student population at the secondary level. The growing professionalism of Catholic educators, spurred by the Sister Formation movement, led to increased contacts with public educators and the Life Adjustment version of the progressive movement.[66]

Catholic authorities continued to view attendance at a Catholic school as an important religious matter. A majority (55 of 104) of Catholic dioceses who responded (104 of 131) to a survey in 1958 replied that there was a statute in their diocese which required Catholic parents to send their children to a Catholic school. Nine of the forty-nine that did not have a statute had some restrictions on attendance at public schools. Twelve of the fifty-five dioceses that had a statutory regulation imposed a reserved sin (one "reserved" to the bishop for forgiveness) on parents who defied the regulation; thirty-eight of the fifty-five required parents to apply formally for permission to send their children to a public school.[67]

The burgeoning Catholic school population, accompanied by increasing costs for new facilities and lay personnel, led to a revival of the question of governmental financial aid to Catholic schools. Arguing from the premises that education is based on morality which in turn is founded on religion, and that parents, not civil authorities, are the primary educators of children, a number of Catholic leaders again called for government assistance to educate their young. Some favored *indirect* aid, such as bus transportation, loan of secular textbooks, or vouchers or tax credits to parents; others wanted *direct* assistance to the schools; while some wanted no aid at all. There were constitutional, as well as political, questions to be answered.

In 1940 the First Amendment became involved in church–state contentions through the Fourteenth.[68] In 1947 the Supreme Court used that decision to hand down a 5–4 ruling that allowed public funds to be used to transport children to church-affiliated schools. The decision was based on the child benefit principle (children, not the church, were primarily assisted), and a public purpose (the safety of the children) was served by the legislation.[69] Cognizant of the emotion engendered over the "separation of church and state" issue, the Court laid down the "Everson Dicta" which were to guide civil government officials in dealing with the establishment and free exercise clauses of the First Amendment. The Court would not rule again on any case that directly affected Catholic schools during this period; that would await 1968.

It was during this period that a new organization, composed mainly of laymen and women, The Citizens for Educational Freedom (CEF), appeared. Virgil Blum, SJ, a political scientist, was the group's leading spokesman. He argued that government's purpose in education was to seek the good of the individual child, which will benefit the common good as well as the child. The child's right to equal treatment under the law is guaranteed by the Fourteenth Amendment. The state may not penalize the child for choice of schools. If the child chooses a religiously affiliated school, the state, bound under the Constitution to be neutral to religion, cannot deny the child his or her benefits.[70] CEF members aggressively sought financial benefits for children to attend what they termed "God-centered" schools.[71]

Archbishop Albert G. Meyer of Milwaukee, President of the NCEA, praised both the quality and quantity of Catholic elementary and secondary education in 1957.[72] Two years later Catholic enrollment stood at 4,101, 792 in elementary schools and 810,768 in secondary schools.[73] Despite the overcrowding and financial strains, the picture was generally regarded as "rosy" for Catholic schools. The historian John Tracy Ellis was among a distinct minority who faulted the schools. Ellis held that there was an overemphasis on the school "as an agency for moral development" which led to an inadequate concern for its intellectual role.[74]

It was a book authored by a lay Catholic, Mary Perkins Ryan, entitled *Are Parochial Schools the Answer?*, which was a harbinger of things to come. Briefly, Mrs. Ryan answered her question with a resounding "No." She maintained that the schools, clerically dominated, had well served a besieged, impoverished immigrant population in the nineteenth century. As a result, parents had never assumed their rightful place in the spiritual upbringing of their children; the parish school had become the center of parish life, which included giving parents the idea that they had fulfilled their responsibility by sending their children to the parish school. In the 1960s, however, Mrs. Ryan described the schools as anachronistic, calling for emphasis on the liturgy, adult education, and instructing the parents on their educative tasks.[75]

The Second Vatican Council

On October 6, 1962, Pope John XXIII convened the Second Vatican Council (Vatican II), an historic event which led to stirrings that shook the very foundations of the Catholic Church and its schools in the United States. Catholic school enrollment reached an all-time high of 5.6 million pupils (elementary and secondary) in 1965–66, when they constituted 87% of the nation's non-public-school enrollment.[76] In the years following 1966 Catholic enrollment plummeted, beset by doubts about Catholic schools' mission and identity as well as undergoing escalating costs due to the substitution of lay teachers for priests and vowed religious in the schools. Indeed, the major challenges to the schools no longer emanated from outside the Church, as had been the case, but from within.

Vatican II was supposed to "open up" the Church, and its institutions, to the modern world. At Vatican II the Fathers declared that the Church's involvement in education is "demonstrated by the Catholic school." They stated that the Catholic school was to be "evidenced by the gospel spirit of freedom and charity;" that it was to prepare the young for this world and for the "advancement of the reign of God;" and reminded parents of their "duty to entrust their children to Catholic schools when and where this is possible."[77] Questions did arise about the justice of the Church practice with so many personnel and so much invested in the schooling of some, and so little committed to the religious education of the many.[78] The American bishops who served on the Education Committee of the Council had a twofold concern: (1) freedom of choice for parents to select the school of their choice for their children assisted financially by government; and (2) the necessity of promoting both Catholic schools and the religious education of those not in Catholic schools.[79]

Questions about the effectiveness of Catholic schools, especially when considered in the context of the heavy investment of personnel and money, were raised in other quarters. Some religious orders, leading prelates such as Cardinal Ritter of St. Louis, and liberal groups of laymen joined in this questioning.[80]

The issue of racial justice reared its head. In the second half of the nineteenth century Catholic parish elementary schools were founded, to a considerable extent, to protect the faith of a poor, immigrant population. Supported by the contributions of dedicated vowed women religious and by the Sunday collection they were, in a sense, Catholic "common schools." In the years following World War II Catholics had moved in considerable numbers from the central cities to the surrounding suburbs. They were replaced by minority groups, mainly blacks, the overwhelming number of whom were not Catholic. The "War on Poverty" of the 1960s, as part of the Civil Rights movement, led to concern that some Catholic schools in the inner cities were serving as racial "escape valves," thwarting attempts to integrate schooling. The closing of other Catholic schools in the central cities led others to allege that the Church was abandoning the poor for the affluent of the suburbs.[81] Statistics reveal that between 1966 and 1968 43% of the Catholic elementary schools that closed were in inner cities, 46% in rural areas, and approximately 11% in the suburbs. Catholic secondary figures reveal that 39% of schools that closed were in inner cities, 44% in rural areas and about 17% in the suburbs. Meanwhile just over half (31 of 60) of the secondary schools that opened were in the suburbs; just under half (72 of 147) of the elementary schools that began were in the suburbs.[82] Even Catholic educational leaders voiced alarm. For instance, Monsignor James C. Donohue, then the Director of Education for the United States Catholic Conference (USCC), the civil arm of the American bishops, thought that the Church would be failing to meet Christ's Second Great Commandment ("Love thy neighbor as thyself"), if it failed to provide educational opportunities for God's poor in the cities. He called on Catholic schools to remain in the urban ghettos and to focus on academic excellence and the development of Christian values.[83]

The difficulties the Church faced in this area were manifold. Nonetheless, there were a number of attempts to bring Catholic education to the urban poor.[84] Among the difficulties the Church faced, as did Protestant churches, in their attempts to combat racial discrimination was the lack of support from their white members, who wanted the Church to "tend to the private religious needs of its members and to stay out of such questions as peace, social justice and human rights." Not only were many of these people prejudiced, as the Berkeley sociologists Charles Glock and Rodney Stark pointed out, they denied "the right of the churches to challenge their prejudice."[85]

The publication of *Inner-City Private Elementary Schools* some years later disproved, in the opinion of its proponents. that Catholic schools were elitist or "racial escape valves." The study, using a randomly selected sample of sixty-four schools in eight cities, fifty-four of which were Title I recipients, and with a minority population of at least 70%, found strong support for these schools by their patrons. Housed in rundown buildings, beset with serious financial problems, mostly Catholic operated but with a third of the student body Protestant, these schools emphasized basic learning skills, fostered moral values in their students, and provided a safe environment. Their existence demonstrates the Church's commitment to the urban poor, their supporters contended (56% of their enrollment was black; 31% Hispanic).[86]

Vatican II had called for more active participation, indeed leadership, by laymen in the affairs of the Church. One of the areas which was to witness an increasing level of such activity were the school boards. Monsignor O'Neil C. D'Amour spearheaded the movement which called for changed governance patterns for Catholic schools that would reflect the social and political realities of American life. He recommended that parish school boards be established with real, not advisory, powers. Distinguishing between the "pastoral" and the "professional," D'Amour found pastoral concern an inadequate substitute for professional competence in school governance.[87] D'Amour developed his model further in the years that followed, calling for diocesan and area boards of education, which he believed could be operated in accord with Church law.[88]

The NCEA also took up the issue of school boards. Arguing that lay boards extended the schools' "base of support" and fostered the "cooperation of the community" on behalf of Catholic schools, the Catholic superintendents in 1967 presented a rationale for the boards' existence as well as guidelines for their functioning.[89] The NCEA was not alone. Other organizations, such as the CEF, supported the board movement.[90] Indeed, the literature records a plethora of articles on the topic, which included consideration of the relative rights of the pastoral and professional to laymen painting a parochial school.[91]

The 1960s witnessed increased Catholic activity in seeking government financial aid for their schools, brought on at least in part by the financial pressures which accompanied the growing number of lay teachers in the schools. In 1963, the Supreme Court had ruled that government must be neutral to religion.[92] Catholics' efforts met with some success when the Supreme Court upheld a New York practice of loaning books which were on the state-approved list for public schools to pupils in church-related schools.[93] Following up on the Court's statement that religious schools fulfilled a secular purpose, Pennsylvania passed a law which provided financial support of these schools for "those purely secular educational objectives achieved through non-public education" such as teachers' salaries, textbooks, and instructional materials.[94] No state funds were permitted for any materials which dealt with worship or religious training

The Court ruled that the Pennsylvania legislation, and the Salary Supplement Act of Rhode Island, were unconstitutional. (The Rhode Island statute called for a 15% supplement to teachers' salaries in non-public schools, provided they did not teach religion and used only materials employed in the public schools.) Fundamentally, the Court found that the legislation fostered "excessive entanglement" between church and state, and hence violated the establishment clause of the First Amendment.[95]

In this decision the Court established the tripartite test which it would use in assessing future aid cases. The test was as follows: (1) the legislation must have a secular purpose; (2) the legislation neither inhibits nor advances religion; and (3) the legislation must not create excessive entanglement between church and state.

In 1967, aware of the crises which had enveloped Catholic schools, the American Hierarchy issued an official pronouncement entitled "Catholic Schools Are Indispensable." The bishops predicted that "not in the too distant future ... the trials and troubles of the present moment will be seen for what they really are, steps toward a new era for Catholic education."[96] The bishops' words notwithstanding, Catholic education in the Untied States was in a state of disarray and pessimism as the decade of the 1960s came to a close.

The 1970s – Reappraisal and Regrouping

In 1972 the bishops published their influential pastoral, *To Teach As Jesus Did*. Writing against the background of Vatican II, they identified a three-fold ministry for Catholic schools: (1) to teach doctrine, the message of hope contained in the gospel; (2) to build community, not simply as a concept to be taught, but as a reality to be lived; and (3) to serve all mankind, which flows from the sense of Christian community.[97] Catholic schools, and their personnel, needed to integrate life, learning, and religious values, which set them apart from other schools and entitled them to the support of the Catholic community.[98] Recognizing the malaise which had infiltrated Catholic schools, the bishops urged their flocks to confront the enormous challenges they faced and above all to "avoid a defeatist attitude."[99]

Catholic elementary and secondary enrollment numbered 4,034,785 in 1971–72, down over 1.5 million from 1965–66; these dwindling numbers reflected the mounting sense of a loss of purpose.[100] Addressing this problem the bishops dealt with the purpose of Catholic schools in 1977 when they wrote that "Catholic schools are unique expressions of the Church's efforts to achieve the purpose of Catholic education among the young. ... Growth in faith is central to their purpose."[101] Pope John Paul II supported the bishops when he penned that:

> The special character of the Catholic school, the underlying reason for
> it, the reason why Catholic parents should prefer it, is precisely the
> quality of the religious instruction integrated into the education of the
> pupils.[102]

The Pope declared that the Catholic school should be the place where the
gospel would "impregnate the mentality of the pupils" with the resulting
"harmonization of their culture" in the "light of faith." The task of developing a "community of believers," he averred, was embodied in the very
mission of the schools.[103]

In 1976, then-President of the NCEA, John F. Myers, suggested that
Catholic educators consider the question "How are we different?" from public
schools, rather than wondering whether Catholic schools were as good as
their public counterparts, a prominent question of the 1950s and 1960s.[104]
The NCEA sponsored workshops for Catholic school superintendents that
were organized around the theme of the school as a Christian educational
community. The superintendents then conducted similar meetings for their
principals and teachers. The NCEA-published *Giving Form to the Vision* was
designed to give Catholic school people tangible assistance to implement the
bishops' message in *To Teach As Jesus Did*.[105]

The theme of the "faith community" was to occupy a prominent place in
Catholic education in the 1970s. Michael O'Neill, picking up on the notion
that Catholic schools should become more of an alternative, concentrating
on their uniqueness, emphasized intentionality as the most critical factor in
the schools becoming faith communities.[106] Intentionality was the sharing of
basic values that conditioned everything that goes on in the school;[107]
"collective intentionality" enabled the school to do all that it did extremely
well, and distinguished it from all other kinds of schools in the process.[108]

Principals were to play a crucial role in developing the "faith community." The *National Catechetical Directory*, for instance, held the principal
accountable for recruiting teachers who were in harmony with the school's
"goals and character." They were also responsible for providing teachers
with the opportunities for spiritual growth, including promoting "community among faculty and students."[109]

Teachers were responsible for instilling religious principles in the students.
With the advent of lay teachers, this task has become more complex. Vowed
religious teachers, who had made up the overwhelming majority of teachers,
were steeped in the traditions of their respective orders, and lived a community life in accord with those traditions. From 1968–69 to 1981–82 the
percentage of religious teachers dropped from 56.7 to 24.8% of the staff.[110]
New means had to be found in order to foster spirituality in the largely lay
staff, indispensable for the schools to be distinctively Catholic, to constitute
"faith communities."

The presence of lay teachers resulted in another new phenomenon in

Catholic schools – collective bargaining agreements. Catholic teaching in labor affairs was based on the encyclicals of Leo XIII and Pius XI, which stated that employers had the duty to respect the rights of workers to organize.[111] This teaching had been reinforced at Vatican II, when the Church fathers recognized the rights of the workers to join associations without "fear of reprisal," and to strike, as the "ultimate means for the defense of the workers' own rights and the fulfillment of their just demands."[112] The position taken by some members of the Church hierarchy, for example in Chicago, seemed at variance with this official social teaching.[113] The strife led to a call by the long-time Catholic labor leader, Monsignor George Higgins, for a "voluntary substitute for the National Labor Relations Board" which would guarantee both that Catholic social teaching would be followed and that the difference between "church-related" and public schools would be taken into account in the arrangement.[114]

Attempts to gain government support for the schools continued throughout the decade of the 1970s. For the most part, with a few exceptions, the "excessive entanglement" criterion established in *Lemon* thwarted such attempts. A number of Catholic sources protested this application of the *Lemon* decision, to no avail. According to the Gallup Polls, however, popular opinion now favored government aid to church-affiliated schools. In 1969 a reported 59% was opposed to such aid, with 38% in favor; in 1974 52% supported such aid, with 35% opposed.[115]

Andrew Greeley et al. reported in 1976 that Catholic schools still enjoyed the strong support of the laity. While only 35% of Catholic parents of school-age children surveyed reported having children in Catholic schools, 38% of the remainder said no parochial school was available. Moreover, 89% of those surveyed rejected the idea that "the Catholic school system is no longer needed in modern day life," and 80% responded that they would contribute more money to save a financially beleaguered parish school. Lastly, the authors said the data indicated that Catholic schools were successful in influencing students in values.[116]

In a controversial "Afterword," Greeley suggested that the Catholic hierarchy get out of the school business and turn control over to the laity who were both able and willing to run the schools. Then, and only then, he argued, would the Catholic schools be healthy.[117] The bishops did not heed Greeley's unsolicited advice.

The bishops did speak out again on Catholic schools in the 1970s, reaffirming their commitment to them. In 1976 they stated that Catholic schools which "realize the threefold purpose of Christian education, to teach doctrine, to build community and to serve, are the most effective means available to the Church for the education of children and young people."[118] Their statement was followed a year later by a publication of the Sacred Congregation for Catholic Education, based at the Vatican. This document focused on the nature and distinctive characteristics of a school that calls itself Catholic, re-emphasized the educational and apostolic value of a Catholic school, developing the ideas of Vatican II:

> all who are responsible for education – parents, teachers, young people and school authorities – and urges them to pool all their resources and the means at their disposal to enable Catholic schools to provide a service which is truly civic and apostolic.[119]

The 1980s – Rebirth and Renewal

In 1981–82 Catholic school enrollment declined further to 3,094,000, down approximately 1 million from 1971–72.[120] In 1982, Alfred McBride, a former NCEA official, identified three major challenges which faced Catholic schools in the 1980s. The "most basic one," according to McBride, was to "keep Catholic schools Catholic, institutionally, morally, and spiritually." The second was to "increase academic excellence competitively, professionally, and creatively." The third, and last, challenge was to "secure a financial basis for ... schools through endowments, development programs, and government aid."[121]

Pope John Paul II addressed the first of these issues in a speech to Catholic teachers in New Orleans in 1987. Speaking encouragingly to his listeners, the Pope called for justice and fairness in all matters; urged the continuance of providing a quality Catholic education to the poor; emphasized the challenge of understanding Catholic identity in education; discussed the opportunity for educators to inculcate correct ethical attitudes and values in young people; and exhorted Catholic educators of all ranks to take Jesus Christ the teacher as their model.[122] The American bishops followed up on the Pope's teaching, in preparation for the twenty-fifth anniversary of *To Teach As Jesus Did*. In a statement that recognized the contribution Catholic schools had made to the Church and nation, they expressed their conviction that the schools must exist for the good of the Church, and, looking toward the future, called on Catholic schools to continue to provide high-quality education for all their students in a context infused with gospel values.[123] The support of Catholic schools by bishops and priests in practice was not overwhelming, however.[124]

The work of James Coleman et al. documents the academic success of Catholic schools during this era, especially when compared with public schools.[125] Not only was student achievement higher in Catholic than in public schools, Coleman claimed that the Catholic schools more nearly met the ideal of the American common school than did their public counterparts.[126] Several years later Coleman argued that Catholic schools have a superior amount of "social capital," community support which assists young people to succeed in school.[127]

The financial crisis which affected Catholic schools generally, with particular emphasis in the inner cities, remained and intensified in the 1980s and on into the 1990s. Parish schools, supported by a combination of tuition and subsidy, often could not meet the spiralling costs connected with education. The schools turned increasingly to professional development efforts, with public relations efforts headed by a development officer, to meet the financial demands.[128]

In 1989–90 there were 8,719 Catholic schools – 7,395 elementary and 1,324 secondary – in the nation.[129] These schools served a number of minority youth, 23% of the total enrollment; 64% of the African–American students enrolled were not Catholic.[130]

In November of 1991 the NCEA sponsored a National Congress on Catholic Schools for the 21st Century. The main goals of the Congress were:

1   To communicate the story of academic and religious effectiveness of Catholic schools to a national audience that includes the whole Catholic community, as well as the broader social and political community.
2   To celebrate the success of Catholic schools in the United States and broaden support for the continuation and expansion of Catholic schooling in the culture.
3   To convene an assembly of key leaders in Catholic schooling as well as appropriate representatives of researchers, business, and public officials in order to create strategies for the future of the schools.[131]

Eleven papers were commissioned on the following five major topics: Catholic Identity of Catholic Schools; Leadership of and on behalf of Catholic Schools; The Catholic School and Society; Catholic School Governance and Finance; and Political Action, Public Policy, and Catholic Schools.[132]

The call for clear identity remained; however, Catholic schools were widely praised in Bryk et al.'s *Catholic Schools and the Common Good*, which appeared in 1993. Decentralization (with parental involvement), a shared set of moral beliefs (by parents, students, and faculty), a shared code of conduct (including "human dignity and the belief that human reason can discern ethical truth"), smallness of size (which promotes interaction between students, parents, and staff), and emphasis on academics (assisted by a concentration on basics) were the traits Bryk et al. identified which marked Catholic schools.[133]

Conclusion

Despite the extraordinary acclaim from outside scholarly observers, such as Coleman and Bryk, and buoyed by slight enrollment increases over the last several years, many Catholic schools still face a troubled future. The basic problem, as Walch describes it, is "money – or lack of it."[134] The financial difficulties are particularly acute in the cities. In the ten years between 1986–87 and 1996–97 Catholic elementary schools declined in these urban areas from a total of 3,424 to 3,139, about 8.3%; their suburban counter-parts meanwhile dropped from 2,232 to 2,150, a decrease of almost 3.75%. At the secondary level, urban schools declined from 750 to 613, a drop of almost 18%, while suburban secondary schools went down slightly from a total of 420 to 413, about 1.5%.[135] For these schools, the future is bleak, unless help is forthcoming.

Where might that help come from? One source is the government. Public vouchers have been employed, as in Cleveland and Milwaukee. Their legal status has not as yet been determined. Legislation to provide parents with choice for their children's schooling is being introduced in Congress as this chapter is being written; its future is equally uncertain. Government aid is not without its dangers. Indeed, along with other religiously affiliated schools, Catholic schools face three common dangers. First, how will these schools manage to remain affordable for families of modest and lesser means? Second, if these schools, embarking on market, consumer-driven strategies, enroll substantial numbers of students who are not members of the sponsoring denomination will they lose their specific religious identity? Third, public aid may cause them to lose the richness of their particular theological soil, and be rendered barren, as has been the case with state-subsidized preaching in several European countries.[136]

Charter schools, whose students included 11% from private schools in one account,[137] 36% of applicants from private schools in another,[138] pose another challenge which is in its infancy as of this writing. The effect that charter schools, which are "free," public schools, unencumbered with the bureaucratic components of traditional public schools, will have on Catholic schools is unclear as of now.

Private sources provide yet another means to assist parents to choose a private (and sometimes public) school for their children. Commonly using the Federal Reduced Lunch Program as the criterion for qualifiers, these programs are now in existence in thirty-three cities nationally. They enroll about 10,000 children with 40,000 more on the waiting lists. The "Parents Advancing Choice in Education" (PACE) program in Dayton, Ohio, is one such program. It includes Catholic, other religiously affiliated schools, and public schools in its operation.[139]

What can we expect in the future? The mission of Catholic schools will remain clear and consistent, but will be shaped according to the exigencies of time and place. We can expect many backers of Catholic schools to join with other Americans in the zealous pursuit of School Choice which seeks to give real power to parents in the selection of schools for their children; we can anticipate increased activity in the area of lay governance of schools; and we can also look for continued emphasis on the mission of the Catholic school in evangelization, in building community, and in apostolic service.[140]

Notes

1 Monica L. McDermott and Thomas C. Hunt, "Catholic Schools: First in Louisiana," *Momentum* xxii, 4 (November 1991): 19.

2 Ibid.

3 Harold A. Buetow, *Of Singular Benefit: The Story of Catholic Education in the United States*, New York: Macmillan, 1970, p. vii.

4 John Carroll, "Pastoral Letter," in Neil G. McCluskey (ed.), *Catholic Education in America: A Documentary History*, New York: Teachers College Press, 1964, p. 48.

5 "Pastoral Letter," First Provincial Council of Baltimore (1829), in McCluskey (ed.), ibid., pp. 52–53; "Pastoral Letter," Second Provincial Council of Baltimore (1833), in McCluskey (ed.), ibid., p. 56; and "Pastoral Letter," Third Provincial Council of Baltimore (1837), in McCluskey (ed.), ibid., pp. 56–58.

6 "Pastoral Letter," Fourth Provincial Council of Baltimore (1840), in McCluskey (ed.), ibid., pp. 58–63.

7 H. Daniel Rops, *The Church in an Age of Revolution*, 2 vols., Garden City, NY: Doubleday, 1967, II, p. 173.

8 *Report on the Population of the United States at the Eleventh Census, 1890*, Vol. I, Part I, Washington, DC: Government Printing Office, p. lxxx.

9 Ibid.

10 Horace Mann, "Twelfth Report" (1848), in Lawrence A. Cremin (ed.) *The Republic and the School: Horace Mann on the Education of Free Men*, New York: Teachers College Press, 1957, p. 105.

11 Diane Ravitch, *The Great School Wars: New York City, 1805–1973*, New York: Basic Books, 1973, pp. 46–76.

12 James A. Burns, *Catholic Education: A Study of Conditions*, New York: Longmans, Green, 1915, p. 15.

13 "Pastoral Letter," First Plenary Council of Baltimore (1852), in McCluskey (ed.), ibid., pp. 78–81.

14 "Pastoral Letter," First Provincial Council of Cincinnati (1855), in Burns and Bernard J. Kohlbrenner (eds), *A History of Catholic Education in the United States*, New York: Benziger Brothers, 1937, p. 138.

15 "Pastoral Letter," Second Provincial Council of Cincinnati (1858), in Burns, *The Growth and Development of the Catholic School System in the United States*, New York: Benziger Brothers, 1912, p. 186.

16 "Pastoral Letter," Third Provincial Council of Cincinnati (1861), in Thomas J. Jenkins, *The Judges of Faith: Christian versus Godless Schools*, Baltimore, MD: John Murphy, 1886, p. 34.

17 *Sadliers' Catholic Directory, Almanac, and Ordo, for the Year of Our Lord 1875*, New York: D.J. Sadlier, 1875, p. 22.

18 R. Freeman Butts, *The American Tradition in Religion and Education*, Boston: Beacon Press, 1950, p. 141.

19 "The President's Speech at Des Moines," *Catholic World* XXII, 130 (January 1876): 433–34.

20 Timothy Walch, *Parish School: American Catholic Parochial Education From Colonial Times to the Present*, New York: Crossroad Herder, 1996, p. 63.

21 "Pastoral Letter," Second Plenary Council of Baltimore (1866), in McCluskey (ed.), *Catholic Education in America*, pp. 82–84.

22 "Instruction of the Propaganda de Fide" (1875), in McCluskey (ed.), ibid., pp. 121–22.

23 Ibid., p. 124.

24 James Conway, "The Rights and Duties of the Church in Regard to Education," *The American Catholic Quarterly Review* IX (October 1884): 669.

25 For example, see "The Catholics of the Nineteenth Century," *Catholic World* XI (July 1870): 436–41; "Are Our Public Schools Free?," *Catholic World* XVIII (October 1873): 9; and "The School Question," *Catholic World* XI (April 1870): 98–100, 104.

26 "The School Question," *Catholic World* XI (April 1870): 106.

27 Peter Guilday, *A History of the Councils of Baltimore (1791–1884)*, New York: Macmillan, 1932, p. 237.

28 "Decrees of the Third Plenary Council of Baltimore," in McCluskey (ed.), *Catholic Education in America*, pp. 93–94.

29 Francis P. Cassidy, "Catholic Education in the Third Plenary Council of Baltimore," *The Catholic Historical Review* XXXIV, Part 1 (October 1948): 305.

30 Quoted in Jenkins, *The Judges of Faith*, p. 122.

31 Mary Perkins Ryan, *Are Parochial Schools the Answer? Catholic Education in the Light of the Council*, New York: Guild Press, 1964, p. 39.

32 William Torrey Harris was among the leaders in articulating this position. See Selwyn K. Troen, *The Public and the Schools: Shaping the St. Louis System, 1838–1920*, Columbia, MO: University of Missouri Press, 1975; Neil G. McCluskey, *Public Schools and Moral Education: The Influence of Horace Mann, William Torrey Harris, and John Dewey*, Westport, CT: Greenwood, 1975; and Thomas C. Hunt, "Public Schools and Moral Education: An American Dilemma," *Religious Education* 74 (July–August 1979): 350–72.

33 David B. Tyack, *The One Best System: A History of American Urban Education*, Cambridge, MA: Harvard University Press, 1974; and Tyack and Elisabeth Hansot, *Managers of Virtue: Public School Leadership in America, 1820–1980*, New York: Basic Books, 1982.

34 Buetow, *Of Singular Benefit*, p. 179.

35 Pope Leo XIII, "Diuturnum" ("On Civil Government"), in Gerald F. Yates (ed.), *Papal Thought on the State*, New York: Appleton-Century-Crofts, 1928, p. 10.

36 Pope Leo XIII, "Immortale Dei" ("The Christian Constitution of States"), in John A. Ryan (ed.), *The State and the Church*, New York: Macmillan, 1922, pp. 4–24.

37 Burns and Kohlbrenner, *A History of Catholic Education*, p. 144.

38 See, for instance, Michael J. Muller, *Public School Education*, New York: D.J. Sadlier, 1872; and Jenkins, *The Judges of Faith*.

39 McCluskey, "America and the Catholic School," in McCluskey (ed.), *Catholic Education in America*, p. 25.

40 Quoted in Anson Phelps Stokes, *Church and State in the United States*, 3 vols., New York: Harper Brothers, 1950, II, p. 653.

41 John Ireland, "State Schools and Parish Schools – Is Union Between Them Impossible?," *National Education Association Journal of Proceedings and Addresses*, Session of the Year 1890, held at St. Paul, Minnesota. Topeka, KS: Clifford C. Baker, 1890, pp. 179–185.

42 See Thomas C. Hunt, "The Bennett Law of 1890: Focus of Conflict between Church and State," *Journal of Church and State* 23 (Winter 1981): 69–94. Catholics were joined by Lutherans, especially those of German background, in this struggle.

43 McCluskey (ed.), *Catholic Education in America*, p. 141.

44 John Ireland, "Clarification to Cardinal Gibbons," in ibid., pp. 141–50.

45 Walch, *Parish School*, pp. 39–40.

46 Pope Leo XIII, "Sapientiae Christianae" ("On the Chief Duties of Christians as Citizens"), in Husslein (ed.), *Social Wellsprings*, I , p. 162.

47 McCluskey (ed.), *Catholic Education in America*, p. 151.

48 "Archbishop Satolli's Fourteen Propositions for the Settling of the School Question," in McCluskey (ed.), ibid., pp. 151–60.
49 Bouquillon's first publication was "Education: To Whom Does It Belong?"; Holaind's response was entitled "The Parent First." For a thorough discussion of the controversy consult Daniel Reilly, *The School Controversy, 1891–1893*, New York: Arno Press and *The New York Times*. Originally published at Washington, DC: The Catholic University of America Press, 1944.
50 Cited in Reilly, ibid., pp. 228–29.
51 For a treatment of Cahenslyism, see Colman J. Barry, *The Catholic Church and German Americans*, Milwaukee, WI: Bruce, 1953, and Gerald Shaughnessy, *Has the Immigrant Kept the Faith?*, New York: Arno Press and *The New York Times*, 1969.
52 John Tracy Ellis, *American Catholicism*, Chicago: The University of Chicago Press, 1956, pp. 118–19. For a thorough study of the "Americanism" controversy consult Thomas T. McAvoy, *The Americanism Heresy in Roman Catholicism 1895–1900*, Notre Dame, IN: University of Notre Dame Press, 1963.
53 McAvoy, ibid., pp. 333–35.
54 James A. Burns, "Catholic Secondary Schools," *American Catholic Quarterly* XXVI (July 1901): 497.
55 Buetow, *Of Singular Benefit*, pp. 182–84.
56 Ibid., p. 179.
57 *Pierce* v. *Society of Sisters*. 268 U.S. 510 (1925).
58 For a concise treatment of Shields and his efforts consult Walch, *Parish School*, especially pp. 119–24.
59 Again, see Walch, ibid., pp. 124–33.
60 Ibid., pp. 134–51.
61 Pope Pius XI, "Divini Illius Magistri" ("The Christian Education of Youth"), in *Five Great Encyclicals*, New York: Paulist Press, 1939, pp. 44–60.
62 Ibid., p. 61.
63 Buetow, *Of Singular Benefit*, p. 226.
64 Neil G. McCluskey, *Catholic Viewpoint on Education*, Garden City, NY: Hanover House, 1959, p. 167.
65 Ibid., p. 107.
66 See Richard Ognibene, "The Influence of Progressivism on Catholic Education after 1945," Paper presented at the American Educational Research Association, March 31–April 4, 1985, Chicago.
67 McCluskey, *Catholic Viewpoint on Education*, pp. 117–18.
68 *Cantwell* v. *Connecticut*. 210 U.S. 296 (1940).
69 *Everson* v. *Board of Education*. 330 U.S. 1 (1947).
70 Virgil C. Blum, *Freedom of Choice in Education*, New York: Paulist Press, 1963, pp. 98–105.
71 See ibid.; CEF Brochure, *Citizens for Educational Freedom*; Blum, *Education: Freedom and Competition*, Chicago: Argus Communications, 1967; and James R. Brown, "Citizens for Educational Freedom," *America*, February 8, 1964, for an understanding of CEF's position.
72 Buetow, *Of Singular Benefit*, p. 276.
73 McCluskey, *Catholic Viewpoint on Education*, p. 100.
74 John Tracy Ellis, *American Catholics and the Intellectual Life*, Chicago: The Heritage Foundation, 1956, p. 46.
75 Ryan, *Are Parochial Schools the Answer?*.
76 *U.S. News and World Report*, August 18, 1975, p. 55; *Education Week*, March 30, 1983, p. 14.

77 "Gravissimum Educationis" ("Declaration on Christian Education"), in Walter M. Abbott (ed.), *The Documents of Vatican II*, New York: America Press, 1966, p. 77.

78 See Mark J. Hurley, *Commentary on the Declaration of Christian Education*, Study Club Edition, Glen Rock, NJ: Paulist Press, 1966.

79 Ibid., p. 23.

80 See *The National Catholic Reporter*, September 27, 1967, p. 5; October 25, 1967, p. 3; and March 5, 1969, p. 5 for an airing of these views.

81 See, for instance, Peter Schrag, *Village School Downtown*, Boston: Beacon Press, 1967; Martin Ahmann, "The Church and the Urban Negro," *America*, February 10, 1968, pp. 181–85; "Are Parochial Schools Racial Escape Valves?," *Christian Century*, October 26, 1968, p. 1298; and John P. Sheerin, "Our Segregated Catholic Schools," *Catholic World*, March 1963, pp. 333–34.

82 *The National Catholic Reporter*, September 4, 1968, p. 3.

83 James C. Donohue, "Catholic Education in Contemporary Society," *National Catholic Educational Association Bulletin* 64 (August 1967): 13–17; Donohue, "New Priorities for Catholic Education," *America*, April 13, 1968, pp. 476–79.

84 See, for example, Robert J. Starratt, "The Parochial Schools in the Inner City," *The National Elementary Principal* 46 (January 1967): 27–33; M. Melathon, "Response to the Challenges of Schools in Disadvantaged Areas," *National Catholic Educational Association Bulletin* 64 (August 1967): 173–79; and Ann M. Wallace, "A New York City Program for Disadvantaged Students," *National Catholic Educational Association Bulletin* 64 (February 1968): 19–26.

85 *The Wisconsin State Journal*, May 31, 1969, p. 10.

86 James C. Cibulka, Timothy J. O'Brien, and Donald Zewe, *Inner-City Private Elementary Schools: A Study*, Milwaukee, WI: Marquette University Press, 1982.

87 O'Neil C. D'Amour, "Parochial Schools without Parochialism," *Ave Maria*, April 24, 1964, pp. 12–14.

88 For D'Amour's thoughts on this subject, consult "Reconstituting Patterns of Education," in C. Albert Koob (ed.), *What Is Happening to Catholic Education?* Washington, DC: National Catholic Educational Association, 1966, pp. 25–37; "School Boards of the Future," *America*, September 25, 1965, pp. 316–17; "The Parish School Board," *National Catholic Educational Association Bulletin* 62 (August 1965): 248–49; "Catholic Schools Must Survive," ibid., 65 (November 1968): 3–7; "The 'Control' Structure of Catholic Education," ibid., 63 (August 1966): 267–74; and "Structural Changes in Catholic Schools," *Catholic School Journal* 66 (June 1966): 27–29.

89 National Catholic Educational Association, *Voice of the Community: The Board Movement in Catholic Education*, Washington, DC: National Catholic Educational Association, 1967, Preface.

90 Stuart Hubbell, "Citizens for Educational Freedom in New York: Outlook for the Future," *National Catholic Educational Association Bulletin* 64 (August 1967): 89–91.

91 The following is a sample of the literature published on school boards in Catholic sources during the mid-1960s: Olin J. Murdick, "Parish School Board," *America*, January 22, 1966, pp. 132–36; Aloysius F. Lacki, "Pastor's Viewpoint on School Boards," *National Catholic Educational Association Bulletin* 64 (August 1967): 161–63; M. Simeon Wozniak, "School Boards in American Catholic Education," ibid., 97–103; William C. Bruce, "A Few Thoughts on Parish School Boards," *Catholic School Journal* 67 (December 1967): 65; "Some Don'ts for a Parish School Board," ibid., 68 (April 1968): 90; "Advice for New School Board Members," ibid., 65 (October 1965): 27; and

Interview with Monsignor J. William Lester, "How a Diocesan Board Upgrades Lay Teachers," ibid., 65 (September 1965): 76–78.

92 *School District of Abington Township* v. *Schempp*. 374 U.S. 203 (1963).

93 *Central School District* v. *Allen*. 392 U.S. 296 (1968).

94 *Lemon* v. *Kurtzman*. 403 U.S. 602, 609 (1971).

95 *Lemon* v. *Kurtzman, Earley* v. *DiCenso, Robinson* v. *DiCenso*. 403 U.S. 602 (1971).

96 National Conference of Catholic Bishops, "Catholic Schools Are Indispensable," *Catholic School Journal* 16, 1 (1968): 25–27.

97 National Conference of Catholic Bishops, *To Teach As Jesus Did*, Washington, DC: United States Catholic Conference, 1973, pp. 1–9.

98 Ibid., pp. 28–29, 31–33.

99 Ibid., p. 34.

100 Kenneth A. Simon and W. Vance Grant (eds.), *Digest of Educational Statistics*, Washington, DC: Department of Health, Education, and Welfare, 1987, p. 56.

101 National Conference of Catholic Bishops, "Sharing the Light of Faith, National Catechetical Directory for Catholics in the United States," Washington, DC: United States Catholic Conference, 1979, p. 143.

102 Pope John Paul II, "Catechesi Tradendae," 1979, paragraph 69. (For the complete English text of "Catechesi Tradendae," see *The Living Light* 17 (Spring 1980): 44–89.)

103 Ibid.

104 *The National Catholic Reporter*, October 22, 1976, p. 8.

105 National Catholic Educational Association, *Giving Form to the Vision: The Pastoral in Practice*, Washington, DC: National Catholic Educational Association, 1974.

106 Michael O'Neill, "Catholic Education: The Largest Alternative System," *Thrust*, May 7, 1978, p. 26; O'Neill, "Toward a Modern Concept of Permeation," *Momentum* 10 (May 1979): 48–49.

107 Ibid., p. 49.

108 Ibid., pp. 49–50.

109 *Sharing the Light of Faith*, p. 131.

110 *Catholic Schools in America: Elementary/Secondary, 1982 ed.*, Englewood, CO: Fisher, 1982, p. xviii.

111 Pope Leo XIII, "Rerum Novarum" ("On the Condition of Labor"), in *Five Great Encyclicals*, New York: Paulist Press, 1939, pp. 1–30; Pope Pius XI, "Quadragesimo Anno" ("Reconstructing the Social Order"), in ibid., pp. 125–67.

112 "Gaudium et Spes" ("Pastoral Constitution on the Church in the Modern World"), in Abbott (ed.), *The Documents of Vatican II*, pp. 277–78.

113 *National Labor Relations Board* v. *The Catholic Bishop of Chicago, et al.* 99 S. CT. 1313 (1979).

114 *The National Catholic Reporter*, September 17, 1982, p. 6.

115 *The New York Times*, June 29, 1969, p. 25; George H. Gallup, "Sixth Annual Poll of Attitudes Toward Public Education," *Phi Delta Kappan*, 56, 1 (September 1974): 20–32.

116 Andrew M. Greeley, William C. McReady, and Kathleen McCourt, *Catholic Schools in a Declining Church*, Kansas City, KS: Sheed and Ward, 1976, p. 301.

117 Ibid., pp. 324–25.

118 National Conference of Catholic Bishops, "Teach Them," Washington, DC: United States Catholic Conference, 1976, p. 3.

119 The Sacred Congregation for Catholic Education, "The Catholic School," Washington, DC: United States Catholic Conference, 1977, p. 3.

120 Simon and Grant (eds.), *Digest of Educational Statistics*, p. 56.
121 Alfred A. McBride, "Major Challenges Facing Catholic Education in the 1980s," *Momentum* 13 (December 1982): 10–11.
122 Pope John Paul II, "The Pope's Address to Teachers," *Origins*, 17, 8: 279–81.
123 United States Catholic Bishops, "In Support of Catholic Schools," *Origins*, 20, 25: 401–406.
124 See J. Stephen O'Brien, *Mixed Messages: What Bishops and Priests Say About Catholic Schools*, Washington, DC: National Catholic Educational Association, 1987, for a thorough study of their attitudes on Catholic schools in the mid 1980s.
125 James S. Coleman, Thomas Hoffer, and Sally Kilgore, *High School Achievement: Public, Catholic, and Private Schools*, New York: Basic Books, 1982.
126 Coleman, "Quality and Equality in American Education: Public and Catholic Schools," *Phi Delta Kappan* 63 (November 1981): 159–64.
127 Coleman, "Social Capital and the Development of Youth," *Momentum* 18 (November 1987): 6–8; Coleman and Hoffer, *Public and Private High Schools: The Impact of Communities*, New York: Basic Books, 1987.
128 Karen Ristau, "Current Concerns," in Mary A. Grant and Thomas C. Hunt, *Catholic School Education in the United States: Development and Current Concerns*, New York: Garland, 1992, p. 237.
129 US Department of Education, Office of Research and Improvement, *Projection of Education Statistics to 2001: An Update*, Washington, DC: December, 1990, pp. 119–20.
130 F.H. Brigham, *United States Catholic Elementary and Secondary Schools 1990–91, Annual Statistical Report on Schools, Enrollment and Staffing*, Washington, DC: National Catholic Educational Association, pp. 10, 14–20.
131 Cited in Ristau, "Current Concerns," in Grant and Hunt, *Catholic School Education in the United States*, p. 242.
132 Ibid., pp. 243–45.
133 Anthony S. Bryk, Valerie E. Lee, and Peter B. Holland, *Catholic Schools and the Common Good*, Cambridge, MA: Harvard University Press, 1993, as cited in Walch, *Parish School*, pp. 244–45.
134 Walch, ibid., p. 245.
135 The National Catholic Educational Association, Mary J. Milks, Comp., *United States Catholic Elementary and Secondary Schools 1996–97. The Annual Statistical Report on Schools, Enrollment and Staffing*, Washington, DC: National Catholic Educational Association, 1997, p. 10.
136 James C. Carper and Thomas C. Hunt, "Epilogue," in Hunt and Carper (eds.), *Religious Schools in the United States K-12: A Source Book*, New York: Garland, 1993, p. 446.
137 Bruno V. Manno, "The Financial, Legal, and Political Context of Private Education," Paper presented at "Private Schools: Partners in American Education – A Research Conference," held at The University of Dayton, November 6, 1997.
138 Bruce S. Cooper, "Comments about the Dayton Conference," *The Religion and Education Forum*, 3, 2 (Spring 1998): 13.
139 Interview with Dr. Theodore J. Wallace, Director, PACE, March 20, 1998.
140 Thomas C. Hunt and Margaret A. Wuelfing, "'Quo Vadis': The Spiritual Journey of American Catholic Schools Since Vatican II," *Private School Monitor*, 19, 1 (Fall 1997): 5.

4 Reclaiming Inquiry in the Catholic Philosophy of Education

William F. Losito

It is patent that Catholic education is confronting a challenging and uncertain future. Financial crises, the dramatic reduction in the number of vowed religious and priests present in the schools, the composition of the student body, and the relationship itself of the Church to a pluralistic society, have all converged in compelling Catholic education leaders to retrieve a vision inspirational and cogent enough to weather the cultural storms of a post-modern society.

Given the richness of the Catholic intellectual tradition, one would expect that there would be a vibrant community of Catholic scholars engaged in lively philosophical inquiry and debate about such a vision. Certainly, there is a deep concern among Catholic educational leaders and scholars which has resulted in excellent individual monographs and presentations. But there is no community of Catholic intellectuals pursuing a coherent agenda of inquiry to serve as a significant resource for educational leaders who are grappling with the formulation of a sacred vision for education in a secular, pluralistic society.

This lacuna has not gone unnoticed by the broader academic community. In 1982, R.F. Dearden, a distinguished educational philosopher, wrote in the *British Journal of Educational Studies*:

> Concerning possible alternatives, one might have expected a distinctive school of Catholic philosophy of education to have developed, but this has not happened. Many philosophers of education are Catholic but they generally follow the mainstream in their choice of topics and methods. The nearest to a distinctive Catholic perspective is probably Jacques Maritain's book *Education at the Crossroads* though this has had very little influence.
>
> (Dearden 1982: 63–64)

In 1995, an essay appeared in the *British Journal of Educational Studies* under the title, "Return to the Crossroads: Maritain Fifty Years On." The authors – David Carr, John Haldane, Terence McLaughlin, and Richard Pring – used the citation from Dearden as a catalyst for their analysis (Carr et al. 1995). (For the sake of brevity, future references will attribute the essay simply to Carr.) Carr accepts Dearden's judgment that the English-speaking Catholic community has not developed a "systematic account of the nature and role of education that could sit alongside those born of Marxism, Pragmatism, and analytic philosophy" (Carr 1995: 163). Carr further accepts Dearden's judgment of Maritain's *Education at the Crossroads* as being the only modern effort to sketch out systematically a Catholic perspective on education. The objective of Carr's essay is to use an analysis of Maritain's book and its Thomistic antecedent as a platform for pursuing the question, "What might be the form of an adequate Catholic philosophy of education?" Carr has a caveat for this pursuit, namely that an "adequate Catholic philosophy of education" is to be interpreted universally as applying to all good education and not exclusively to Catholic schools.

Introduction

In general, I agree with the initial points affirmed by Dearden and Carr. While there are a number of papal documents and pastoral letters which address directly the characteristics and importance of Catholic schools, a community of Catholic intellectuals and leaders has not emerged to engage in a sustained dialogue about the content of these documents and other substantive documents. The papal documents and pastoral letters are directed explicitly at qualities of Catholic education in general terms. An inquiring community of Catholic scholarship devoted to the philosophical task is needed to craft a comprehensive educational perspective that contextualizes the principles into praxis. After articulating the most fundamental tenets – such as the transcendent destiny of humans and the Incarnation – the real philosophizing commences in trying to draw out the relevance for multicultural settings, students with special needs, and expectations for educational professionals. Perhaps the absence of sustained philosophical inquiry from the Catholic perspective is due to the laity having been overly reliant on thinking being done by vowed religious and clerical leaders. Dearden and Carr do not speculate about this matter.

George Marsden (1994), in his magisterial *Soul of the American University*, develops a thesis which can offer a partial explanation for the Catholic academy's lack of attention to the development of a distinctly Catholic perspective on education, at least as it applies to the situation in the United States. Marsden argues that over the past century the liberal scholarly academy, in a misguided effort to respond to intellectual pluralism, has gradually marginalized religious frameworks for scholarly research.

Even though Marsden does not apply his argument directly to Catholic educational philosophy, his account provides a more general explanation, in part, for Catholic philosophers and educational leaders neglecting inquiry about education from the Catholic perspective. While Dearden does not offer an explanation in his essay, he does note that "Many philosophers of education are Catholic but they generally follow the mainstream in their choice of topics and methods" (Dearden 1982: 63). On Marsden's account, the behavior is clearly understood as an instance of the contemporary academic canons taking priority over the scholar's personal value commitments. In the case of educational philosophy, the academy's misguided sensitivity toward matters of religious pluralism, coupled with my speculation of overdependence on clerical intellectual leadership, has left a serious gap in the contemporary debate about educational reform.

Carr's strategy in developing the "form of an adequate Catholic philosophy of education" is to find the Cartesian axiomatic principles in the Catholic intellectual tradition and proceed to unpack their educational implications. Carr proposes the systematic philosophical thought of Thomas Aquinas as the essential point of departure for developing a distinctly Catholic educational perspective. Notwithstanding the striking diversity of views among Catholics, Carr asserts that "important resources for the rational articulation and defence of a distinctly Catholic conception of education are indeed to be found in the philosophy of St. Thomas" (Carr 1995: 176). Carr devotes the main body of his essay to identifying the tenets of Thomistic philosophy which are most promising for developing a Catholic philosophy of education.

Carr acknowledges that only occasionally does Thomas focus his investigation explicitly on the educational process. For that reason, Carr extends his analysis of Aquinas to include the consideration of the educational thought of Jacques Maritain, especially his *Education at the Crossroads* (1943). Maritain was an avowedly neo-Thomist intellectual who worked out the views of Thomas and extended their implications for contexts and areas not explicitly addressed in the original investigations of Aquinas. Because of Maritain's extension of Thomism to contemporary education, Carr includes Maritain as integral to the overall argument about the fittingness of Thomism as a primary text for rejuvenating the development of a Catholic educational philosophy.

My own objectives here are to offer a critique of Carr's general argument and to suggest ground rules and strategies for developing a Catholic philosophy of education. I do acknowledge an intellectual sympathy with the initial Dearden–Carr judgment that no significant work in the Catholic philosophy of education has been done since Maritain's *Education at the Crossroads*. The caveat here is that we are referring to systematic philosophical inquiry, since there are clearly many examples, notably the documents of Vatican II and selected pastoral letters, which have contributed to the legacy of Catholic educational thought. Just as troubling, and central to my own concern, is that a community of Catholic intellectuals has not emerged devoted to philosophical inquiry about education that finds its wellspring in the Catholic intellectual tradition. Any development of a distinctly Catholic perspective presupposes the formation of such a community so that the inquiry can proceed with energy and focus. About this, I will comment further a little later.

Carr Critique

Let us proceed to considering the general features of Carr's argument. My intention is not to provide a detailed critique of Carr's analysis of the ideas of Aquinas and Maritain. In the main, I assume that the major points of interpretation are not contentious. But I do want to take issue with or suggest refinements to some of his assumptions – assumptions which turn out to have serious implications for the field or boundaries of a distinctly Catholic educational philosophy.

For starters, consider Carr's contention that Catholic philosophical inquiry about education should commence with an examination of the Thomistic texts. Carr argues this point largely from the historical influence of Thomism in official church documents and intellectual tradition (p. 164). He comments that "it is hardly possible even to entertain the idea of Catholic philosophy without thinking of Thomism" (p. 163).

I think that Carr's claim that for intellectuals steeped in the Catholic tradition the ideas and name of Thomas will readily be invoked in serious reflection about Catholic philosophy. But Carr takes the claim further where he asserts, "It is reasonable, therefore, particularly in the present context, to interpret 'Catholic' as Thomist and to ask 'what would be a Thomist philosophy of education?'" I am not sure what about the "present context" justifies the reduction of "Catholic" philosophy to "Thomist philosophy." Surely, one would hope that the Thomistic texts (authored by Aquinas and adherent to his thought) would be an invaluable part of the canon for philosophical inquiry in the Catholic tradition. But it is premature to identify a priori a Catholic educational philosophy with the Thomistic framework. It may be the case that we discover Catholic *philosophies* of education.

To be sure, we would legitimately contend that even these plurality of forms have a common bond, so that the search for a distinctively Catholic philosophy of education is still in order. Nonetheless, it may be the case that the Thomistic framework is only one of several that satisfy the dictates of a common bond. There is nothing to presume that Thomism and Thomism alone captures the essential features of a distinctly Catholic educational philosophy. Just "as reasonable" (to invoke Carr's phrase), phenomenological and process philosophical orientations, or perhaps philosophical perspectives embedded in or emanating from liberation theology, might also capture the distinguishing characteristics. This is not to dismiss or disparage Carr's contention that Thomistically grounded educational philosophy is fruitful and reasonable. I simply want to ensure that the rejuvenated inquiry does not foreclose the range of reasonable systematic philosophical approaches to quandaries in Catholic educational philosophy.

It needs to be iterated that while Carr's emphatic reduction of the Catholic intellectual tradition *vis-à-vis* educational philosophy to Thomism is flawed, nonetheless Carr does point to Thomistic themes which, indeed, do merit special consideration as privileged ideas for helping to characterize a Catholic philosophy of education. But it is possible to identify these themes and advocate them as central tenets in a Catholic educational philosophy without exclusively locating them in the Thomistic texts, as they are likewise found in other philosophical orientations in the Catholic intellectual tradition.

What is it, in Carr's view, that makes Aquinas such a commendable resource for developing a Catholic philosophy of education? In fact, it is that Aquinas has such a rich philosophy of human nature that leads to a powerful conception of education. Aquinas conceptualizes humans as rational animals with a transcendent destiny (p. 165). There is a unity to the human person as a being in which spirit and body are integrated. Reason is the integrating feature of human nature and becomes, then, the focus for purpose of education (p. 177). The uniquely Christian aspect of education in Aquinas's account derives from the telos he builds into human nature. We are created so that we are destined toward completion in the risen Christ (p. 165). This goal not only specifies a philosophy of human nature, in general, but also a goal for education – trying to develop toward union with the risen Christ.

Maritain

As a consequence of Carr's partiality for Thomism as the privileged philosophy within the Catholic tradition, Carr points to Maritain as the best contemporary philosopher for a segue into the thought of Aquinas as it pertains to education. In *Education at the Crossroads*, Maritain gives a systematic account of education. Following Aquinas, Maritain grounds his educational view in the human telos – union with the triune God. Maritain contextualizes his account of educational purpose in ways that Aquinas simply could not because of cultural differences. For example, Maritain works out his account in contrast with contemporary "secular philosophies" that "too rarely have anything to offer by way of an ennobling self-conception" (Carr 1995: 166). In particular, he selects Dewey as *bête noire* who is guilty of a "reductive naturalism" that denies any spiritual qualities to humans and their transcendent destiny (p. 168). Like Aquinas, Maritain underscores the centrality of moral education.

There are at least two other implicit assumptions that are worthy of comment. Throughout Carr's essay, he uses the term "Catholic philosophy of education" and he uses the texts of Thomas Aquinas as the necessary resource for developing the distinctively Catholic perspective. Now, it is clear that many of the key ideas in Aquinas are explicitly theological in nature or at least theological in derivation. Thus, an educational perspective generated from this source is more accurately designated as a theological/philosophical perspective. The very human telos proposed by Aquinas and Maritain – union with the risen Christ – is itself theologically grounded.

About this point, Carr himself would be in agreement, I think. In the latter part of the essay, he points out that the distinctive Catholic vision of the spiritual, moral, and social life relevant to developing an educational philosophy is itself "grounded first and foremost in divine revelation … refined and developed in the course of a long tradition of patristic and doctrinal reflection into an ideal of human flourishing" (Carr 1995: 176). The grounding in divine revelation and tradition, of course, situates the source, in large part, in theological reflection. I suspect that for the sake of simplicity Carr uses the term "philosophy" even when other disciplinary perspectives, especially theology, are actually included.

Rather than call for disciplinary purity, I applaud the inclusion of multi-disciplinary perspectives under the rubric of "philosophy." There is a common bond in philosophical discourse – namely, the use of disciplined reason to speculate about ideal states-of-affairs – but the post-modern intellectual polemics have amply demonstrated that there is not disciplinary purity in any of the academic fields, especially philosophy.

So, as a strategy I suggest that we continue to name the effort to develop a distinctive educational perspective as a project in "educational philosophy" even though key ideas and assumptions are derived from other disciplines. In fact, we should welcome the interdisciplinary nature of the project, as the perspectives of theology, anthropology, psychology, and literature, to name just a few, will greatly enrich the project.

Agenda for a Catholic Philosophy of Education

In this section, I want to speculate about what might be the items on a Catholic philosophy of education agenda. Indeed, these items might, in fact, be derived from the Thomistic philosophy, but is not necessarily so and certainly not exclusively so. Our effort here is first to identify the core ideas that characterize the Catholic perspective on life in general. These core ideas, in fact, may be doctrines central to the theological system, or they may just be central ideas within the intellectual tradition. Also, it may be the case that the core idea, or doctrine, may be shared with other traditions and, therefore, is not prima facie a distinctive characteristic of a Catholic theology. Likewise it may be, although it is unlikely, that all the characteristically Catholic core ideas are shared in more or less a congruent way with one or more other identifiable Christian perspectives. The notion of personal redemption and the Incarnation are examples of core ideas which would be widely shared, albeit articulated distinctly in different Christian traditions, therefore being characteristic of Catholic thought but not necessarily distinctive of the Catholic perspective.

In some areas, one does not seek so much core ideas that are doctrinally defined but are explicitly part of the intellectual tradition, such as the notion of service. Clearly, Jesus was a servant savior, but the notion is not doctrinely defined in theological language. In these cases, what we are about is seeking thematic strands or questions for the agenda in Catholic educational philosophy.

Once these core Catholic theological ideas are identified, then attention can be directed toward identifying questions that are important on a Catholic philosophy of education agenda. Carr does not address this task in a detailed manner. Rather, he starts from the caveat that the most fruitful ideas will be found in the writings of Aquinas and the contemporary explication in educational contexts from the writings of Maritain. This implicitly gets at some of the central issues, such as questions about the telos of education, but it does not explicitly address or identify the questions themselves.

Terry McLaughlin, one of Carr's co-authors does, in another place, identify several of the important questions on a Catholic education philosophy agenda. For example, McLaughlin identifies several issues which he considers especially worthy of inquiry from the perspective of the Catholic intellectual tradition – aims of education, the personal autonomy of the individual, moral education, and religious education (McLaughlin 1996: 139). McLaughlin points out that these topics are already extensively investigated in educational philosophy but without the benefit of Catholic concepts and arguments.

For McLaughlin, as for Carr in the first piece, the overriding goal is to develop a distinctive Catholic philosophy of education. He translates this objective into the overarching question: What is distinctive of Catholic education? (McLaughlin 1996: 139). And for him, likewise as it is for Carr, the notion of a "Catholic education" is not limited to Catholic schools but any school which tries to embody its characteristics. For McLaughlin, there are at least three distinctive features of a good Catholic school: the embodiment of a view about the meaning of human persons and of human life; an aspiration to holistic influence; and religious and moral formation (pp. 140–44).

For present purposes, I will not explore a detailed analysis of what McLaughlin means by each of those features. A few comments are in order, however. First, even though McLaughlin's initial concern is in formulating a Catholic educational philosophy perspective applicable generically to schools, his analysis quickly moves to focusing on Catholic schools. For instance, in explicating the first feature, McLaughlin identifies the distinctiveness of Catholic education as consisting in its relationship to the Catholic faith in which all aspects are related to Christ (p. 141).

This contention seems to undermine his earlier stated intention of working toward a "Catholic philosophy of education which seeks to illumine the nature not merely of Catholic education, but of education as such" (p. 139).

It is problematic as to whether McLaughlin is pursuing the development of a philosophical perspective which applies uniquely to Catholic schools or to "education as such," as he previously avows. Surely, his three general features of a Catholic education, as initially stated, can arguably be applicable for education as such, although there may be questions concerning religious formation as a universally illuminating feature of education. But when McLaughlin starts explicating the features, it becomes clear that his focus is on a philosophy of Catholic schools.

McLaughlin's analysis does uncover several dimensions of the problem of articulating a Catholic philosophy of education. First, there is the difference between defining characteristics and distinctive features of Catholic education. The three features that McLaughlin identifies may very well be characteristics of Catholic education which are shared with other educational perspectives, especially with other Christian perspectives. Defining what is distinctive and unique is a different and more difficult intellectual discernment. And finally, there is the problem of identifying what aspect of the Catholic perspective has relevance for illuminating education generally.

Developing Rules for the Road

Given the difficulty in separating these different aspects of the issue, I suggest the following rules of the road. As a caveat, I acknowledge that I think the primary objective is to develop a Catholic perspective on education that has pertinence paradigmatically to Catholic schooling but also to education generally. But that objective is "down the road," so to speak.

My first recommendation is for the inquiry to proceed by trying to identify the ideal characteristics of a Catholic school. Discerning the distinctive features and what is generally relevant is a subsequent form of inquiry. After determining the characteristics and distinguishing features, then one must elaborate on what is appropriate for generic education.

In trying to identify the ideal characteristics and distinctive features of Catholic schools, certainly Church documents and texts written by Catholic authors should be consulted. But works written by non-Catholics, such as Parker Palmer and David Purpel, likewise should be consulted. In Palmer's latest book, *The Courage to Teach*, he develops the theme that to "educate is to guide students on an inner journey toward more truthful ways of seeing and being in the world" (1998: 6). Surely that is a theme that can resonate with a reasonable exposition of a characteristic of Catholic education. David Purpel, in *The Moral and Spiritual Crisis in Education*, describes the prophetic dimension that should permeate good education. Likewise, this idea of teacher as prophet is arguably a candidate for one important characteristic of Catholic education. This simply illustrates that the pertinent texts can be found outside the Catholic canon.

After articulating characteristics of Catholic education, the subsequent task is one of discernment – discerning the distinctive features of Catholic education. These become the paradigm features of Catholic education that are then used to generate implications for education in general. Several authors, most notably Thomas Groome, have proposed distinguishing criteria for Catholic education. Groome's list of "distinguishing characteristics" are as follows:

> its positive anthropology of the person;
> its sacramentality of life;
> its communal emphasis regarding human and Christian existence;
> its commitment to tradition as a source of its Story and Vision; and
> its appreciation of rationality and learning, epitomized in its commitment to education.
>
> (Groome 1996: 108)

Of course, Groome gives a fuller explication of each criteria. And within the explication, ideas distinctive to Catholic education may be apparent. But on the face of it, the criteria can arguably apply to other Christian traditions as well.

In addition to a strategy for sorting out educational characteristics from distinctive features, it is essential that there be a community of individuals dedicated to inquiry about the Catholic philosophy of education. This community needs to be inclusive of both academics and practitioners. A coherent set of problems need to be addressed but not always with a common philosophical syntax. A multiplicity of philosophical lenses should be used, as well as multidisciplinary insights. No longer is it desirable, if it ever was, for the academics to set themselves apart for esoteric conversations. Both a community and an agenda need to emerge for Catholic education to meet the challenging and uncertain future and make its contribution to the public common good.

References

Carr, David, Haldane, John, McLaughlin, Terence, and Pring, Richard (1995) "Return to the Crossroads: Maritain Fifty Years On," *British Journal of Educational Studies*, XXXXIII, 2 (June): 162–78.

Dearden, R.F. (1982) "Philosophy of Education, 1952–1982," *British Journal of Educational Studies*, 30 (1): 57–70.

Groome, Thomas H. (1996) "What Makes a School Catholic?," in McLaughlin, Terence H., O'Keefe, Joseph, and O'Keefe, Bernadette (eds.) *The Contemporary Catholic School: Context, Identity, and Diversity*, London: Falmer Press.

Maritain, Jacques (1943) *Education at the Crossroads*, New Haven, CT: Yale University Press.

Marsden, George (1994) *Soul of the American University*, New York: Oxford University Press.

McLaughlin, Terence (1996) "The Distinctiveness of Catholic Education," in McLaughlin, Terence H., O'Keefe, Joseph, and O'Keefe, Bernadette (eds.) *The Contemporary Catholic School: Context, Identity, and Diversity*, London: Falmer Press.

Palmer, Parker (1998) *The Courage to Teach*, San Francisco: Jossey-Bass.

Purpel, David E. (1989) *The Moral and Spiritual Crisis in Education*, New York: Bergin & Garvey.

5 The Law and Catholic School Policy

An Overview

Charles J. Russo

The United States Supreme Court's 1925 decision in *Pierce* v. *Society of Sisters* is the most important ruling in the history of Catholic, and other non-public, schools in American history. *Pierce* involved a successful challenge to Oregon's compulsory attendance law which required parents or guardians of "normal" children to send them "to a public school for the period of time a public school shall be held during the current year" (p. 530). In a suit filed by the Society of Sisters and the Hill Military Academy, the Court unanimously affirmed that Oregon's compulsory attendance law was unconstitutional because it "unreasonably interfere[d] with the liberty of parents and guardians to direct the upbringing and education of children under their control" (pp. 534–35).

Along with upholding the right of Catholic schools to operate, *Pierce* established a key principle in the relationship between non-public schools and the state. In *Pierce*, the Court acknowledged the power of the state "reasonably to regulate all schools, to inspect, supervise, and examine them, their teachers and pupils" (p. 534). A myriad of subsequent opinions by federal and state courts have interpreted *Pierce* to mean that while individual States, and the federal government, may regulate non-public schools, they may not do so to any extent greater than they impose on public institutions. In fact, if anything, Catholic, and other non-public, schools have significant freedom from most forms of governmental oversight.

The freedom that Catholic schools have from most forms of governmental regulation notwithstanding, administrators need to be mindful of the parameters of the legal system as it should help them to maintain effective, efficient, and safe learning environments. As such, this chapter is divided into four sections. The first part reviews the nature and structure of the American legal system. The next section examines the rights and duties of teachers and other personnel in Catholic schools. The third section looks at the rights of students (and their parents). The final section briefly reflects on two emerging legal issues that are likely to impact upon Catholic schools in the near future.

Sources of Law

In reviewing the sources of law that affect the daily operations of Catholic schools, it is important to recognize that understanding the legal system is not an end in itself. Rather, knowledge of the law comes into play as the most important factor in developing sound policies that contribute to the smooth, efficient, and safe operations of the schools.

Simply stated, the United States Constitution is the law of the land. As the primary source of American law, the Constitution provides the basic framework within which our entire legal system operates. To this end, all actions taken by the federal and state governments, including state constitutions (which are supreme within their jurisdictions as long as they do not contradict or limit rights protected under their federal counterpart), statutes, regulations, and common law are subject to the Constitution as interpreted by the Supreme Court.

As important as education is, it is not mentioned in the Constitution. Consequently, under the Tenth Amendment, which decrees that "[t]he powers not delegated to the United States by the Constitution, nor prohibited by it to the States, are reserved to the States respectively, or to the people," education is primarily the concern of individual states. It is important to note that the federal government can intervene in disputes, such as *Brown* v. *Board of Education* (1954), when the government deprives individuals to rights protected under the Constitution.

In *Brown*, the Supreme Court struck down state-sanctioned racial segregation on the ground that it violated the students' rights to equal protection under the Fourteenth Amendment.

The Constitution also protects Americans from arbitrary and capricious acts of the government. This is essential insofar as public schools are extensions of the government; the full weight of the Constitution protects their students and teachers. However, since Catholic schools are private entities, students and teachers generally do not have constitutional protections. The major exception is that the federal government can become involved when protected constitutional rights, such as the right of parents to direct the upbringing of their children, as in *Pierce*, are involved, or when rights are explicitly extended by statute such as Title I, which offers educational services for specifically identified children based on socio-economic need.

In addition to delineating the rights and responsibilities of Americans, the Constitution establishes the three co-equal branches of government that exist on both the federal and state level. The legislative, executive, and judicial branches of government, in turn, give rise to the other three sources of law.

The legislative branch makes the law. In other words, once a bill completes the legislative process, it is signed into law by a chief executive who has the authority to enforce the new statute. Keeping in mind that a statute is not unlike the frame of a house, the executive branch fleshes a law out by providing details in the form of regulations. For example, a typical compulsory attendance law requires that "[e]xcept as provided in this section, the parent of a child of compulsory school age shall cause such child to attend a school in the school district in which the child is entitled to attend school" (Ohio Revised Code, 3321.03 (1997)). Even in recognizing exceptions for parents who wish to send their children to attend Catholic schools, statutes are typically silent on such important matters as the content of the curriculum and the length of the school day. Consequently, these essential elements are addressed by regulations which are developed by personnel at administrative agencies who are well versed in their areas of expertise. Given their extensiveness, it is safe to say that the professional lives of educators, at least in public schools, are more directly influenced by regulations than by statutes.

The fourth and final source of law is judge-made or common law. Common law refers to judicial interpretations of the law that have evolved over time when dealing with issues that may have been overlooked in the legislative or regulatory process or that may not have been anticipated when the statute was enacted. In the landmark case of *Marbury* v. *Madison* (1803), the United States Supreme Court asserted the authority to review the constitutional validity of actions taken by the other branches and in so doing has the ability to establish precedent. Although there is an occasional tension between the three branches of government, the legislative and executive branches generally defer to judicial interpretations of their actions.

Precedent stands for the proposition that a majority ruling of the highest court in a given jurisdiction is binding on all lower courts within its jurisdiction. In other words, a ruling of the United States Supreme Court is binding throughout the nation while a decision of the Supreme Court of Ohio is binding only in Ohio. Persuasive precedent, a majority ruling from another jurisdiction, is actually not precedent at all. For example, a ruling of the Supreme Court of Ohio is only persuasive precedent in Indiana. In other words, as judges in Indiana seek to resolve a novel legal issue, they typically review precedent from other jurisdictions to determine whether it has been addressed elsewhere. However, a court is not bound to follow precedent from another jurisdiction.

Two forms of common law are especially important for Catholic schools: contracts and torts. Although a full discussion of these two vital areas of law is well beyond the scope of this chapter, a few words are in order.

Contracts are significant because unlike the public schools, where education, as a matter of right, is controlled by the state, most of the rights of teachers, students, and parents are created by entering into contracts. In order to be binding, a contract must consist of an offer and acceptance on mutually agreed terms, the parties must offer consideration (such as tuition in return for an education or salary in return for teaching), the parties must have the authority to enter into the agreement, the subject matter must be legal, and, depending upon its length and what it addresses, a contract may have to be in writing. Oral contracts are valid but, in the absence of a written agreement, the burden of proving their existence falls upon the party seeking its enforcement.

Torts are civil, as opposed to criminal, wrongs other than breaches of contracts. Intentional torts and negligence are the two most important types of torts that occur in the schools. Intentional torts include assault (fear of unwanted physical contact), battery (the actual contact), false imprisonment, and concerns over defamation (which may overlap with free speech). In order for a school (or its employees or volunteers) to be liable for negligence, or inadequate supervision, which is, by definition, not intentional, the party bringing suit must prove four related items. First, the party must show that a school had a duty which required it to take reasonable steps to foresee and prevent an injury from taking place. Second, the school must have breached, or failed to meet, its duty. Third, there must be an injury for which compensation can be awarded. Finally, the school must be the proximate, or actual, cause of the injury. However, even if a school appears to be at fault, it may escape liability if it applies a defense such as assumption of risk, contributory negligence, or charitable immunity.

In sum, other than applicable federal and state anti-discrimination laws that may have limited applicability, Catholic schools operate largely free of governmental regulation. Even so, personnel manuals and student policies would be wise to mirror practices that are followed in the public schools as they typically have been developed over time and are sensitive to safeguarding the rights of both the schools and their personnel.

Rights of Employees

Insofar as the rights of Catholic school personnel are largely grounded in contract, it is important to maintain sound employment policies that provide a detailed review of the rights of all parties. With that in mind, this section briefly reviews the salient features of key federal statutes dealing with employment-related matters.

Perhaps the most important federal law dealing with hiring is Title VII. This far-reaching statute, which applies regardless of whether an employer receives federal financial assistance, prohibits practices that discriminate in hiring, firing, or classifying workers based on race, color, religion, sex, or national origin (1998). At the same time, Title VII does permit religious employers to set bona fide occupational qualifications that include religion and also allows them to limit hiring in key areas to members of their faith.

Other important federal statutes that apply regardless of whether a school receives financial aid include the Equal Pay Act of 1964 (EPA) (1998), Age Discrimination in Employment Act (ADEA) (1998), and the Family and Medical Leave Act (FMLA) (1998). Subject to a number of exemptions including seniority and merit, the EPA requires employers to pay women and men at the same rate for the same job. The ADEA, which applies to workers who are 40 or older, prohibits employers from using age as the determining factor in hiring, firing, classifying, or paying employees. The FMLA, which is designed to protect workers who may be forced to choose between caring for their families or themselves and job security, requires employers to establish leave policies to cover such circumstances.

A second category of federal laws applies based on whether a school receives federal financial assistance. Perhaps the most important of these laws, and one which also applies to students, is Section 504 of the Rehabilitation Act of 1973 (1998). Section 504 declares that "[n]o otherwise qualified individual with a disability ... shall, solely by reason of her or his disability, be excluded from participation in, be denied the benefits of, or be subjected to discrimination under any program or activity receiving Federal financial assistance." Section 504 requires schools to provide reasonable accommodations to individuals with disabilities. Accommodations may involve modest adjustments such as permitting an employee to sit rather than stand while teaching or to allowing a student with a visual impairment to occupy a seat in the front, rather than the back, of a classroom. However, schools are not required to make accommodations that are unduly costly, create an excessive monitoring burden, expose others to excessive risk, or fundamentally alter the nature of a program. Similarly, Title I of the Americans with Disabilities Act (1998), which deals with employment, and Title III, which deals with public accommodations (including education), may also impact upon the operation of Catholic schools.

Other statutes that may cover Catholic schools that receive federal financial assistance include Titles VI (1998) and IX (1998). Title VI, which does not contain an exemption for religious practices, prohibits discrimination based on race, creed, or national origin. Title IX outlaws discrimination based on gender.

Unfortunately, the other end of the hiring spectrum involves discipline or dismissal of employees. The most common grounds for adverse employment actions in public schools are incompetence, neglect of duty, and conduct unbecoming an educator. While state laws do not apply to Catholic schools, administrators would at least be wise to borrow from the procedures they outline and thoroughly document their acts as this will make them more legally defensible. Further, to the extent that many Catholic schools do not confer tenure, the rights of teachers are governed by their contracts and policy manuals. Even where tenure is not available, the evolving common law doctrine of the expectation of continuing employment may apply. Under this legal construct, the longer that an employee has provided satisfactory service, the greater the evidence that a school will have to produce in dismissing an individual.

Tenure seems to be granted most frequently in Catholic high schools that are represented by some form of teachers' union or association. Yet, the

Church's stance with regard to unions is curious. Beginning with Pope Leo XIII's *Rerum Novarum* in 1891, the Church has consistently affirmed the right of all workers to organize and bargain collectively. Even so, the Church has consistently relied on the Supreme Court's ruling in *National Labor Relations Board* v. *Catholic Bishop of Chicago* (1979) which held that since church-related institutions are outside of the scope of the National Labor Relations Act, they are not required to bargain with their employees.

More recently, in 1986, the American Catholic Bishops, in their pastoral letter, *Economic Justice for All*, explicitly extended this right when they proclaimed that "[a]ll Church institutions must also fully recognize the rights of employees to organize and bargain collectively with the institution through whatever association or organization they freely choose" (p. 176). Despite the eloquent language of *Economic Justice for All*, leaders in Catholic schools have continued to oppose teachers who sought to assert their right to organize and bargain collectively. However, relying on state, rather than federal, law, the High Courts of New York and New Jersey, in *New York State Labor Relations Board* v. *Christ the King Regional High School* (1997) and *South Jersey Catholic School Teachers Organization* v. *St. Theresa of the Infant Jesus Church Elementary School* (1997), respectively, rejected arguments advanced by Catholic school officials that permitting teachers to organize and bargain collectively would have impacted negatively on their managerial authority and missions. While neither supporting nor opposing the right of teachers to organize, one can only wonder why Church leadership has been so reluctant to put its espoused teachings into practice.

Student Rights

Just as educators in Catholic schools are not protected by the full array of federal laws, the same is true of students. Perhaps the most significant issue affecting students is how administrators in Catholic schools apply discipline. As such, the heart of any discipline policy should focus on procedural due process and fairness. In other words, consistent with a wide variety of Supreme Court cases applicable to public schools, most notably *Goss* v. *Lopez* (1975), administrators should not only outline the range of unacceptable behaviors, but must also detail any penalties that might attach for violations.

Based on growing problems with substance abuse, violence, and weapons, administrators in Catholic schools would be wise to familiarize themselves with the two Supreme Court cases involving searches and/or seizures of students.

New Jersey v. *TLO* (1985) addressed searches of students in public schools. In *TLO* the Court held that the Fourth Amendment's prohibition against unreasonable searches and seizures applies to officials in public school. The Court devised a two-part test to evaluate the legality of a search. According to the Court, "[f]irst, one must consider 'whether the … action was justified at its inception;' second, one must determine whether the search as actually conducted 'was reasonably related in scope to the circumstances which justified the interference in the first place'" (p. 341).

The Court added that a search is ordinarily justified at its inception when school officials have reasonable grounds for suspecting that a search will uncover evidence that the student has violated or is violating either school rules or the law. A subjective measure that must be based on specific facts, reasonable suspicion is a significantly lower standard than the probable cause standard that is applied to the police. Insofar as school, also known as administrative, searches are designed to ensure safety where there are generally large numbers of young people and reasonably few adults present, educators need only articulable justification before searching.

In considering the totality of circumstances, school officials may have to depend on the reliability of witnesses in determining whether to search. Keeping in mind that there is a wide spectrum of possibilities, it is more likely that a principal would proceed in searching a student or his or her locker based on a tip from a teacher who is well regarded than a student who is frequently in trouble.

Turning to the scope of a search, the Court ruled that a search is permissible if its goals are reasonably related to its objectives and is not excessively intrusive in light of the age and sex of a student and the nature of an infraction. For example, school officials will have to adopt less intrusive methods when searching younger students and may act in a more invasive manner if they are looking for a gun rather than a child's missing lunch.

Ten years after *TLO*, the Supreme Court revisited the Fourth Amendment rights of students in examining the implications of mass and suspicionless searches. In *Vernonia School District 47J v. Acton* (1995), the Court addressed the question of individualized suspicion that it left unanswered in *TLO Acton* involved a seventh-grade student in Oregon who was suspended from interscholastic athletics because he and his parents refused to comply with a district policy requiring them to sign a consent form allowing him to be tested for drug use. The family challenged his suspension claiming that the district violated his Fourth Amendment rights and the state constitution since there was no reason to believe that he used drugs.

Responding to the perception of increased drug use on campus, the board created a policy that required all students trying out for interscholastic athletic teams to submit to a urinalysis drug test. As part of the policy, student athletes were tested individually at the beginning of each season and randomly throughout the year. The district also adopted elaborate procedures to safeguard the privacy rights of students. Students who tested positive were required to undergo a second examination. Those who tested positive on a second test were suspended from the team and sent for counseling. Subsequent violations led to mandatory suspensions from athletics.

The Supreme Court applied a three-part balancing test in affirming the constitutionality of the policy. First, it found that students have a lesser expectation of privacy than ordinary citizens. In fact, the Court reasoned that student athletes in particular have diminished privacy expectations because they are subject to physical examinations before becoming eligible to play and dress in open areas of locker rooms. Second, the Court indicated the urinalysis was minimally intrusive since it was coupled with safeguards that allowed little encroachment on students' privacy. Finally, given the perception of increased drug use, the Court maintained that there was a significant need for the policy. However, a caution is in order since *Acton* applies only to drug testing of student athletes. Consequently, it is unclear whether drug testing of any other groups would pass constitutional muster.

Even though these cases do not apply in Catholic schools, administrators would be wise to implement policies that are consistent with their rationales. Moreover, any policy dealing with searches of students, their lockers, and possessions should be clearly stated in the school's handbook as a means of avoiding problems when or if a search becomes necessary.

Emerging Issues

Two emerging, related, issues – vouchers and that status of programs conferring federal aid – may present Catholic schools with interesting alternatives. In *Jackson* v. *Benson* (1998), the Supreme Court of Wisconsin reversed an appellate tribunal and upheld the constitutionality of the Milwaukee Parental Choice Program (MPCP). The Court reasoned that the MPCP, which was designed to provide publicly funded vouchers that enable low-income parents to send their children to private schools, including those that are religiously affiliated, did not violate the Establishment Clause of the First Amendment to the United States Constitution or the establishment provisions of the Wisconsin constitution. Insofar as opponents of the MPCP are planning an appeal to the Supreme Court (Walsh 1998), it will be interesting to see how this issue plays itself out. While many Catholic school leaders are reluctant to accept public funds for fear of subjecting themselves to increased levels of state oversight, the status of vouchers is an issue that certainly bears watching.

The Supreme Court's 1997 ruling in *Agostini* v. *Felton* reversed its earlier ban against New York City's on-site delivery of services under Title I of the Elementary and Secondary Education Act (1996). Based on the majority's conclusion that there were sufficient safeguards in place to avoid constitutional difficulties with separation of church and state, the Court ruled that since Title I, a federally funded program that provides supplemental, remedial instruction to economically disadvantaged students on a neutral basis, the practice did not violate the Establishment Clause. Combined with its earlier ruling in *Zobrest* v. *Catalina Foothills School District* (1993), wherein the Court ruled that a deaf student in a Catholic high school was entitled to a sign language interpreter, the Court seems to be expanding the permissible parameters of aid to students regardless of where they attend classes. With such a precedent in place, it will be most interesting to observe how the Supreme Court rules if it addresses the constitutionality of the voucher program from Milwaukee.

Conclusion

By relying on a thorough knowledge of the law in developing sound policies, educational leaders in Catholic schools will help to ensure that their schools continue to operate effectively. Moreover, to the extent that these leaders are not constrained by the same regulatory processes as the public schools, then they can seek to follow the spirit, rather than the letter, of the law, in making sure that Catholic schools remain a gift to the nation.

References

Age Discrimination in Employment Act, 29 U.S.C. 623 (1998).

Agostini v. *Felton*, 117 S. Ct. (1997).

Americans with Disabilities Act, 42 U.S.C. §§§12201 *et seq*. (1998).

Brown v. *Board of Education of Topeka, Kansas*, 347 U.S. 483 (1954).

Elementary and Secondary Education Act, 20 U.S.C. §§&2701 *et seq*. (1996).

Equal Pay Act of 1964, 29 U.S.C. § 206 (d) (1998).

Family and Medical Leave Act, 29 U.S.C. §§ 2601 *et seq*. (1998).

Goss v. *Lopez*, 419 U.S. 565 (1975).

Jackson v. *Benson*, 578 N. W. 2d 602 (Wis. 1998).

Leo XIII, Pope. (1891; 1987 reprint) *Rerum Novarum, On the Condition of the Working Class,* Boston: Daughters of St. Paul.

Marbury v. *Madison*, 5 U.S. 137 (1803).

National Labor Relations Bd. v. *Catholic Bishop of Chicago*, 440 U.S. 490 (1979)

New Jersey v. *TLO*, 469 U.S. 325 (1985).

New York State Labor Relations Bd. v. *Christ the King Regional High School*, 660 N.Y.S. 2d 359 (N.Y. 1997).

Ohio Revised Code, §3321.03 (1997).

Pierce v. *Society of Sisters*, 268 U.S. 510 (1925).

Section 504 of the Rehabilitation Act of 1973, 29 U.S.C. §794 (1998).

South Jersey Catholic School Teachers Org. v. *St. Theresa of Infant of Jesus Church School*, 696 A.2d 709 (1997).

Title VI, 42 U.S.C. §2000d (1998).

Title VII, 42 U.S.C. §2000e-2(1) (1998).

Title IX, 42 U.S.C. §1681 *et seq*. (1998).

United States Constitution, Amendment X.

United States National Conference of Catholic Bishops (1986) *Economic Justice for All: Pastoral Letter on Catholic Social Teaching and the United States Economy*, Washington, D.C.

Vernonia School District 47 J v. *Acton*, 515 U.S. 646 (1995).

Walsh, M. (1998) "Court Allows Vouchers in Milwaukee: Religious Schools Included in Ruling," *Education Week*, June 17, pp. 1, 16.

Zobrest v. *Catalina Foothills School District*, 509 U.S. 312 (1993).

6 Key Issues for the Future of Catholic Schools

Michael J. Guerra

It is not especially difficult to build the case for a strong future for American Catholic schools. As the new millennium approaches, Catholic schools are reporting annual enrollment increases and new schools are opening. Researchers continue to praise Catholic schools for achieving strong academic results at relatively modest costs. Growing coalitions of business and community leaders see inner city Catholic schools as shining examples of the power of high expectations and personal interest to educate the children of the poor. If the recent past is prologue, Catholic schools can look to a future of continued growth and increasing moral and fiscal support.

The research literature that looks at Catholic school outcomes has been largely positive, and on occasion almost embarrassingly enthusiastic. The late James Coleman's first study comparing public and private schools[1] provoked great controversy, and for a time, it supported a small industry of contrarian scholarship.[2] Five years later, Coleman published a second book[3] which analyzed additional data from the same students included in the US Department of Education's longitudinal study, *High School and Beyond*. The second study confirmed all of the assertions about academic achievement described in the first study, and went on to postulate a unique source of social capital in the relationship between the Catholic school and the Catholic community in which it was rooted. Strangely, this time there were few scholarly or political counterattacks. When Coleman's first study was reported at a scholarly meeting, a sympathetic colleague observed that one could hear minds snapping shut. It is difficult to determine why reactions to the more sweeping conclusions of the later work were muted, although a case could be made that the political interests opposed to Coleman's findings decided that silence served their cause better than counterattack.

When Anthony Bryk and his colleagues published *Catholic Schools and the Common Good* in 1993, they broke new ground.[4] These scholars went beyond the claim that Catholic schools offered many students greater opportunities for personal academic success. They argued that the basic mission of the Catholic school, the gospel imperative to love and serve, was in fact more consistent with the appropriate role of schooling in civic society than a focus on personal advancement and economic gain, goals which they found dominating the agenda for public education.

Researchers were not alone in their discovery of Catholic schools as civic assets. Many dioceses asked for and received substantial support from corporate leaders for their annual funds, often linking their appeals explicitly to diocesan commitments to support inner city Catholic schools.[5] New initiatives by major donors in Indianapolis, New York, and Milwaukee established privately funded scholarship programs that were not Church sponsored.[6] Operating in much the same way that publicly funded voucher programs would function, these non-sectarian groups made scholarships available for poor families, most of whom found places for their children in Catholic schools. Currently, over thirty programs fund scholarships for more than 12,000 students throughout the United States, and commitments have been made that would increase the number of participating cities to more than fifty and the number of participating students to more than 50,000. While these donors are motivated by their commitment to help poor families educate their children in schools of their choice, there is good reason to believe that these privately funded voucher programs could not have succeeded were it not for the availability of Catholic schools, their willingness to work with children from disadvantaged backgrounds, and their record of academic achievement.

In spite of all the good news about Catholic schools, it seems prudent to revisit some past predictions before suggesting that projections based on the current status of Catholic schools will provide reliable indicators of their future. It was only ten years ago that Andrew Greeley described the glowing research record as a "golden twilight,"[7] the brilliant conclusion to an era of Catholic school accomplishments that had gone unacknowledged and certainly unappreciated, a condition that he predicted would lead inexorably to the closing of many more schools. That has not happened.

Optimists do not necessarily fare any better as prophets. The early 1960s saw a great expansion in the number of Catholic school buildings. Dioceses and parishes launched capital campaigns that were largely successful because the Catholic community believed in the importance of their schools and the capacity of religious communities to administer them and staff them. But 1965 turned out to be the high-water mark. Changes in attitudes, demographic shifts in population, reductions in the numbers of vocations, and the introduction of new ministries for religious put the optimists to flight and left the bully pulpit to those who saw the Catholic school as a symbol of what they called the cramped vision of an immigrant Church.[8] Advocates of Catholic schools rallied their forces for one great noble effort to obtain government support to finance schools whose budgets were being stretched by growing numbers of salaried lay teachers replacing religious who had worked for modest stipends. When the United States Supreme Court rejected the constitutionality of some state-level legislative successes,[9] many Catholic school advocates were brought to the brink of despair. In a valiant effort to remind the Catholic community of the importance of their schools, the American bishops offered a powerful statement of support for Catholic schools in 1972.[10] Some took heart from this strong episcopal endorsement of Catholic schools that were true to their mission of preaching the gospel message, building community, and encouraging a commitment to service. But the pessimists were more audible and more numerous. Some schools closed, many continued with reduced numbers of students, a few thrived.

And then a strange thing happened. As the last decade of the century began, the Catholic community seemed to rediscover its schools, and recover its pride and passion for their place in the Church. The bishops issued another statement in support of schools and expanded their commitment to work with parent organizations and others to promote school choice.[11] Catholic educators around the country came together in an unprecedented National Congress convened by the National Catholic Educational Association in 1991, and developed a shared vision of Catholic schools for the twenty-first century. Marketing became a respected professional activity for Catholic schools, and development became more than bingo and bake sales. And so, the past forty years have seen large and usually unpredicted shifts in the life of American Catholic schools (see Figure 6.1). While there was never a shortage of prophets, both the optimists and pessimists have had comparably bad records in predicting the future of Catholic schools.

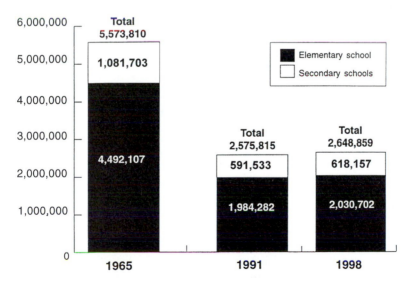

Figure 6.1   Catholic school enrollments, 1965–98

Sources: Bredeweg, F., *A Statistical Report on Catholic Elementary and Secondary Schools For the Years 1967–68 to 1969–70*, NCEA, 1970; Brigham, F., *United States Elementary and Secondary Schools, 1990–91*, NCEA, 1991; McDonald, D., *United States Elementary and Secondary Schools, 1997–98*, NCEA, 1998.

Michael J. Guerra

The Future of Catholic Schools

After scorning the work of earlier prophets, it takes more than a dollop of hubris to offer my own predictions about the future of Catholic schools. But hubris is at the heart of all temptation, and predicting the future of Catholic schools represents a particularly tempting apple. For now, I propose to limit myself to a description of the apple's possibilities; eventually I may take a small bite.

The Issues

I suggest the future of Catholic schools will be determined by the extent to which the schools and their supporters respond to challenges posed by three major issues. I propose to name each of these issues, to restate it in the form of one or two simple questions, and then to explore the complexity of the issue in some greater detail, without exhausting the issue or the reader.

Issue 1: Authenticity

How Will Catholic Schools Understand, Explain, and Support Their Unique Religious and Educational Mission?

This question is often described as the Catholic identity issue. Throughout their history, Catholic schools have been seen as instruments of the Church. The Holy See has consistently described Catholic schools as integral to the teaching ministry of the Church.[12] The American bishops repeatedly condition their strong support for Catholic schools on the schools' acknowledgement of and fidelity to their religious mission. On the surface, this seems to present no great challenge for Catholic schools. For Catholic educators, their religious mission and their educational mission are inextricably linked as aspects of a singular reality. The belief statements of the National Congress make this point:

The Catholic Identity of Catholic Schools

We believe that:

- The Catholic school is an integral part of the church's mission to proclaim the Gospel, build faith communities, celebrate through worship and serve others.
- The commitment to academic excellence, which fosters the intellectual development of faculty and students, is an integral part of the mission of the Catholic school.
- The Catholic school is an evangelizing, educational community.

- The spiritual formation of the entire school community is an essential dimension of the Catholic school's mission.
- The Catholic school is an experience of the church's belief, tradition and sacramental life.
- The Catholic school creates a supportive and challenging climate, which affirms the dignity of all persons within the school community.

To put our beliefs into practice, we make these commitments:

- We will guarantee opportunities for on-going spiritual formation for Catholic school faculties, staff and leadership.
- We will challenge our faculty, staff, students and families to witness to their belief in Jesus Christ.
- We will champion superior standards of academic excellence.
- We will commit ourselves to teach an integrated curriculum rooted in gospel values and Catholic teachings.
- We will welcome and support a diverse cultural and economic population as a hallmark of our Catholic identity.[13]

Rhetoric is not necessarily practice. As Catholic schools continue to examine their curricula, staffing, and co-curricular programs in light of their mission, they are subject to scrutiny from a number of different sources. Catholic schools live in two worlds. Understanding the claims of these two worlds, and offering appropriate responses to God and to Caesar, are unique and important tasks for Catholic school leaders.

As an integral part of the teaching mission of the Church, the schools are accountable to the Catholic community and its leaders. Some in the Catholic community measure the efficacy of the schools' religious mission solely in terms of the religious knowledge, attitudes, and practices of students and staff. While the measurement of these outcomes is essential, the shortage of content, assessment, and performance standards leaves Catholic schools open to criticism for any and all perceived imperfections. There is some research to support the claim that Catholic schools make a measurable difference in the adult lives of their graduates, but some critics are unwilling to accept this evidence of efficacy and impact.[14]

At the same time, Catholic schools are an integral part of a multifaceted American educational system in which all schools – public, private, and religious – serve a public purpose and are, as a consequence, subject in various ways to public scrutiny and public accountability. There are some libertarians and *independentistas* who argue for the complete separation of education and the state and the radical privatization of schooling, but they count few Catholic educators among their allies. On the contrary, the history of Catholic schooling in the Unites States suggests a preference on the part of

Catholic educational leaders for collaboration and integration within the larger American educational world, as long as Catholic identity is not threatened or diluted.

But our history has also been complicated by ambiguity and ambivalence about the place of religion and religious institutions in American life. We have gone through painful times during which explicitly anti-Catholic attitudes subjected our people and our schools to prejudice, ridicule, even violence. The great expansion of Catholic schools in the late nineteenth century was led by American bishops who decided, after prolonged debate, that the hostility of the larger society to Catholic values, inevitably reflected in the way in which public schools were educating Catholic children, meant the Church would have to build its own alternative system of schools. This debate was not easily resolved, and there were some, a minority, who believed accommodations should be negotiated.

For many years, Catholic schools were considered educationally suspect. With hindsight it is not at all clear that they were in fact educationally inferior, since they succeeded in facilitating the extraordinarily successful socio-economic development of several immigrant communities within a relatively short time. Nevertheless, the perception of second-class educational status was shared by many educators, including some in the Catholic leadership community who launched their own school improvement programs. Their efforts included many small but significant initiatives, and two giant steps: the Sister Formation movement, which provided women religious with opportunities to complete full educational and professional preparation programs; and the regional accreditation movement, which encouraged Catholic secondary schools to apply for membership in the appropriate regional associations. Catholic educators were determined to insure that Catholic schools would become full and respected partners in American education. Their teachers and their schools would meet the highest professional standards. Today the evidence suggests that they succeeded.

The age of blatant anti-Catholicism has passed, but fundamental questions are far from settled. What is the role of the religious school in a secular society? To what extent does the larger society support, resist, or ignore the choices some families make to send their children to a religious school? In 1925, the United States Supreme Court stopped the state of Oregon from insisting that all children go to public schools,[15] but in the current debate about publicly financed vouchers, opponents who claim a privileged status for public schools sometimes suggest that religious schools are divisive and un-American. Whether they are unfamiliar with or simply unwilling to acknowledge Bryk's research suggesting that Catholic schools are uniquely true to American democratic ideals, their position forces Catholic school leaders to confront a basic question: how do we participate as partners in the larger American educational enterprise, while bringing our own faith-inspired values to critique and challenge the secular order?

Assimilation can be a seductive and subtle threat to authenticity. Today the most powerful forces driving American educational reform are the school choice movement and the standards movement. While many Catholic educational leaders have been active in the school choice movement, few have played prominent roles in the standards movement, which has attracted an unusual mix of advocates and adversaries. Standards come in three inter-related categories: content, assessment, and performance. Since superficial arguments and occasional paranoia can be found among both supporters and opponents of standards-based reform, Catholic educators are chal-lenged to sort out the arguments thoughtfully in order to balance a variety of claims for institutional accountability from the Church and civic society.

Questions abound. Content standards for history: are they appropriately sensitive to inclusion of groups whose roles in our shared story have been underdeveloped, or are they models of political correctness that subvert traditional values and underscore flaws rather than heroism? Assessment standards for mathematics: should they incorporate the use of calculators and original problem solving, or should they stress mastery of basic skills? Performance standards: if criterion-referenced testing inevitably reflects judgments about what students *should* know and be able to do, whose judg-ments should set these standards? Can/should student performance standards be extended to include religious knowledge, religious values, reli-gious practices? In the interrelationship between norm-referenced and criterion-referenced assessments, how will we best account for develop-mental differences? How do we include students who are challenged in fair and helpful assessments? At what point do assessment programs make unreasonable claims on the time available for academic instruction and reli-gious formation?

Issue 2: Access and Affordability

Who Will Attend Catholic Schools?

At the National Congress on Catholic Schools for the Twenty-first Century, the late Archbishop James Lyke was asked to identify the people Catholic schools were expected to serve. His answer: "All Catholic families who want their children in Catholic school, and those of other faiths who understand what our schools are all about and who want them for their children."[16] Archbishop Lyke's response is both encouraging and challenging, because it is fundamentally inclusive. He underscores our schools' commitment to serve the Catholic community, but he describes a community whose minds, hearts, and doors are open. Evangelization as an invitation is meaningless if all the doors are closed. If schools are not available and affordable, the open invitation is at best a sign of good intentions, at worst a form of hypocrisy. Current data on enrollments, tuitions, and financial aid offer strong evidence that Catholic school leaders are committed to serving a diverse population (Figures 6.2 and 6.3).

But tuitions are increasing at rates that exceed inflation. Unless financial assistance increases at comparable rates, the socio-economic profile of many Catholic schools may shift upward. Privately funded scholarship programs have made Catholic schools available to the children of low-income families in a growing number of cities, and the prospects for publicly funded school choice initiatives in a growing number of states are promising. Nevertheless, Catholic schools will not be able to serve all the families who would choose them unless schools establish development and endowment programs that either reduce the percentage of their operating budgets supported by tuition or increase their capacity to provide financial aid to middle- as well as low-income families.

It will also be necessary to build new schools. In the last ten years over 170 new schools have been opened, most of them as the result of diocesan initiatives, some the product of parent initiatives with diocesan and parish encouragement. The capital costs for new school construction are daunting, especially for larger secondary school campuses, but the successes of recent years demonstrate that strong leadership can raise capital as well as spirits.

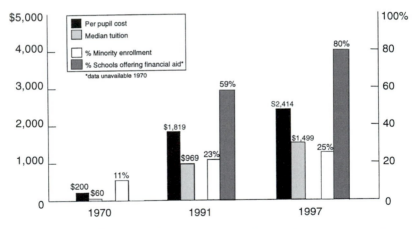

Figure 6.2   Per pupil costs, median tuition, minority enrollment, and financial aid in Catholic elementary schools

Sources: Bredeweg, F., *A Statistical Report on Catholic Elementary and Secondary Schools For the Years 1967–68 to 1969–70*, NCEA, 1970; Kealey, R., *United States Catholic Elementary Schools and Their Finances 1991*, NCEA, 1992; Brigham, F., *United States Elementary and Secondary Schools, 1990–91*, NCEA, 1991; Kealey, R., *Balance Sheet for Catholic Elementary Schools: 1997 Income and Expenses*, NCEA, 1998; McDonald, D., *United States Elementary and Secondary Schools, 1997–98*, NCEA, 1998.

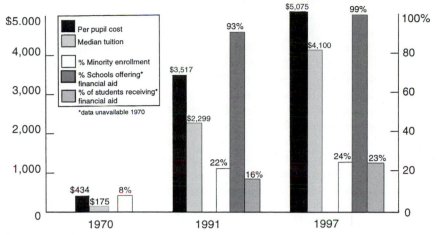

Figure 6.3: Per pupil costs, median tuition, minority enrollment, and financial aid in Catholic secondary schools

Sources: Bredeweg, F., *A Statistical Report on Catholic Elementary and Secondary Schools For the Years 1967–68 to 1969–70*, NCEA, 1970; Guerra, M. and Donahue, M., *Catholic High Schools and their Finances 1990*, NCEA, 1991; Brigham, F., *United States Elementary and Secondary Schools, 1989–90*, NCEA, 1990; Guerra, M., *CHS2000: A First Look*, NCEA, 1998.

Issue 3: Leadership

Who Will Lead Catholic Schools?

There seems little doubt that the quality of leadership will have a decisive influence on the future of Catholic schools. Andrew Greeley's pessimism in 1989 was based on his evaluation of Church leadership at the highest levels. One can argue that Greeley underestimated the leadership of the American bishops or that he overestimated the impact of the bishops' leadership on the future of a largely decentralized network of schools. I suggest there is some evidence to support both arguments.

The American bishops' 1990 statement[17] "In Support of Catholic Schools" was followed by important initiatives at local levels throughout the country. Strategic planning and development efforts were encouraged at school and diocesan levels. The National Conference of Catholic Bishops funded an office for Catholic school parent organizations within the United States Catholic Conference. Although there are certainly schools and regions struggling to sustain and support the current level of enrollments, there has been aggregate growth in American Catholic school enrollments each year for the past six years.

Diocesan leadership has been vitally important in providing vision and encouragement as well as support for capital expansion, but research invariably links the success of individual schools in both the public and private sectors to the school leader. Administrative titles and structures are changing, especially at the high school level. Presidents, principals, pastors, and boards share responsibility, credit, or blame for the current status and future prospects of Catholic schools. While all leaders are important, like the great theological virtues of faith, hope, and love, there is one, the administrative head of the school, that is pre-eminent.

If the current status of Catholic schools is, in general, strong, then it seems reasonable to assume that the current cadre of school leaders is strong. The questions – Who are they? Where did they come from? How were they trained? – are more than research exercises if they can inform our understanding of the next generation of school leaders. Who will they be? Where will they come from? How will they be trained? There is some helpful information about the incumbents,[18] and there are growing numbers of successful preparation programs sponsored by Catholic colleges.[19] But because Catholic schools are largely decentralized and funded at the institutional level, cross-institutional and regional efforts to identify and train school leaders are difficult to initiate and sustain, since they depend on collaborative planning and shared funding. A number of religious communities have had some success in building leadership development programs, and some dioceses have developed partnerships with Catholic colleges, often sharing costs in order to make professional formation programs accessible to teachers and other potential school leaders.

There are no comprehensive national programs in place, and *ad hoc* solutions may prove short sighted or short lived. Some Catholic educational leaders have begun to question the wisdom of hiring personnel with public school backgrounds to fill leadership roles. Nevertheless, a predominantly lay cohort has taken on leadership roles at the school, diocesan, and national levels with no discernible slippage in commitment to the religious mission of Catholic schools. Of course, as mutual funds must, by law, remind us, past performance is no assurance of future results.

Conclusion

Authenticity, access, and leadership – what are Catholic schools about, whom do they serve, and who will lead them? In my view, these are the most important issues for the future of Catholic schools. Admittedly, there are many other important questions. The faculty is the heart and soul of the school. Who will teach? How will they be prepared? How will they be supported professionally and spiritually, and how will they be compensated?

Governance is a critical issue. Who will be responsible for nurturing the vision of the school for the future? While many schools report that they have developed effective boards, there are still unresolved debates about the extent to which the trust for a Catholic institution can/should be broadly shared. The evidence suggests that strong schools tend to have strong boards, but schools with strong boards need to be particularly attentive to the way a full understanding of mission is passed on to succeeding generations of board members. Schools without boards need to consider how their mission can be institutionalized in ways that transcend the idiosyncratic gifts of the school administrator, pastor, or diocesan leader.

Curriculum, instruction, and technology trigger a set of critically important questions. What will be taught? How will technology be integrated into curriculum, instruction, and management? What impact will the opportunities that emerging technologies offer for non-campus learning programs have on the Catholic school's commitment to integrate experiences of community, service, and worship in its mission?

Without diminishing the importance of any of these questions, I remain convinced that the most fundamental issues for the future of Catholic schools are those that consider the authentic mission of the school, the community it serves, and the competence, commitment, and faith of its leadership. If these issues are resolved wisely, Catholic schools will thrive and multiply in the next millenium. Surely, some Catholic schools will prosper because they are beneficiaries of strong and creative local leadership. Whether these successful Catholic schools are exceptional or typical will depend on strong and creative leadership at the local, diocesan, and national levels.

Catholic leaders can give God and Caesar their due, as long as they are sensitive to the concerns of the Catholic community for authenticity and the educational community for excellence, and are willing to negotiate standards and assessments that respond to the legitimate requests for accountability from both sectors.

Catholic leaders will keep the doors of their schools open to all, if they continue to accept major responsibility for sophisticated development efforts, and if they are informed and passionate advocates for children and families in public policy debates about school choice.

New generations of strong and faithful leaders will create a bright future for Catholic schools, if the current generation has the wisdom and generosity to find them, encourage them, train them, and support them.

Catholic schools are not mutual funds. Although their past is no guarantee of their future, their historical resilience and their ability to confound both their adversaries and their doubting friends should remind us that the spirit animating this enterprise is more enduring than the market.

Notes

1 Coleman, J.S., Hoffer, T. and Kilgore, S., *Public and Private High Schools & High School Achievement*, New York: Basic Books, 1982.
2 For example, Alexander, K., and Pallas, A., "School Sector and Cognitive Performance," *Sociology of Education*, April 1985, pp. 115–27.

3 Coleman, J.S. and Hoffer, T., *Public and Private High Schools: The Impact of Communities*, New York: Basic Books, 1987.

4 Bryk, A.S., Lee, V.E., and Holland, P.B., *Catholic Schools and the Common Good*, Cambridge, MA: Harvard University Press, 1993.

5 For example, BLOCS (Business Leadership Organized for Catholic Schools), Archdiocese of Philadelphia; The Big Shoulders Fund, Archdiocese of Chicago.

6 Educational CHOICE Charitable Trust, Indianapolis, IN; Student Sponsorship Partnership, New York City, NY; Partners Advancing Values in Education, Milwaukee, WI.

7 Greeley, A., "Catholic Schools: A Golden Twilight?," in *America*, February 1989, pp. 106–108, 116–118.

8 Ryan, Mary Perkins, *Are Parochial Schools the Answer? Catholic Education in the Light of the Council*, New York: Holt Rinehart and Winston, 1964.

9 *Lemon* v. *Kurtzman* and *Rhode Island* v. *Di Censo*, 403 U.S. 602 (1971).

10 *To Teach As Jesus Did: A Pastoral Message on Catholic Education*, Washington, DC: National Conference of Catholic Bishops/United States Catholic Conference, 1972.

11 *In Support of Catholic Elementary and Secondary Schools*, Washington, DC: National Conference of Catholic Bishops/United States Catholic Conference, 1990.

12

> The complexity of the modern world makes it all the more necessary to increase awareness of the ecclesial identity of the Catholic school. It is from its Catholic identity that the school derives its original characteristics and its "structure" as a genuine instrument of the Church, a place of real and specific pastoral ministry. The Catholic school participates in the evangelizing mission of the Church and is the privileged environment in which Christian education is carried out.
>
> (From *The Catholic School on the Threshold of the Third Millennium*, Vatican City: Congregation for Catholic Education, 1998)

13 Guerra, Michael, Haney, Regina, and Kealey, Robert J., *Catholic Schools for the 21st Century: Executive Summary*, Washington, DC: National Catholic Educational Association, 1992, pp. 17–18.

14 Greeley, A. et al., *Young Catholics in the United States and Canada*, Los Angeles: Sadlier, 1981; Guerra, M. et al., *Heart of the Matter*, Washington, DC: National Catholic Educational Association, 1990.

15 *Pierce* v. *Society of the Sisters of the Holy Names of Jesus and Mary*, 268 U.S. 510 (1925).

16 Unpublished transcript of proceedings: *National Congress of Catholic Schools for the 21st Century*, Washington, DC: National Catholic Educational Association: 1991.

17 *In Support of Catholic Elementary and Secondary Schools*, Washington, DC: National Conference of Catholic Bishops/United States Catholic Conference, 1990.

18 Harkins, William, *Introducing the Catholic Elementary School Principal*, Washington, DC: National Catholic Educational Association, 1993.

19 Directory of the Association of Catholic Leadership Programs. See also *CACE/SPC Directory*, Washington, DC: National Catholic Educational Association, Department of Chief Administrators of Catholic Education, 1997, p. 65.

Part II
Teacher Preparation and Development

7 Staff Development in the Catholic School

The Caring Response of a Community

Louise Moore

The Catholic school is unique because it provides a religious community within a learning community. As learning communities, Catholic schools work to maintain high academic standards and practices. Appropriate programs and methods support the academic learning of students. At the same time, the life of Jesus Christ becomes the model for all who participate in the Catholic school community. Students, teachers, and parents are called to follow Jesus. As followers, they are asked to love others as Jesus did. This call to follow forms the basis for the Catholic school goal to respect the dignity of every human being. Catholic schools integrate faith, life, and culture into an effective educational endeavor (Crave 1974; McCormick 1985; McDermott 1986).

What does staff development mean for Catholic schools? In Catholic schools we care for people because of their intrinsic value. This, then, is the starting point or fundamental assumption which underlies all staff development efforts in the Catholic school. The purpose of this chapter is to present current thinking in the field of staff development, address unique characteristics of staff development in Catholic schools, and discuss practical ways to implement staff development in Catholic schools. Staff development in Catholic schools is the caring response of a caring community.

Staff Development Theory

Staff development is a process designed to foster personal and professional growth of individuals within a respectful, supportive, positive, and organized climate. The ultimate aim of staff development is better learning for students while at the same time encouraging continuous, responsible self-renewal for educators and schools (Joyce and Showers 1988). This definition of staff development embraces many of the beliefs and values which are widely recognized as distinguishing qualities of Catholic schools. Essential attributes of the Catholic school include: a positive anthropology which assumes a basic goodness of its members, a sense of sacramentality or worship, a spirit of inquiry, a strong sense of community which fosters an openness to people and ideas, Christian tradition, and a belief that revelation and reason are congruent partners in the education of the total person (Convey 1992). In addition, research indicates that when these organizational and environmental factors are present in any school, public or Catholic, measurable differences in outcomes occur. In schools that are organized as functional communities, high expectations of students result in high student achievement; service to others flows naturally from beliefs about being members of a community; high levels of collegiality and collaboration are observed; a common sense of vision and mission is shared by members; and appreciation for the unique gifts and talents of individuals leads to the celebration of the dignity of each person in the community (Bryk et al. 1993; Convey 1992).

Why is staff development, which is so widely recognized as critical to school improvement, so challenging an undertaking? Staff development addresses the culture of the school. School culture involves a complex system of attitudes, relationships, and behaviors among many individuals. In order for the culture of a school to support growth and self-renewal, it must exist in an environment that makes people intrinsically want to be there. The culture of the Catholic school is unique because Christ is at the center of all belief and activity. In our struggle to become more like Christ, Catholic school educators must constantly strive to grow both personally and professionally in ways that are consistent with the teachings of Jesus (*To Teach As Jesus Did*, 1972).

Even in schools where the goals and beliefs are explicit, important questions must be addressed for effective staff development to occur. These questions are complex but critical to the heart of the business of developing human resources. Unanswered, these questions will serve as serious impediments to the growth of individuals and the school. What is really important to teachers in Catholic schools? What inspires them? What motivates them? What discourages them from readily embracing staff development efforts? All teachers want to give students the best they can. The moment when student and teacher "meet" can be a powerful, rewarding experience for both student and teacher. Researchers have identified, however, several characteristics of the school culture which can undermine positive growth in the school environment. It is important to understand these factors if a sound program of staff development is to be developed.

The sociologist Dan Lortie (1975), in his landmark study of teachers in public schools in Florida, asked teachers what it was that attracted them to teaching. The themes which dominated their responses included serving others and working with people. Although teachers chose interpersonal themes as strong reasons for entering teaching, they soon found the reality of teaching to be a largely private ordeal which reinforces individualism and isolation. Teachers expressed high degrees of teacher uncertainty and described a weak and poorly defined technical culture. Lortie concluded that teachers never did gain control of any area of practice. However, the challenge for teachers in Catholic schools is to continue to maintain our motivation of serving others and working with people.

Other researchers echo the belief that the social organization and culture of the school environment often work against effective staff development. The effect of the "classroom press" is one with which many teachers can identify. Exerting a daily influence on teachers, the classroom press draws focus on day-to-day efforts, isolates teachers from other adults, exhausts energy, and limits opportunity for sustained reflection (Huberman 1993). Schools have been identified as loosely coupled organizations (Pajak 1989). Communication within schools is limited because of the way in which schools are organized and administered. Teachers have little opportunity to talk with colleagues about teaching. This lack of opportunity for communication contributes to isolation and individualism. Again, these realities of the life of the teacher are challenges to those in Catholic schools who value just the opposite qualities. We count community and communication as central to our existence. Therefore, it is imperative that Catholic school leaders work tirelessly to promote and preserve the qualities of community and communication in our schools.

Successful staff development must address the current social environment in schools and work to move school cultures toward a new way of thinking and behaving. New attitudes must be created before staff development can truly succeed. Rather than basing activity in schools on "doing things right," current educational thinkers challenge teachers and administrators to concentrate on "doing the right thing." For many years, teachers have been expected to comply with rules and regulations in schools. Teachers and all educational leaders are now being called, both individually and collectively, to base teaching practice on sound moral and educational principles. Schools are encouraged to become learning communities in which all members share in the development of goals and can work each day in a climate of trust and respect. (Fullan 1993; O'Toole 1995; Rosenholtz 1991; Rost 1993; Sergiovanni 1992). In the context of a caring community, teachers can be supported in their efforts to work collaboratively and can create a climate in which all members are empowered to grow both personally and professionally. This research reaffirms what we in Catholic schools believe to be part of our school culture and supports our core beliefs.

Sound, well-planned staff development programs can assist teachers by providing increased skills and knowledge, as well as increased opportunities for collegiality and communication. It is important to view staff development as a complex ongoing process, rather than merely a series of isolated events. Staff development efforts must consider the long-term growth of individuals and the gradual transformation of the school culture itself. Staff development efforts must care for the individual teachers in the immediate sense, and ultimately for the well-being of each and every student in the school.

As with any process of change, staff development efforts will flow through a series of stages (Rogers 1995). The initial stages of change usually include fear and resistance. Individuals resist change and the organization of schools can work against successful change. In the social context of a committed, caring environment, however, individuals can more easily adopt new attitudes and practices. The staff development process is one of human resource development. As such, each individual will take on personal responsibility for his or her own personal and professional growth. Teachers must be willing to conquer their individual fears of change and reluctance to part with some current practices in the name of greater personal and school-wide growth. If the well-being of the students remains the ultimate goal of staff development, teachers will rise to this challenge.

The Catholic school, with its strong sense of community and commitment, is well positioned for staff development efforts. Rooted in the belief that each individual is a valuable member of the school community, it is natural that the development of each individual's full potential is of deep concern to all members. This moral purpose of education transcends individual activities, and reaches for the greater goal of making a difference in the lives of all (Fullan 1993). Although strong traditions may sometimes seem to discourage change and more open communication in schools, they should not be viewed as obstacles. Instead, the strong traditions of Catholic schools should be seen as foundations or supports for new ideas and attitudes.

Unique Characteristics of Staff Development in Catholic Schools

Staff development in Catholic schools requires a unique dimension in addition to those of personal and professional growth. In the Catholic school, an institution whose mission is to be a faith community which integrates religious instruction, value formation, and faith development into the lives of its students (Convey 1992), teachers must also attend to their own faith formation. Faith formation thus calls for a third area for staff development. If teachers intend to influence the lives of their students in the area of faith, it is important for teachers themselves to be models of Christian thought and action.

In addition to being an academic community, the Catholic school represents a faith community. All members of the Catholic school community share a belief that Christ is central to their purpose. The prime responsibility for creating these unique Christian school climates rests with the teachers, as individuals, and as a community. The ecclesial declaration *Gravissimum educationis* encourages all those involved in Catholic school education to continue their work, even in the face of challenges. The work of the Catholic school teacher is viewed by the Church as a response to God's call. More than an occupation, teaching in a Catholic school is a vocation. It is a special ministry to God's children. How, then, can Catholic schools support and encourage the important spiritual work of their teachers?

For many years, priests and religious men and women found their spiritual formation through the religious communities that ran Catholic schools. Living daily in a spirit of community, these religious men and women generously shared their lives and wisdom with the children who were entrusted to their care. Having dedicated their lives to the Catholic Church in a very visible way, these courageous men and women withstood many hardships as they forged ahead to remain faithful to preserving Christ's presence in every aspect of the Catholic school experience.

A strong sense of community remains a distinguishing characteristic of Catholic schools. The Declaration on Christian Education, *Gravissimum educationis*, declares that what makes the Catholic school distinctive is its religious dimension which is found in its educational climate, the personal development of each student, the relationship established between culture and the gospel, and the illumination of all knowledge with the light of faith (Flannery 1984). The climate in a Catholic school is based on the dignity of each individual and that individual's relationships with others in the community and with Christ. All academic learning is set in the context of these key relationships among members of the school community. Placing learning in a values and relational context enhances intellectual efforts for students and teachers. The goals of Catholic schools reach beyond purely academic learning to the more enduring end of ultimate salvation based on a life which centers on Christ (Nelson 1988). Catholic school communities help students become aware that a relationship exists between faith and human culture.

Understanding the distinctive qualities of the Catholic school assists teachers and other school leaders in developing staff development processes, which support the spiritual purposes of the Catholic school. In addition to a strong sense of community, Catholic schools are recognized for their strong historical sense, which is very much a part of the school culture. Awareness of all who have preceded them gives students and teachers today a rich historical context upon which to understand their own places in the educational process of Catholic schools (Heft 1991) and in society as a whole. They are part of something larger and stronger than the present reality.

Ritual and symbol play an important part in the Catholic Church. This is also the case in Catholic schools where this rich heritage of ritual and symbolism can be extended to the areas of art and drama (Heft 1991). Ritual and symbol, along with the sense of community in a Catholic school, work to produce a sort of social and cultural fabric which provides a very powerful, yet often difficult to measure, quality of the Catholic school (Bryk et al. 1984; Charron 1980; Mutschler 1974).

The importance of service is another distinguishing characteristic of

Catholic schools. This call to service follows naturally from the philosophy and goals of the school. Service is the tangible outreach of the development of the Christian spirit. It is Christ at work in the world.

The overarching religious atmosphere in the Catholic school is a product of the school climate and the religious ethos. The religious development of teachers, then, should be a primary concern of Catholic educators. It is critical that teachers in Catholic schools perceive themselves as ministers of the Church. The content of preparation and continued spiritual formation of Catholic school teachers is necessary to maintaining the ministerial effectiveness of Catholic school faculties and staffs.

During the past three decades, the number of religious in Catholic schools has decreased markedly. The religious formation of teachers, which was once taken for granted since virtually all teachers in Catholic schools were men and women who lived in religious communities, has become a topic which Catholic educators must seek to better understand. How will Catholic school teachers now and in the future develop their own faith both individually and as a community within a school?

Catholic school leaders must take a hard look at this very important issue facing Catholic schools today. How will we preserve and continue to transmit the critical faith dimension of our Catholic schools? What programs, experiences, and models can we provide for teachers and administrators that will support their own faith journey? There are undoubtedly many answers to this very complex question. One thing which is certain, however, is that the question must be asked now. Catholic school teachers respond to their own faith-calling by choosing to work in Catholic schools. They acknowledge publicly their belief in the value of a Christ-guided school community. It is the responsibility of those teachers and their administrators to insist upon and contribute to those elements which will strengthen their own commitment to faith and to the total Catholic school community.

All staff development efforts in the Catholic school must integrate the essential element of spiritual formation. This spiritual dimension of teacher growth is crucial to the overall development of teachers in Catholic schools and every effort must be made to integrate spiritual formation into any and all staff development programs.

Practical Ways to Implement Staff Development in Catholic Schools

Reflecting on my many years as a Catholic school teacher and principal, I see my own journey in staff development as one marked by stages and signposts which reflect my own growth as a person, as a teacher, and as a follower of Christ. My progress was not always swift nor was it easy. It has been, however, valuable because it has deepened my commitment to a ministry in Catholic schools and to the children we serve. And, having struggled with my own personal and professional development as a Catholic school teacher, it has become very important to me to help others become good teachers in a faith community.

By sharing some of my own experiences as a Catholic school teacher for eighteen years and a principal of a Catholic school for seven years, I hope to illustrate for you that staff development is a very personal experience for the members of any individual school. It is not something that can be mass produced or easily transplanted from one environment to another. Effective staff development efforts must take the form of a response to the individual school community. Although certain principles of effective staff development can provide direction for planners, the design for each school must reflect the individuals who work together there each day and must be unique to that school. In the Catholic school, any staff development efforts must embrace the spiritual dimension of its members.

Some of the staff development activities that the teachers and I have undertaken over the past several years have been successful while others have had little effect. Initial efforts at staff development were the most challenging. In the first few years, we all had fears and resistance to overcome. Our school culture was typical of that found in many other Catholic schools. Teachers felt a sense of isolation and uncertainty which marked much of our daily activity. Little time was available for teachers to talk about teaching and learning. It is not surprising, then, that my initial efforts at staff development were met with no interest by my colleagues. While still active as a classroom teacher, I had become excited about high-quality research articles through my own participation in teacher education and educational administration classes as well as through work with a professor from a local Catholic university. I wanted to share this valuable information with my colleagues. The absence of reactions of the teachers caused me to face the realization that these articles were not of interest to them. After much reflection, I came to understand that I had to seek out the teachers' own needs and interests.

One of the other attempts at staff development in my early years as a principal included the writing of in-house grants. Each teacher was asked to submit a one-page grant request for some activity or project that he or she would like to try in the classroom. The grants were developed by individual teachers in consultation with doctoral education students from a local Catholic university. A panel of faculty representatives then reviewed proposals and three grants were provided monetary awards. In addition, all teachers who submitted a grant were compensated for their participation. This activity was repeated for two years. It, too, was a positive step in encouraging teachers to take charge of their own learning and professional growth. Still, this was an activity imposed upon and required of teachers rather than one which originated from a response to their own interests and needs.

The real challenge for us was to develop shared ownership of faculty professional development activities. How could teachers themselves grow to recognize and trust their own ideas and needs? Over time and with the help of an outside facilitator, we tried to ask the teachers what it was that they wanted to do. Initially, this was a difficult question to address. Teachers were used to being told what to do and how to do it. They were not used to expressing their own learning and growth needs. After many efforts and much discussion, the teachers and I concluded that we needed to talk more about teaching with one another. We eventually realized that we could trust our own experiences as teachers as an important source of ideas and questions for our professional development activities. Through this long and tedious process, we became not only a learning community, but also a Christian community.

As we began to listen to one another and teachers were encouraged to share freely their own ideas, hopes, and fears, we began to identify shared goals and activities that would assist us in reaching those goals. It is important to mention that the spiritual goals of teachers in Catholic schools must be addressed both in the spiritual formation sense and in application of the curriculum. One particularly valuable activity for me was a series of individual interviews with teachers, asking them why they initially chose to teach in a Catholic school and why they had decided to remain in Catholic schools. The teachers spoke of their deep commitment to their faith and their feeling of being called to pass on that rich Catholic tradition to others. They truly viewed their teaching role in the Catholic school as a ministry. That activity provided for me a rich new insight into the depth of commitment of Catholic school teachers and it reminded me of the important reasons that any staff development must necessarily include a faith dimension.

As we deepened our commitment to staff development, we realized that our faculty meetings needed a new focus. Teachers began to take turns preparing and leading the gathering prayer for our faculty meetings. We began to read and discuss spiritual books as a staff. For example, each teacher was given his or her own copy of Henri Nouwen's *Reaching Out* and asked to read and reflect upon one chapter prior to the faculty meeting. At the meeting, the book discussion became the first order of business. Other times, we selected a book which focused on teaching techniques such as *Inspiring Active Learning*, or asked faculty members to give short presentations to the faculty on areas which interested them and in which they might have specific knowledge. Hearing about current research on teacher isolation or student retention from peers made the introduction of research much more personal and credible for teachers. By beginning our faculty meetings by tending to our own spiritual and professional growth, we placed a new priority on our time spent together as a faculty. Our own development as persons and as teachers was elevated to a new position of importance as witnessed in our professional conduct.

As we began to grow closer as a faith community, we began to gather occasionally for informal prayer. This tended to be a spontaneous gesture, often in response to a specific need or request for prayers from a member of the school or parish community. Although completely voluntary, these spontaneous prayer sessions have continued to be very popular and well attended by faculty and staff alike. We may only spend a few moments together, but we all place great value on our precious moments of shared prayer.

Religious retreat and in-service days are another way in which we like to come together as a faculty. Recently, such days have included a retreat day in a beautiful wooded setting in which we learned and prayed about the spiritual aspects of outdoor education. This provided us all with an experience which meshed our important religious and spiritual selves with the science curriculum. On another occasion, we were guided by a facilitator in a day-long reflection of the ministry of teaching.

The teachers and I have included a mentoring program for new teachers in our program over the past few years. This mentoring program has been successful in several ways. In addition to providing support for beginning teachers, the mentoring program acknowledges and affirms the value of the experienced teacher. Both mentor and mentee find the mentoring program expands their ideas about teaching and helps build a collegial atmosphere in the school. Teachers are talking about teaching with each other!

Another form of staff development which we have utilized and enjoyed as a faculty is peer observation. Through the peer observation program, volunteer teachers attend several sessions in which they learn various strategies which can be used when conducting formative evaluations of teachers. Each teacher then pairs with another teacher and they take turns observing one another's teaching. Teachers feel comfortable with another teacher in the classroom and respect one another's opinions since, as colleagues, they have a high degree of trust for each other. Following the observations, teachers engage in very lively discussions about teaching and learning and acknowledge that they learn a great deal from one another. Peer observation opportunities add to the knowledge base of teachers and provide increased opportunities for collaboration among teachers. Teachers work together, which reduces teacher isolation and uncertainty and contributes to both community and communication.

Pre-service teachers from a nearby Catholic university work with faculty and provide many ideas and opportunities for talking about teaching. In addition, the campus supervisors often meet with classroom teachers and provide support and encouragement relating to the many challenges involved in teaching.

Offering graduate courses in conjunction with a local Catholic university for teachers at the school site has met with success at our school. One semester teachers came together regularly, for example, for a child study course. This two-hour graduate course was conducted under the supervision of a university professor and was facilitated by a member of the elementary school faculty who had been trained in the process. Again, teachers enjoyed the formal opportunity to come together to learn new skills which would aid them in more effectively discussing young learners.

Another opportunity for graduate credit was a two-day workshop on formative teacher evaluation techniques. This workshop was part of the Professional Development School activities conducted with a nearby Catholic university. In this case, a professor, who had already met with teachers on an informal basis, trained them in teacher assessment techniques. The entire faculty participated in this activity which was held at the end of the school year. The enthusiasm of the teachers was contagious, as we, once again, enjoyed learning more about effective teaching strategies.

It is important to remember that, much like the parable of the sower and the seed (Mark 4: 1–20, *The New American Bible*), staff development efforts will have varying effects on the growth of individual teachers. In that parable, Jesus tells about the farmer who went out sowing. Some of what he sowed landed on the road, where the birds came along and ate it. Some of the seed landed on rocky ground, where it had little soil; it sprouted immediately because the soil had no depth. Then, when the sun rose, it scorched the seedling, and it began to wither because of lack of roots. Some seed landed among thorns, which grew up and choked it off, so it did not grow. Finally, some seed landed on good soil, where it took root and yielded a bountiful crop. Depending upon levels of teacher readiness and willingness to take on a new perspective toward teaching and learning, activities will have different results for different teachers. Drawing a parallel with the parable of the sower and the seed, we should be aware that even the most effective programs of staff development will meet with different results depending upon the culture of the school and the developmental stages of teachers. Like the seed that fell on the road, some staff development efforts will fail to take root because teachers are preoccupied with other matters which seem more urgent. In other cases, like the seed that fell on rocky ground, staff development activities will create a big initial splash with some individuals but will not develop and take root and will eventually be replaced by other activities. They will whither because of lack of roots – the school culture has not provided a strong community and communication which could serve as good soil for the development of teachers. Being rootless, these efforts have limited effect and are not shared deeply by teachers. Some staff development efforts will fall upon thorns. In that case, teachers will see themselves as overwhelmed and overburdened, choked by the seemingly impossible demands of time and energy required for growth and change.

In a school culture which has worked to maintain a strong sense of community and communication, staff development efforts will take root and flourish, just as the seed that fell on good soil. In such a rich school culture, teachers will be open to the exciting possibilities of growth and willing to endure the various stages and challenges which growth requires. The harvest for those teachers and their students will be bountiful.

Some teachers will welcome a new challenge, while others will prefer to wait and watch at first. Once the momentum has begun, however, most teachers will be inspired and encouraged by the enthusiasm of those around them. Staff development can be most exciting and rewarding. The Catholic school leader and teachers must keep in mind, however, that great patience and commitment to developing a Christian community are essential. In the Catholic school, staff development efforts must address all three of the critical dimensions which inform teacher performance and motivation: professional, personal, and spiritual. In this way, Catholic schools will be able to engage in professional development which will be congruent with and inspired by their beliefs about Christianity and about teaching. Such manner of professional development, then, will truly be the caring response of a caring community.

References

Bryk, A., Holland, P., Lee, V., and Carriedo, R. (1984) *Effective Catholic schools: an exploration* (Executive Summary), Washington, DC: National Center for Research in Total Catholic Education.

Bryk, A., Lee, V., and Holland, P. (1993) *Catholic schools and the common good*, Cambridge, MA: Harvard University Press.

Charron, R. (1980) *Parental perceptions of the unique qualities of Catholic schools: an exploratory study*, Doctoral Dissertation, Michigan State University.

Convey, J. (1992) *Catholic schools make a difference*, Washington, DC: National Catholic Educational Association.

Crave, M. (1974) *The leadership structure of a Catholic community and the purposes of Catholic schools*, Doctoral Dissertation, Marquette University.

Flannery, A. (ed.) (1984) *Vatican Council II: the conciliar and post conciliar documents*, Northport, NY: Costello.

Fullan, M. (1993) *Change forces*, Bristol, PA: Falmer Press.

Groome, T. (1998) *Educating for life*, Allen, TX: Thomas More.

Heft, J. (1991) *Catholic identity and the future of Catholic schools. Catholic schools for the twenty-first century*, Washington, DC: National Catholic Educational Association, pp. 5–20.

Huberman, M. (1993) *The lives of teachers*, trans. J. Neufield, New York: Teachers College Press (originally published 1989).

Joyce, B. R. and Showers, B. (1988) *Student achievement through staff development*, New York: Longman.

Lortie, D. (1975) *Schoolteacher: a sociological study*, Chicago: University of Chicago Press.

McCormick, P. (1985) *A comparison of the school's Catholic identity, the principal's instructional leadership, and the overall school effectiveness in Catholic elementary schools administered by members of religious institutes with those schools administered by lay principals*, Doctoral Dissertation, University of Cincinnati.

McDermott, E. (1986) *Distinctive qualities of the Catholic school*, Washington, DC: National Catholic Educational Association.

Mutschler, M. (1974) *Effective Catholic schooling: an organizational analysis*, Doctoral Dissertation, Fordham University.

Nelson, J. (1988) "Academic development or faith formation?," *Momentum* 19(4): 41–44.

O'Toole, J. (1995) *Leading change*, San Francisco: Jossey-Bass.

Pajak, E. (1989) *The central office supervisor of curriculum and instruction: setting the stage for success*, Boston: Allyn and Bacon.

Rogers, E. (1995) *Diffusion of innovations*, New York: Free Press.

Rosenholtz, S. (1991) *Teachers workplace: the social organization of schools*, New York: Teachers College Press.

Rost, J. (1993) *Leadership for the twenty-first century*, Westport, CT: Praeger.

Senge, P. (1990) *The fifth dimension: the art and practice of the learning organization*, New York: Doubleday.

Sergiovanni, T. (1992) *Moral leadership: getting to the heart of school reform*, San Francisco: Jossey-Bass.

8   The Challenge of Teaching Religion in Catholic Schools

William J. Raddell

Teaching religion is a unique enterprise. It is an academic subject, yet the transmission of knowledge alone fails to achieve the goal of educating a student in the Catholic faith. It is difficult to gauge whether a student has successfully learned the lessons taught in the religion classroom. The full effect of the religious educator's efforts may not become apparent for decades or even a lifetime. Religion teachers not only transmit a body of knowledge but give witness to their most deeply held values and convictions. A student who fails to achieve academically may nevertheless have a profound spirituality and a close, personal relationship with Jesus. The distinctive nature of religious education makes it one of the most difficult subjects to teach. Many challenges confront those who teach religion in Catholic schools.

Ideally, students in Catholic schools would already have developed a relationship with God and the task of the religion teacher would be to help them deepen that relationship and to grow in understanding of the Catholic faith tradition. The reality, however, is that students come from a variety of backgrounds and with vastly differing degrees of knowledge and experience. Parents send their children to Catholic schools for many different reasons. Their purpose may be a desire for greater discipline, a solid academic program, for sports, to avoid a particular public school system, to maintain a family tradition, or numerous other motives. Religious education may only be one, if any of the motives, and not necessarily the predominant one.

For this reason religious education programs must continually provide a balance between evangelization and catechesis in their approach. There must be an ongoing call to conversion. There is no assurance that a response will take place and no strategy that can guarantee results. Religion teachers may feel they are building on sand. Without a relationship with God religious ritual makes little sense and may appear to students to be simply going through the motions. The task of evangelization is often made more difficult when there are a lack of models of meaningful faith in their experience. Parents who fail to set an example through worship, participation in the sacramental life of the Church, or applying the teachings of Jesus to their lives may make it difficult to believe that the spiritual life is important.

Likewise, when students do not have models of a dynamic faith community in their parishes or congregations, or, even if there is, find no place to fit in or to play an active part in their churches, they may find the encouragement to become involved in the life of the Church lacking in credibility. If students' experiences with the institutional Church have been negative, the level of difficulty increases. Many students fail to differentiate between relationship with God and relationship with the Church and end up rejecting both. Distinguishing between the two and helping students to address each of these significant but separate issues is a necessary step in the evangelization process and prerequisite for effective catechesis.

Another area which requires attention is in developing a program which balances information and formation. There is an obvious need for religious and biblical literacy among young people today. During the era when the Baltimore Catechism was the basis for religious education students had a high degree of religious literacy, but little emphasis was given to integrating this instructional foundation into the students' lived experience. During the 1970s and early 1980s the pendulum swung in reaction from a focus on the intellectual dimension to emphasize personal development and faith experience. Today the goal is to build a program which addresses not only the intellect but the heart, soul, and will as well.

Beyond the difficulties presented by the multifaceted nature of the subject, religion teachers must deal with the issues their students bring to the classroom with them. The research of theorists like Lawrence Kohlberg, Carol Gilligan, Erik Erikson, John Westerhoff, James Fowler, and others gives insight into the developmental tasks students are going through and the implications of those stages in religious instruction. Erikson helps the educator to understand the process of identity formation wherein the young adult begins to form values and develop his or her own attitudes and opinions. This may involve rejection of those values with which the student was raised, trying on alternative choices, and seeking greater independence in thought and action, all of which may surface in the religion classroom as the educator seeks to teach about Christian values and the Christian lifestyle. This may be particularly difficult when dealing with issues of authority whether they be biblical or magisterial. Westerhoff and Fowler indicate that questioning is normal and healthy as students go through the phase of Searching Faith (Westerhoff)/Individuative–Projective Faith (Fowler) which begins in the teen years and continues into early adulthood. Doubt, questioning, struggling with new concepts, and rejection of traditional assumptions are typical as the student searches for understanding, truth, and relevance to life. It is important that the teacher both recognize and convey to students that such questioning is normal and may also be an indication of the process of moving to a personally owned faith. Much of the work of religious education must take an apologetic approach seeking to make faith rational and relevant to the student's experience.

Typically, adolescents have a tendency to compartmentalize various aspects of their lives. They may see little connection between how they act with their friends and the moral teaching of the gospels. What one does on Sunday may be entirely disassociated with what happens during the remainder of the week. While the Catholic tradition has four basic components – faith, worship (sacraments), moral life, and prayer – young people tend to pick and choose those they see as meaningful rather than viewing them as an integrated whole.

Dealing with earlier religious education experiences can be a source of frustration when trying to help students mature their religious viewpoint. Many basic concepts are developed during what Fowler calls the stage of Mythic–Literal Faith which occurs about the ages of 6 to 11 or 12. Interpretation of scripture and religious concepts regarding things like afterlife tend to be literal with no understanding of deeper symbolism or better ways to conceptualize these realities. This occurs because children are incapable of abstract thought; they can only perceive things on a concrete level. It is only when a young person reaches puberty that the intellectual ability to think abstractly becomes possible. Whereas in other subjects like math and English there is a graduated program of learning which helps the student make the transition from simple concepts to more complex ones as the student's intellectual capabilities grow, no such standardized curriculum exists in the field of religious education. When the student enters the high school classroom comments such as "That isn't what my grade school teacher taught us", or "Then they lied to us," or "How can we know who to believe?" become commonplace as the high school teacher seeks to help students to broaden their understanding or expose them to better or more complex ways of viewing religious concepts.

Most grade school teachers are trained in elementary education or an area of specialization but not in theology or religious studies. Unless they have taken the responsibility to stay current about their faith they may pass on outdated theological concepts, misinformation or misunderstanding of what they were taught, and the like. Often their familiarity with Catholic teaching is limited to what is in the textbook. Those who did not attend a Catholic high school or university may be forced to call upon their own primary school religious education to answer questions. Few high school teachers are familiar with grade school religion curriculum and resources, and since high schools may draw students from a wide assortment of feeder schools, both parochial and public, there may be vast differences in both the quality and quantity of religious knowledge among students entering high school. This necessitates starting with some type of overview course, which may seem to some students needless repetition while to others it may be their first exposure to such material. Creating a course of studies which will address this diversity of needs is not easy.

Baggage from students' family backgrounds is interjected into the religion classroom. The fragmented nature of the contemporary family – the financial necessity of both parents working outside of the home, single-parent house-holds, families fractured by divorce, struggles with addiction, or abuse, competing and at times conflicting demands on time and energy – may present obstacles to students' understanding biblical/spiritual concepts such as community, commitment, fidelity, and unconditional love and give rise to the question of where God is in the midst of difficulties. Those who lack effectual fathering may have difficulty grasping or relating to the image of God as a loving father. Moral teaching about areas such as divorce, premar-ital sex, and related areas may be seen as a criticism of parents whose lives have been touched by these issues.

A factor which has had a significant impact on the effort to teach religion is the American culture. The Age of Enlightenment brought a shift in models of knowing reality used in earlier eras. The need for rational expla-nations and an emphasis on scientific method and empirical proof were applied to the area of religion. These brought about attitudes of skepticism, individualism, and relativism. These cultural filters are brought into the reli-gion classroom. The concepts of objective truth and universal moral absolutes are rejected and everything is seen as an opinion. Students believe that what they think is as valid as what anyone else believes, without seeing the necessity that their beliefs must be grounded in an objective reality. Religion is perceived as a subjective domain where everyone's belief has merit. Religion teachers are frequently accused of trying to impose their "opinion" on students when they convey the teachings of the Church.

In the spirit of rugged American individualism many students have devel-oped a "Lone Ranger" approach to religion. "Why do I need to go to church to worship God? Why can't I just pray at home on Sunday?" are typical questions asked by students. There is no sense of the importance of commu-nity or the fact that the Christian faith makes little sense outside of the communal dimension. As stated earlier, this is in part due to the lack of meaningful models in their experience. Community is, in many cases, a concept given lip service but little expression in Catholic parishes. Even when schools have dynamic programs for spiritual formation, opportunities for peer ministry, creative forms of expression in liturgical and para-litur-gical worship, the students find little of this in their parishes or anywhere outside of the school setting. When combined with the American belief that we are sufficient in ourselves, teaching about the values of community, inter-dependence, communal witness, etc., is an uphill battle.

The media is a powerful influence in the lives of students. The talk show model reinforces the belief that everyone's opinion is equally valid; emotion tends to take precedence over logic and information. Materialism is raised to supreme importance. The glorious is trivialized and the trivial is glorified. Immorality and moral ambiguity are commonplace and religious values are ridiculed. Excitement and entertainment are the standards by which the value of something is judged. The religious educator must compete with this distorted value system and may be told he or she is "boring" since learning about a religious tradition cannot compare to the attraction of today's media approaches. Because of their limited experience, lack of historical background, and the exposure to media which makes the present supreme, students are mistakenly led to believe that things have always been this way or that the Church is outdated and cannot speak to contemporary culture.

Increasing numbers of non-Catholic students have enrolled in Catholic schools in recent years, particularly in large urban areas where a significant number of students may come from non-Catholic backgrounds. Frequently this is because the parents of these students believe that they will receive a better education in a private school than in troubled urban schools in the public system. The presence of these students can be both problematic and providential.

Of primary concern is the issue of Catholic identity. When a significant percentage, or at times a majority, of the students enrolled in a Catholic school are from non-Catholic backgrounds, how does a school retain its distinctively Catholic character? Will all students be required to take religion class? How does one sensitively handle liturgical celebrations when a significant number of students are unable to partake of Eucharist, particularly when many of their churches allow intercommunion? This pastoral sensitivity must also be exercised in the religion classroom when students challenge Catholic teaching and practice based on what their religious tradition teaches. This is especially true for those from fundamentalist backgrounds in terms of their approach to Scripture interpretation and understanding the role tradition plays in Catholic teaching. The Catholic approach seeks to help students recognize God already present in their midst, whereas many evangelicals believe there must be a clear and concise embracing of a formula of conversion in order to develop a relationship with God.

While dealing with these pastoral concerns may be a source of distraction or frustration for some religious educators, they can also be an opportunity which will benefit all students – Catholic and non-Catholic alike. This can lead to an exploration of the uniqueness of differing Christian traditions, recognizing what these traditions share in common and on what points there are departures in agreement in how to best interpret Jesus' teaching and its application to one's life. It presents a situation which can lead to a recognition of how most Christian faiths share a common history up until the Reformation. It can be an occasion for promoting ecumenism as well as having the potential of attracting students from other traditions to the Catholic faith.

A more difficult challenge is presented by those students who are unchurched, where there is no common background or any points of departure. These students are more likely to be openly skeptical or even antagonistic in regard to religious instruction, seeing little value in exploring the spiritual dimension of life. Moral concerns may appear to be unrealistic or naive to them. Such students present a distinct opening for evangelization, an ongoing need for students from a Catholic background as well. In the 1970s the American bishops said the greatest need among American Catholics was to be evangelized. That insight is as true today as when the bishops made that statement decades ago.

Those who teach religion often face obstacles or must deal with certain handicaps in terms of preparedness for teaching. Most of those who teach religion are theology or religious studies majors. Because universities which train future religion teachers in both their discipline as well as the art of teaching are rare, many of those who teach religion have little background in educational theory and methods and often have no student teaching experience unless they were certified in another academic area. As a result, they enter the classroom with solid subject backgrounds but few educational skills. Or the converse may be true. A person may have been trained in another educational discipline with a limited background in theology and be asked to teach religion. In either case these individuals are at a distinct disadvantage in comparison to those who have a solid foundation in both their subject area and educational methodology. To offset this problem there is a need for mentoring relationships between novice religion teachers and those experienced teachers who display mastery in this field. Often this falls under the responsibility of department chairpersons who may not have adequate time to give the beginning teacher the attention he or she needs.

One final concern which teachers of religion in Catholic schools face is that of teacher morale. Because of the unique character of religious education, parents and even administrators or other educators frequently fail to comprehend the difficulties and stresses peculiar to teaching religion.

Often there are biases toward religion as an academic subject. There are still individuals who believe only priests or religious are truly competent to teach religion. Lay persons, no matter how solid their professional credentials, are seen as a reluctant necessity due to the declining numbers of religious in school ministry. Parents make comments like, "How could anyone fail (or do poorly) in religion? It's such an easy subject," as though religion was not an academic subject like other courses in the program of studies.

Administrators, too, can be guilty of similar biases. The notion that "anyone can teach religion" or the belief that any vowed religious is automatically qualified to teach religion is all too common even today. The religion program, along with campus ministry and retreat programs, are seen as secondary in terms of priorities, funding, and support from administrators. Other faculty members may see these activities as a distraction from or interference with the academic programs of the school.

Unless religion departments take a firm stance wherein they convey to the administration, faculty, and staff that catechesis is the primary duty of the department but evangelization is the responsibility of the entire school community, it is likely that anything with a spiritual or religious dimension will be delegated to the religion department. In addition to a full teaching schedule, religion teachers are expected to plan liturgies, put on retreats, run mission collections and supervise service programs, and conduct charitable drives. With schools increasingly introducing campus ministry programs and hiring campus ministry directors, this burden is being shared more equitably, but many schools still place this responsibility solely on the religion department, leading people to become overextended and burned out. Oftentimes, too, there is no additional compensation for these additional duties.

Another morale issue results from what occurs in the classroom. As previously mentioned there is the frustration that accompanies the perception that what is being taught is just the teacher's opinion. More devastating still is the fact that student opposition or verbal confrontation frequently attacks the teacher's most deeply held personal values and convictions. It can be difficult to separate the rejection of a particular area of Catholic teaching from personal rejection of the teacher since these beliefs have become an integral part of the teacher's very identity.

Conclusion

Lest the challenges of teaching religion in Catholic schools give the misimpression that those who embark on this mission face a hopeless or overwhelming task, it is important to conclude this chapter with the blessings and hope that those committed to this endeavor possess. First, religion teachers have the conviction that they have a message that others need to hear. They have been entrusted with the mission to share the Good News; share in the mission of Jesus himself. They can take heart in reflecting upon Jesus' public ministry. Frequently, his closest disciples misunderstood what he sought to teach them. Their lives often reflected disorder and confusion and they, too, tried to tell the Teacher how he should do things. In the end, only eleven of Jesus' apostles stayed the course. Eventually, though, they finally saw the light and carried on with what they were taught. Teachers of religion can take comfort in reflecting on the Paschal Mystery: after the passion and death, resurrection finally comes.

Religious educators are in the unique position of having a significant influence at a critical juncture in their students' lives. They can be catalysts in the process of moral development and value formation. They can provide the instruction, feedback, encouragement, and support which will guide the student in a positive direction which will continue over the course of a lifetime. In the same way as St. Paul wrote that one plants, another waters, and still others bring in the harvest, religion teachers know that what they do in the classroom is an investment in the future. The joy of these dedicated individuals is when they encounter graduates years later and see that they have turned out well and that some of them have indeed become men and women of faith.

Finally, there is the sense that what they do is not just an occupation, it is a calling. Teaching is indeed a form of ministry. And since it is God's enterprise, God has an investment in the outcome and will, therefore, provide the grace and gifts necessary to accomplish the task to which he calls those who teach religion. Their call is not primarily to be successful; it is to be faithful. The rest is in God's hands.

References

Congregation for Catholic Education (1977) *The Catholic school*, Boston: Daughters of St. Paul.

Congregation for Catholic Education (1988) *The religious dimension of education in a Catholic school*, Boston: St. Paul's Books & Media.

Congregation for Catholic Education (1997) *The Catholic school on the threshold of the Third Millennium*, Vatican City, Rome: Vatican Library.

Declaration on Christian Education (1965), Boston: St. Paul's Books & Media.

Erikson, Erik H. (1902) *Identity, youth and crisis*, New York: W.W. Norton.

Fowler, James W. (1984) *Becoming adult, becoming Christian: Adult development and Christian faith*, San Francisco: Harper & Row.

Fowler, James W. (1997) *Weaving the new creation: Stages of faith and the public church*, San Francisco: Harper.

Gilligan, Carol (1982) *In a different voice: Psychological theory and women's development*, Cambridge, MA: Harvard University Press.

Kohlberg, Lawrence (1981) *The philosophy of moral development: Moral stages and the idea of justice*, San Francisco: Harper & Row.

National Conference of Catholic Bishops (1972) *To teach as Jesus did*, Washington, DC: United States Catholic Conference.

National Conference of Catholic Bishops (1976) *Teach them*, Washington, DC: United States Catholic Conference.

National Conference of Catholic Bishops (1990) *In support of Catholic elementary and secondary schools*, Washington, DC: United States Catholic Conference.

Westerhoff, John H. (1980) *Bringing up children in the Christian faith*, Minneapolis, MN: Winston Press.

Westerhoff, John H. (1994) *Spiritual life: The foundation for preaching and teaching*, Louisville, KY: John Knox Press.

9 Teaching and Learning in the Catholic School

Grounded in Sacred Soil[1]

Gini Shimabukuro

During the final quarter of this century, information technologies have changed the traditional Catholic school. Mullin wrote that "new information is being discovered so fast that it is probable that a student (as well as his teacher) will know a smaller percentage of all human knowledge when he graduates than when he entered secondary school."[2] Church literature on education since the Second Vatican Council echoes this same concern:

> Recent years have witnessed an extraordinary growth in science and technology; every object, situation, or value is subjected to a constant critical analysis. One effect is that our age is characterized by change; change that is constant and accelerated, that affects every last aspect of the human person and the society that he or she lives in. Because of change, knowledge that has been acquired and structures that have been established are quickly outdated; the need for new attitudes and new methods is constant.[3]

The perception of curriculum as a finite body of information to be learned by students, and instruction as the transmission of that information into students who are viewed as *empty vessels*, is outdated from a secular educational, as well as a Catholic, perspective. The essence and beauty of Catholic education, since the paradigmatic shift brought about by Vatican II, is to promote the growth of the individual, the development of the *whole person*. This call to formation of the *whole person* in students is one with far-reaching implications for curriculum and instruction in the Catholic school. It places special emphasis upon learner outcomes, but in the balanced context of a faith community that insists upon the continuous formation of the teacher[4]and subject matter that is organized relevantly to the wholistic development of the student (Figure 9.1).

Today's teacher, including the Catholic school teacher, is called to become a reflective practitioner,[5] an instructional designer who, according to Wiggins, is dedicated to students' achievement of "progressive understanding" through teaching. He suggests that:

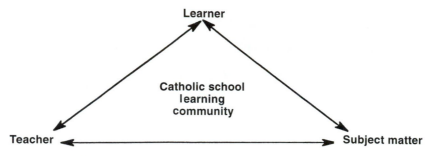

Figure 9.1   Balance required among learner–teacher–subject matter in a learning
community

> Effective learning and school improvement are possible only when we
> grasp that curricula must be built backward from authentic assessment
> tasks, the latter providing a rationale and a basis for selecting content,
> skills, modes of instruction, and sequence.[6]

This perspective of *working backwards*, i.e., of adjusting the instructional
focus to the desired performance outcomes of the student rather than
teaching from the isolated logic of content, requires, according to Wiggins,
"wholesale changes in our habits and curricular frameworks."[7]

A process of curriculum and instruction that incorporates the changes
needed to promote a wholistic approach to teaching and learning in the
Catholic school lies in seven steps of curriculum development (Figure 9.2).[8]
In general, they are: (1) to define the philosophy underlying the curriculum;
(2) to create the learning climate; (3) to delineate intended learning
outcomes; (4) to design instruction; (5) to deliver instruction; (6) to assess
the intended student outcomes; and (7) to improve the instructional design.
This model, when applied to Catholic education with the integration of faith
and values throughout the process, is dynamic, i.e., in continuous motion,
cyclical, and, when the growth of the learner is at stake, not always sequen-
tial. It is dynamic in the sense that it is question generated, thus inviting the
teacher to continuous discernment and improvement. Each step of this
process will be examined and will include valuable input from Church documentation on education (Table 9.1).

Step 1: Define Philosophy Underlying Curriculum

Key curricular questions: *What is the teacher's philosophy of Catholic education? To what extent is the teacher's philosophy of Catholic education
operationalized through his or her curriculum and instruction? To what extent
is the teacher's philosophy congruent with the school philosophy?*

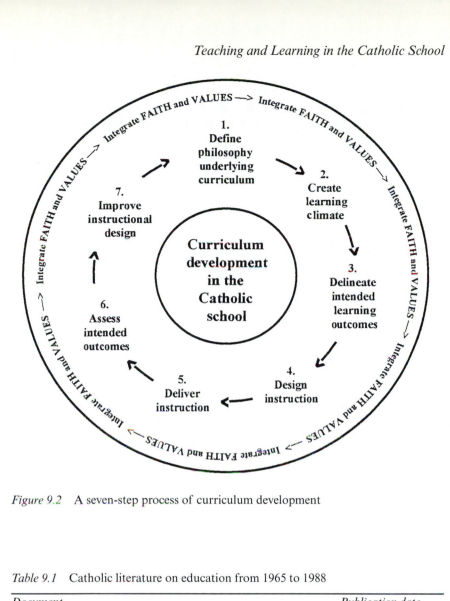

Figure 9.2   A seven-step process of curriculum development

Table 9.1   Catholic literature on education from 1965 to 1988

Document	Publication date
Declaration on Christian Education	1965
To Teach As Jesus Did	1972
Teach Them	1976
The Catholic School	1977
Sharing the Light of Faith	1979
Lay Catholics in Schools: Witnesses to Faith	1982
The Religious Dimension of Education in a Catholic School	1988

The individual teacher's philosophy of Catholic education is essential to meaningful curriculum development. Wiles and Bondi maintain that a philosophy serves the curriculum leader in four primary ways: (1) to suggest purpose in the educational endeavor; (2) to clarify objectives and subsequent learning activities in the school; (3) to define the roles of individuals involved in the school; and (4) to guide the selection of learning strategies in the classroom.[9] A potentially unfortunate teaching and learning situation involves the teacher who is not aware of his or her philosophy. For example, the teacher who blindly accepts that all intelligence is innate, static, and easily represented by an IQ score will structure the learning environment and relate to students differently from one who believes in student potential and who perceives intelligence as developmental and multifaceted. Involving teachers in dialogue about their philosophies on an ongoing basis is necessary to ascertain the extent to which the school philosophy is actualized in classrooms. Individual teachers' philosophies that counter the school philosophy constitute a *hidden curriculum*, a covert message that undermines the functionality of the school. A shared vision for the school does not imply that everyone must think alike, which would reduce the school to an institution whose administration controls the thinking and beliefs of its members. It does mean that members individually, consciously, decide to participate in a vision that they have helped to create. A functional Catholic school community depends upon the creative input of its members.

A conglomeration of relativistic teacher philosophies throughout a Catholic school fragments the necessary shared vision among teachers, the desired *unity* that is contained in the word *community*. However, teachers may inform their visions of the Catholic nature of education through a series of forward-thinking documents that have been written explicitly for Catholic school educators by Roman and American Church authorities since the Second Vatican Council (Table 9.1). Such documents serve as reliable links to the Catholic Church, thus preventing relativistic philosophical stances. A valuable in-service for faculty is to select one, or more, of these documents to read and discuss prior to revisiting the school's philosophy statement.

In order to develop a philosophy of Catholic education, the teacher must understand those educational dimensions that are distinctively Catholic. Many solid educational concepts are contained in the Roman and American Church documents, urging Catholic schools to foster: lifelong learning for both students and teachers; academic excellence; personalized student learning; social skill development of students; service; the ethical use of technology; student dignity; an appreciation for student diversity; community; the development of relationships with students; education for peace and justice; collaboration among colleagues, parents, and the outer community of the school; and other factors implicit in the effective education of youth.[10] These elements contribute to the potentially productive education of students of any orientation, public as well as private. However, the distinctiveness of the Catholic approach, according to Church authors, remains solidly in the integration of faith and values with life throughout each aspect of the curriculum. The Roman authors of *The Religious Dimension of Education in a Catholic School* illuminated the connection between faith and secular studies in a poignant manner:

> Intellectual development and growth as a Christian go forward hand in hand. As students move up from one class into the next, it becomes increasingly imperative that a Catholic school help them become aware that a relationship exists between faith and human culture. Human culture remains human, and must be taught with scientific objectivity. But the lessons of the teacher and the reception of those students who are believers will not divorce faith from this culture; this would be a major spiritual loss. The world of human culture and the world of religion are not like two parallel lines that never meet; points of contact are established within the human person. For a believer is both human and a person of faith, the protagonist of culture and the subject of religion. … Helping in the search is not solely the task of religion teachers. … Everyone should work together, each one developing his or her own subject area with professional competence, but sensitive to those opportunities in which they can help students to see beyond the limited horizon of human reality.[11]

Thus, successful integration of the religious dimension into a secular curriculum hinges upon the developing spirituality of educators who have made "integral human formation their very profession."[12] The value of initiating an instructional plan with a clear awareness of one's beliefs about teaching and learning in a Catholic school cannot be overstated. Monitoring the development of one's curriculum from the vantage point of one's philosophy is key in achieving congruence throughout the instructional process.

Step 2: Create the Learning Climate

Key curriculum questions: *To what degree is the teacher's philosophy expressed through the classroom climate? Does the climate consistently enhance each student's self-concept? To what extent does the classroom atmosphere foster student learning? Is the classroom climate microcosmic of the school climate?*

At the heart of Catholic education is the call to build community among all members of the school. Authors of *The Catholic School* profoundly wrote, "Christian faith, in fact, is born and grows inside a community."[13] Clearly, the religious identity of the Catholic school rests in the creation and nurturance of community. In his book *The Different Drum*, M. Scott Peck described authentic community with themes that share commonalities with Church writings:

> Community is integrative. It includes people of different sexes, ages, religions, cultures, viewpoints, life styles, and stages of development by integrating them into a whole that is greater – better – than the sum of its parts. Integration is not a melting process; it does not result in a bland average. Rather, it has been compared to the creation of a salad in which the identity of the individual ingredients is preserved yet simultaneously transcended. Community does not solve the problem of pluralism by obliterating diversity. Instead it seeks out diversity, welcomes other points of view, embraces opposites, desires to see the other side of every issue. It is "wholistic." It integrates us human beings into a functioning mystical body.[14]

Educational research strongly supports the correlation between the self-concept of a student and his or her school success.[15] This implies that a nurturing classroom climate, a classroom community that cooperatively strives for success for each of its members, is essential to student learning. Moreover, Church authors consistently have emphasized that the primary role of the teacher is that of a community-builder, even so far as to state "that the atmosphere and relationships in the school are as much the focus of the Catholic school as is the formal religious education class."[16]

Therefore, the curricular starting point *with students* in the Catholic school is in building a community atmosphere in the classroom. Roman authors of *The Religious Dimension of Education in a Catholic School* went so far as to encourage the Catholic school teacher to create a "school-home," i.e., a simulation of a home atmosphere in his classroom, demonstrating the extent to which the teacher is urged to develop a unique, caring, classroom climate. They wrote, "[students] should come to think of the school as an extension of their own homes, and therefore a 'school-home' ought to have some of the amenities which can create a pleasant and happy family atmosphere."[17] Martin developed this metaphor of a "school-home" for public schools into a book carrying that precise title. She emphatically stated that: "Our challenge is to turn the schoolhouse into the Schoolhome: a moral equivalent of home for our young that will be ... responsive to the needs and conditions of children and their parents at the end of the twentieth century."[18]

This step in the curriculum development process, often trivialized due to academic pressures, is foundational to effective instruction and must be ongoing throughout the instructional process. In order to begin to create a community in the classroom, the teacher must assess three vital areas: him- or herself, the social forces that encroach upon the school community, and his or her students within their individual contexts. Although such assessment requires focus, time, and dialogue with students, other teachers, and parents, it provides valuable information that forms the basis for true community building.

Teacher Self-assessment

Key curricular questions: *Does the teacher perceive his or her professional role in the context of a "vocation" to Catholic education? What is the identity and self-concept of the teacher? Do these aspects of the teacher support a positive classroom climate?*

The Catholic dimension of the school finds its roots in each teacher's commitment to spiritual growth. Intrinsic to the Catholic approach is the perception that the teacher's identity includes that of *minister*, of one who possesses a *vocation* to Catholic education. Several of the Church documents explicitly urge the teacher to routinely engage in self-evaluation on the authenticity of his or her vocation to Catholic education.[19] As stated in the *Declaration on Christian Education*, "This vocation requires special qualities of mind and heart."[20] Teachers are called to "teach by what they are,"[21] presupposing a healthy teacher self-concept, for it is impossible to nurture students' self-concepts without positive self-regard. Thus, successful community building hinges upon a positively oriented teacher–leader, particularly one who routinely fosters his or her spiritual and psychological growth and professional skills development.

Assessment of Social Forces

Key curricular questions: *What social forces impact students? How do these social forces affect their learning?*

Social forces, such as the permeation of technology throughout society, the explosion of information, the breakdown of the nuclear family, the rise of violence among children, drug usage, the media, and so on, impact students' lives in dramatic ways. In a successful learning community, the teacher communicates with his students and seeks to understand how they are influenced by the larger society. This information equips him to relate relevantly to their lives and to customize the curriculum to better meet their needs.

Assessment of Learners

Key curricular questions: *What is the identity of each learner? How does each student learn best?*

Establishing relationships with students is at the core of community building, and the crux of the Catholic approach to educating students. Authors of *Lay Catholics in Schools: Witnesses to Faith* advised:

> A variety of pedagogical theories exists; the choice of the Catholic educator, based on a Christian concept of the human person, should be the practice of a pedagogy which gives special emphasis to direct and personal contact with the students ... the relationship will allow for an openness and a dialogue.[22]

This direct and personal contact is not just a methodology by which the teacher can help in the formation of the students; it is also the means by which teachers learn what they need to know about the students in order to guide them adequately.[23]

For the teacher, relationship with students transforms an objectified *student body* into a diverse group of *persons*, each possessing unique family circumstances, cultural backgrounds, individual learning needs, specific strengths and weaknesses, likes and dislikes. Relationship with students provides the teacher with the necessary human data to address their learning needs, and, ultimately, to design appropriate and potentially effective curriculum and instruction. Such interest in students, which extends beyond the record keeping of their academic performance and into the diversity of their lives, invites a qualitative change in the classroom atmosphere, one which welcomes knowers to be known. This shared knowledge, which reveals the identity of each student, ignites a sense of community, typified by human connections that must be nurtured in a context of security and trust.

The classroom as a community forms the culture for the development of the whole person. If the philosophy of the teacher emphasizes the acquisition of information, then this step in the curriculum development process may be viewed as inconsequential. However, if the teacher's philosophy is truly a Catholic approach, that of assisting in the development of the whole person, including the spiritual, emotional, intellectual, moral, and social dimensions, then this preliminary (and ongoing) step of assessing students is critical to the relevant development of curriculum.

Step 3: Delineate Intended Learning Outcomes

Key curricular questions: *What knowledge is of most worth? What are the desired outcomes of instruction? What will learners be able to do after instruction that they could not do prior to it? Considering the diversity of learners, what methods of assessment will most accurately reflect their knowledge and levels of understanding?*

With the implosion of information in today's technological world, the most difficult, and, at the same time, vital, curricular question for today's Catholic educators at all levels of schooling is *What knowledge is of most worth?* This question is further complicated by the accelerated development of technologies which makes it virtually impossible to predict the many occupations that will appear in the workplace in the next quarter-century.

Thus, teaching students the skills that will enable them to function as self-reliant, lifelong learners takes precedence to, but does not exclude, transmitting to them bodies of knowledge that will qualify them as learned. Educational prognosticators during the 1980s conceptualized the *Basics of Tomorrow* as skills that would equip students to function in a society of unknowns, i.e., in a society in which the only constant would be that of change. These skills included: higher order thinking abilities, including application, analysis, synthesis, and evaluation; critical thinking; coping strategies; problem-solving techniques; organization and reference skills; creativity; decision making given incomplete information; and communication skills through a variety of modes.[24] The *tomorrow* of the 1980s has quickly become the reality of today.

This reality requires teachers, prior to preparing instruction, to devote serious thought to the learning outcomes that they desire their students to realize, which should be congruous with their educational philosophies. These intended outcomes in the Catholic school should reflect the development of the *whole child*, i.e., the student's intellectual, religious/spiritual, emotional, and social growth. The Catholic school teacher is thrust into the formidable role of an instructional decision-maker who is continuously discerning *What knowledge is of most worth?* to his or her students and their future lives. This is not a simple task given the pressures of *teaching to tests* versus *teaching for understanding* that teachers, public as well as private, routinely encounter. Most importantly, the Catholic school teacher must address this knowledge dilemma in the context of the religious formation of his or her students, "to inform, form, and transform ... who they are and how they live – with the meaning and ethic of Christian faith."[25]

Mager claimed that instruction that does not change anyone in desired directions is ineffective. He advised teachers: "In other words, first you decide where you want to go, then you create and administer the means of getting there, and then you arrange to find out whether you arrived."[26] This step of *deciding where you want to go* involves the formulation of learning outcomes (behavioral objectives) that specifically delineate desired performances to be exhibited by learners to demonstrate their competencies. This step challenges the teacher to formulate learning outcomes that promote higher order thinking skill development in students, as well as to stimulate the expression of their *multiple intelligences*.[27]

The articulation of learning outcomes to students prior to instruction assists in the community aspect of the learning process, i.e., it promotes a unity of teacher and student understanding of the intended destination of instruction. Sadly, students have been known to express their confusion as to the purpose of learning in certain classes, unable to discern the intended instructional direction of their teachers. In such cases, teachers either assume that students understand their instructional intentions or, worse yet, are unclear themselves about student learning outcomes; hence the importance of clearly establishing relevant learning outcomes from the start with students.

After delineating learning outcomes, the teacher-as-curricular-designer devises assessment procedures that will permit students to demonstrate their achievement of the intended learning outcomes. These tasks include a variety of methods through which students may exhibit their levels of knowledge and understanding in performance-based ways. Assessment tasks, such as portfolios, products, and performances, can be integrated easily into the learning process. When students are introduced to assessment tasks prior to instruction and involved in these tasks during instruction, the mystery is removed from assessment and learning becomes less result oriented and more enjoyable. Thus, the lines between curriculum and assessment become obscured, with student learning consequently more focal in the instructional process and assessment more aligned with learning.

Assessments that are performance based and geared to a variety of students' learning styles create a more wholistic profile of students' progress. According to Roman authors of *Lay Catholics in Schools: Witnesses to Faith*, "The entire effort of the Catholic teacher is oriented toward an integral formation of each student."[28] They elaborate this concept of wholistic formation:

> The integral formation of the human person, which is the purpose of [Catholic] education, includes the development of all the human faculties of the students, together with preparation for professional life, formation of ethical and social awareness, becoming aware of the transcendental, and religious education.[29]

When learning outcomes are designed to address the development of the *whole child* in the Catholic school, but the use of standardized and "paper-and-pencil" tests are the sole measurement of student learning, a subversive message is conveyed. This message communicates that all students learn in basically the same ways and that learning is primarily a linguistic and logical enterprise. To aspire to individualize instruction and to subsequently assess students in multiple ways creates congruency in curriculum development and compatibility with the Catholic approach to education.

Step 4: Design Instruction

Key curricular questions: *To what extent does the curriculum in the Catholic school integrate the religious dimension? What are the characteristics of an effective instructional design?*

As noted earlier, the integration of the religious dimension into curricular areas constitutes the distinctive feature of a Catholic school. This does not imply that every subject area become doctrinal. However, it does mean that the teacher be alert, in his or her instructional planning, to opportunities that connect the religious and spiritual with the secular. *The Religious Dimension of Education in a Catholic School* devotes significant text to this topic. Its Roman authors discuss the integration of the faith dimension in specific subject areas, such as science and technology, literature and the arts, and the social sciences. The crux of this methodology lies in the following:

> A Catholic school must be committed to the development of a program which will overcome the problems of a fragmented and insufficient curriculum. Teachers ... all have the opportunity to present a complete picture of the human person, including the religious dimension. Students should be helped to see the human person as a living creature having both a physical and a spiritual nature; each of us has an immortal soul, and we are in need of redemption. The older students can gradually come to a more mature understanding of all that is implied in the concept of *person*: intelligence and will, freedom and feelings, the capacity to be an active and creative agent, a being endowed with both rights and duties, capable of interpersonal relationships, called to a specific mission in the world.[30]

While designing instruction *to present a complete picture of the human person*, Catholic school teachers, likewise, have the opportunity to further reinforce a value for the *complete person* by applying this methodology to their students. On a practical level, designing learning activities that allow for the expression of the *multiple intelligences* of students assists in this endeavor. The more completely students experience a value for their multi-faceted beings, the more readily they will transfer this value to others in the world.

Effective instructional content is designed to assist students to make the connections that foster understanding. There are many components that contribute to an effective instructional design. For example, sequence, the order in which learning outcomes, the content, and learning activities are introduced, can affect the extent to which students comprehend the content. This includes the appropriate integration of technologies, such as computers, videos, music, manipulatives, overheads, and other learning tools. Assuming that students understand concepts, when in reality they do not, can create gaps in the curriculum and subsequent learning difficulties.

Another component of effective instructional design lies in assisting students to make connections for understanding at every teachable moment. For example, connecting content with previous learning, or demonstrating how content areas are related by means of thematic instruction, permits students to establish meaningful contexts for future learning. In addition, connecting content to students' lives personalizes the curriculum and creates relevancy in the learning process. Designing learning activities that stimulate higher order thinking in students, i.e., application, analysis, synthesis, and evaluation, is crucial in preparing them to function in an information-generated workplace.

Step 5: Deliver Instruction

Key curricular question: *How must instruction be delivered to best facilitate learning?*

Of primary consideration in the delivery of instruction is the deliverer. Effective teachers in Catholic schools embrace the Catholic approach to education, which includes a lifelong commitment to the development of their interior,[31] as well as their professional, lives. They realize that their interior lives are displayed to their students every minute of the school day and that the most powerful teaching strategy lies in the modelling of positive behaviors. Consequently, effective teachers are dedicated to continuous self-improvement, both spiritually and professionally.[32]

Teachers who honor learner diversity strive to diversify their delivery of instruction to accommodate the variety of learners in their classrooms. The educational literature is filled with professional materials describing the multitude of teaching strategies available to teachers at all levels,[33] such as cooperative learning techniques, synectics, concept development models, inquiry methodologies, conflict-resolution models, and so on. Of particular interest to the Catholic educator may be the teaching methodologies formulated by two Protestant educators, Thom and Joani Schultz. They proposed four powerful learning techniques of Jesus, which can be applied to Catholic school instruction and which complement the methodology suggested in the Church literature. They reported that Jesus: (1) started with the learner's context, realizing that effective learning builds upon what the learner currently knows; (2) facilitated learners to discover truth for themselves; (3) took advantage of teachable moments, creating lessons out of the circumstances that surrounded him; and (4) provided his learners with opportunities to practice what they learned.[34] The effective teacher, one who sincerely values his or her learners, devises creative ways to engage them continually in the act of learning, as Jesus did.

Step 6: Assess Intended Outcomes

Key curricular question: *To what extent were the intended learning outcomes achieved?*

As discussed earlier, Wiggins proposed that effective schools have undergone an adjustment of instructional focus from teaching from the isolated logic of content to the desired performance outcomes of students. This shift was elucidated by Lazear who elaborately compared *the old* with *the new* assessment paradigms and described the instructional consequences of such a shift. Table 9.2 provides a sample of Lazear's model.[35] Although the new assessment paradigm indicates a shift to qualitative measurement, it does not dictate that quantitative approaches, such as "paper-and-pencil" testing, should be abandoned. Rather, a combination of quantitative with qualitative measurements should be utilized thoughtfully in the pursuit of a comprehensive, wholistic learning profile of each student.

During step 3 of the curriculum development process, the teacher delineated the intended learning outcomes and, additionally, devised the tasks in which to collect data about student performance, early on informing the students of these activities. Displaying *benchmarks* to students, i.e., examples of excellent work for their ability levels, assists them to comprehend performance expectations. Sharing with students clearly delineated *rubrics*, the actual standards to be used for assessment, clarifies communication between students and teacher, thereby eliminating a host of unknowns associated with the administration of grades. Further, engaging students in the assessment of their work builds their self-evaluation skills, as well as conveys to the teacher students' perceptions of expectations and the extent to which they believe they achieved them.

Table 9.2 The paradigm shift in assessment, as characterized by Lazear

The old assessment paradigm	*The new assessment paradigm*
"Assessment is separate from the curriculum and instruction; that is, there are special times, places, and methods for assessment."	"The lines between the curriculum and assessment are blurred; that is, assessment is always occurring in and through the curriculum and daily instruction."
"Outside testing instruments and agents provide the only true and objective picture of student knowledge and learning."	"The human factor, that is, people subjectively involved with students (for example, teachers, parents, and the students themselves), holds the key to an accurate assessment process."
"There is a clearly defined body of knowledge that students must master in school and be able to demonstrate or reproduce on a test."	"Teaching students how to learn, how to think, and how to be intelligent in as many ways as possible (that is, creating lifelong learners) is the main goal of education."
"If something can't be objectively tested in a uniform and standardized way, it isn't worth teaching or learning."	"The process of learning is as important as the content of the curriculum; not all learning can be objectively tested in a standardized manner."

Step 7: Improve Instructional Design

Key curricular questions: *Precisely what elements in the instructional design, as well as in its delivery, promoted student learning? ... hindered student learning? What student factors advanced learning? ... impeded learning? How might the curriculum and instruction be improved?*

This final step of the curriculum development process, improvement, marks the beginning of a new instructional cycle. Ideally, the teacher, at points throughout the cycle, ponders effective as well as ineffective aspects of the curriculum and its delivery, and initiates needed adjustments along the way. However, this juncture represents an opportunity for a more wholistic and objective assessment of the process. It may involve the evaluative input from students which informs the teacher of their perceptions of their learning and further draws them into the curriculum development process.

During this reflective undertaking, the teacher might consider such issues as whether continuity was exhibited between each step of the cycle; which curricular areas could have been developed further, eliminated, or rearranged to better promote student understanding; to what extent the religious dimension was meaningfully integrated throughout the process; and the degree to which the students were engaged in learning. With the insight derived from a dedicated reflection on factors that either hindered or advanced student learning, the teacher then proceeds to implement necessary changes for instructional improvement, and, thus, concludes a complete cycle of learning and instruction among his or her students.

These seven steps are essential to meaningful curriculum development in Catholic education. The formation of the *whole child* is clearly a key Catholic pedagogical concept, echoed throughout the documents on education. Commitment to this worthy goal necessitates that the planned curriculum, its delivery, as well as student assessments, be designed in a diversified manner with the intent of meeting the learning needs of each student. It also requires that instruction occur in the context of authentic community making in which each member, including the teacher, is valued on the basis of personal identity. Finally, and most importantly, meaningful instruction in the Catholic school assumes a *grounding in sacred soil*, i.e., the blending of religion and spirituality, in which the shared faith dimension of the learning community permeates every aspect of curriculum development.

Notes

1 This metaphorical phrase, referring to teaching and learning as *grounded in sacred soil*, was taken from Parker Palmer, *The Courage To Teach*, San Francisco: Jossey-Bass, 1998, p. 111.

2 Mark H. Mullin, *Educating for the 21st Century*, Lanham, MD: Madison Books, 1991, p. 5.

3 The Congregation for Catholic Education, *Lay Catholics in Schools: Witnesses to Faith*, Boston, Daughters of St. Paul, 1982, p. 67.

4 Gini Shimabukuro, *A Call to Reflection, A Teacher's Guide to Catholic Identity for the 21st Century*, Washington, DC: National Catholic Educational Association, 1998.

5 Donald A. Schon, *The Reflective Practitioner*, New York: Basic Books, 1983.

6 Grant Wiggins, *Educative Assessment*, San Francisco: Jossey-Bass, 1998, p. 205. Another excellent resource is Wiggins' earlier text, *Assessing Student Performance*, San Francisco: Jossey-Bass, 1993.

7 Ibid.

8 The curriculum development model proposed in this chapter was derived from the works of the following curricularists: Ralph Tyler, *Basic Principles of Curriculum and Instruction*, Chicago, University of Chicago Press, 1949; Hilda Taba, *Curriculum Development: Theory and Practice*, New York: Harcourt Brace Jovanovich, 1962; Derek Rowntree, *Educational Technology in Curriculum Development*, San Francisco: Harper & Row, 1982; Lorraine Ozar, *Creating a Curriculum That Works*, Washington, DC: National Catholic Educational Association, 1994.

9 Jon Wiles and Joseph Bondi, *Curriculum Development, A Guide to Practice*, Upper Saddle River, NJ: Merrill, 1998, p. 35.

10 Virginia Shimabukuro, *Profile of an Ideal Catholic School Teacher: Content Analysis of Roman and American Documents, 1965 to 1990*, Unpublished Doctoral Dissertation, University of San Francisco, 1993.

11 The Congregation for Catholic Education, *The Religious Dimension of Education in a Catholic School*, Boston: Daughters of St. Paul, 1988, p. 51.

12 *Lay Catholics in Schools: Witnesses to Faith*, op. cit., p. 15.

13 The Congregation for Catholic Education, *The Catholic School*, Washington, DC: United States Catholic Conference, 1977, p. 53.

14 M. Scott Peck, *The Different Drum*, New York: Simon & Schuster, 1987, p. 234.

15 *Curriculum Development, A Guide to Practice*, op. cit., p. 133.

16 National Conference of Catholic Bishops, *Teach Them*, Washington, DC: United States Catholic Conference, 1976, pp. 7–8.

17 *The Religious Dimension of Education in a Catholic School*, op. cit., p. 27.

18 Jane Roland Martin, *The Schoolhome, Rethinking Schools for Changing Families*, Cambridge, MA: Harvard University Press, 1992, p. 33.

19 The Church documents on education that advise that the Catholic school teacher engage in self-evaluation on the authenticity of his or her vocation to Catholic education are *The Catholic School* (1977), *Sharing the Light of Faith* (1979), and *Lay Catholics in Schools: Witnesses to Faith* (1982).

20 Austin Flannery (ed.), *Declaration on Christian Education (Gravissimum educationis)*, in *Vatican Council II*, Vol. 1, rev. ed., pp. 725–37, Northpoint, NY: Costello, #5.

21 *Teach Them*, op. cit., p. 3.

22 *Lay Catholics in Schools: Witnesses to Faith*, op. cit., p. 21.

23 Ibid., p. 33.

24 The skills cited as the *Basics of Tomorrow* were derived from The Education Commission of the States (1982) as cited in *Teaching Thinking Skills: Theory and Practice*, edited by Joan Boykoff Baron and Robert J. Sternberg, New York: W.H. Freeman, 1987, and a 1988 study conducted by the Society for Visual Education, Inc., entitled *Preparing Schools for the Year 2000*, Chicago.

25 Thomas Groome, "What Makes a School Catholic?," in T. McLaughlin, J. O'Keefe, and B. O'Keefe (eds.), *The Contemporary Catholic School: Context, Identity and Diversity*, Guildford and King's Lynn: Biddles, 1996, p. 118.

26 Robert Mager, *Preparing Instructional Objectives*, Belmont, CA: Lake, 1984, p. 1.

27 Recommended readings on the topic of multiple intelligences include the works of: Howard Gardner (*Frames of Mind*, New York: Basic Books, 1985); Thomas Armstrong (*In Their Own Way*, Los Angeles: Jeremy P. Tarcher, 1987); and Ronald Nuzzi (*Gifts of the Spirit: Multiple Intelligences in Religious Education*, Washington, DC: National Catholic Educational Association, 1996).
28 *Lay Catholics in Schools: Witnesses to Faith*, op. cit., p. 28.
29 Ibid., p. 17.
30 *The Religious Dimension of Education in a Catholic School*, op. cit., p. 55.
31 Gini Shimabukuro, "The Authentic Teacher: Gestures of Behavior," *Momentum*, XXIX (2), 1998, 28–31.
32 *A Call to Reflection*, op. cit.
33 Helpful resources include *Models of Teaching* by Bruce Joyce and Marsha Weil (Englewood Cliffs, NJ: PrenticeHall, 1986) and *Instruction, A Models Approach* by M.A. Gunter, T.H. Estes, and J. Schwab (Boston: Allyn & Bacon, 1995).
34 Thom and Joani Schultz, *Why Nobody Learns Much Of Anything At Church: And How To Fix It*, Loveland, CO: Group, 1993, pp. 33–35.
35 David Lazear, *Multiple Intelligence Approaches to Assessment*, Tucson, AZ: Zephyr, 1994, p. 5.

10 Preparing for the Journey

Teachers for Catholic Schools

Karen Ristau and Margaret Reif

Preparing effective teachers for Catholic schools is a high priority in Catholic education circles. The issue is surrounded by goodwill, support from official Church documents, and hopes for solution. However, in reality the goal is fraught with problems of logistics, perceptions of scarce resources, lack of palpable progress, and needs reframing. This chapter raises questions and attempts to suggest a different view of the perceived problems; it is written in the hope of staffing every school with teachers competent in the subject matter and willing to learn more; well versed in pedagogy; and "prepared to be role models and effective sources of religious formation for our children" (Baum 1989: 709).

The Journey to Teaching

Preparing to be a teacher presents a metaphor, like other "preparing" exercises, of getting ready for a journey – and like other journeys, this one may present safe traveling as well as bumps, turns, and detours. William Ayers (1993) used the same metaphor to describe the challenge of the teaching experience:

> Much of what I know of teaching is tentative, contingent and uncertain. I learned it by living it, by doing it and so what I know is necessarily ragged and rough and unfinished. As with any journey, it can seem neat and certain, even painless, looking backward. On the road, looking forward, there is nothing easy or obvious about it. It is hard, grinding, difficult work. ... The collective, ongoing conversation with them (student and families) about teaching allows me to glimpse something of the depth of this enterprise, to unearth the intellectual and ethical implications beneath the surface.
>
> (Ayers 1993: xi)

Asking how a person prepares for the hoped-for and the unexpected at the same time will not guarantee a sure answer; instead it leads the questioner into the arena of paradox. People planning to enter any profession are at this same place during college preparatory years. Some knowledge and skills can be acquired, but the first job usually requires adaptability, flexibility, and openness to present reality. Young people want to make the world a better place; they remember inspiring teachers and poignant experiences in class-rooms when they were students. College students presently enrolled in a teacher education program at the University of St. Thomas (UST) in Minnesota verify this:

> Children are our future; teach them well and let them lead the way. Ever since I can remember, helping others has been an important area in my life. As a senior in high school, I volunteered in a community service program called the PALS Program. In this program I had the privilege of working with and tutoring a first grader in reading, writing and math. Not only did I help Alvina in these academic areas, but I also reached out to her as a friend, big sister, and adult role model. I want to teach so I can offer troubled, sad, and lonely students a haven for their discomforts. A haven where they can come and talk to me not only for academics but also for different kinds of support and guidance. Although most of one's guidance and support should come from home, in some cases it doesn't. My other motivation for becoming an educator in the 21st century is to provide information and education to young people in hopes that they would someday use it to prepare for their goals and dreams in life.
>
> (Erin Ward)

> While I was in high school I had so many teachers who did all they could to help students and push them to succeed. When I look back at those teachers I want to be able to make other students feel like they made me feel.
>
> (John Stewart)

Future teachers may have decided on some grade level or subject they might like to teach. They know they do not have the skills to work with very young children or they do. Perhaps they picture themselves as high school teachers. The exact school in the exact town is uncertain. At this time of career prepa-ration, the old adage "If you don't know where you're going, that's where you'll end up" holds true for many. The job market at any given time influ-ences, as well, in what classroom and where the new teacher will work. Quite clearly, then, to identify people in this liminal stage who have actually set Catholic school teaching as their goal is unrealistic.

The Unique Path for Catholic Educators

This, then, makes establishing a prescriptive form of pre-service education for those who become Catholic school teachers quite problematic. Yet the role of the Catholic school teacher differs from the public teacher in significant ways, so preparation for that responsibility should differ. *The Religious Dimension of Education in a Catholic School* (1988) points out that a teacher's primary task is to give witness, so students appreciate the unique environment of the Catholic school. The Vatican II Declaration on Christian Education says:

> let the teachers realize that to the greatest possible extent they determine whether the Catholic school can bring its goals and undertakings to fruition. They should, therefore, be trained with particular care so that they may be enriched with both secular and religious knowledge, appropriately certified, and may be equipped with an educational skill which reflects modern-day findings. Bound by charity to one another and to their students, and penetrated by an apostolic spirit, let them give witness to Christ, the unique Teacher, by their lives as well as by their teachings.
>
> This holy Synod asserts that the ministry of such teachers is a true apostolate which our times make extremely serviceable and necessary, and which simultaneously renders an authentic service to society.
>
> (pp. 646–47)

The Catholic school teacher, then, is uniquely placed to influence the next generation of society's Catholics. Not only are these educators responsible for teaching the classical three R's, they are charged with the fourth R, religion, as well.

Teaching within the Catholic elementary school is special and unique as a faith teaching experience. The effective teacher brings gospel values into all areas of classroom life, and this implicit faith formation curriculum of the Catholic school is powerful (Schuttloffel 1998: 304).

If one accepts the stereotypical attitude that lay persons are less able to serve as real, unordained ministers, the present statistics about who is teaching in Catholic schools may impede the possibility of that powerful education being provided.

In 1986, 81.2% of teachers in Catholic schools were lay persons; in 1996 that figure had increased to 91.6% (National Catholic Educational Association, 1997). Galetto (1996) provided a profile of Catholic elementary teachers in his article "Building the Foundations of Faith." The group surveyed was predominately lay persons (98%). This stands in sharp contrast to data from 1965 which found "65% of teachers in Catholic elementary schools were members of religious congregations or were diocesan priests" (p. 32).

The group in the Galetto (1996) study was 95% female, 94% white, and 96% Catholic. In age, 24% were 24 to 34, 30% were 35 to 44, 29% were 45 to

54, and 11% were 55 or older. Further, 25% of the teachers never attended Catholic elementary school, although 57% attended for seven to nine years; 49% attended Catholic high school; and more than 30% of those who did not belong to a religious community never attended Catholic high school. Also, 30% had four or more years in Catholic college, while 44% had no Catholic college education. Finally and importantly when considering the role of the teacher in Catholic schools, about 8% of the teachers surveyed had no formal (school-based or parish-based) religious education.

Identifying people – ahead of time – so that they might receive the education which will prepare them for the call to ministry in a Catholic school is a challenge which has been addressed previously. As an example, a monograph, published in 1982 by the National Catholic Educational Association, *The Pre-Service Formation of Teachers for Catholic School: In Search of Patterns for the Future*, was written by a group of US Catholic school leaders from elementary, secondary, and higher education. The program the authors recommended, the questions raised, and the solutions offered are still appropriate more than fifteen years later. The qualities of the person, the components of the proposed program, even the planning and implementation considerations, hardly need revision. The issues and concerns remain. Since the issues still exist and no substantial progress has been realized, a serious question for the Catholic educational community remains. Either the proposed solution is impossible, or there is not the will to solve it – which is highly unlikely – or a more workable solution must be found.

The Invitation

If the solution is seen to rest more perfectly in pre-service education then before adequate teacher preparation programs can be fully prescribed, the problem of identification must be solved. Diocesan superintendents, local school leaders, and school teachers have been hesitant, perhaps even remiss, about encouraging young people to consider teaching in a Catholic school. Fearful that invitation means a promise of a job – which it does not have to imply – no call is offered. The decision to remain inactive does not correlate with the history of Catholic education and the spirit of the religious orders who staffed the schools of former generations. The founders of the religious orders were bold in recruiting and inviting others to join their work. The same kind of altruistic young people with generous spirit still exist. Today's high school and college students are service oriented: 45 of 100 teacher education students recently surveyed at UST indicated that they volunteer 5–15 hours weekly (Reif 1997) and the Director of Student Service at UST indicated that 12 to 15% of all 5,000 undergraduates volunteer yearly (Kevin Busco, personal communication, May 4, 1998). The words of these young people in teacher education speak strongly to their motivation:

I want to be an early example and influence in the classroom that can affect a child for life. I want to make a difference. If I can encourage one child to reach their potential in life, then I have done my job. I know a difference can be made early on in life. I would like to be an example and educate the children of the future. When you hold the future generations in your hand, you hold a great challenge, but a great responsibility.

(Kiesha Wetterberg)

I have always known that I wanted to be a teacher, but I was sometimes unsure that teaching would be the career through which I could make the greatest contribution to the world ... when I was a senior in high school, I did some serious deliberation. I found out while doing a research paper on international business and entrepreneurs, that there really is no alternative career for me. I had to teach. I think it is what I was born to do.

(Cara Crawford)

These students reflect a close match to Catholic school ministry and appear ready for an invitation to teach in the schools. The hesitancy or shyness, born perhaps of lack of confidence in the lay person, to invite educators to teach does not serve Catholic education well. The history of religious communities doing the educative work of the Church and the generosity of those members has perhaps masked a problem Church leaders have been reluctant to address in a serious and concrete way. The Church has always been articulate about the role of the laity in its work but slow to put words to action, particularly in non-ordained ministerial roles. Church leaders then must take seriously and, more importantly, provide concrete support to the laity in their role as transmitter of faith to generations of future Catholics.

Partners

Finding future teachers for the schools should be a partnership activity. Some of the partners can already be found in parishes, in their youth groups, in Catholic high schools, and in Newman clubs. We often fall prey to the misguided notion that if we (whoever that might be) do not teach a person ourselves that person cannot possibly know anything or know it correctly. Church personnel would find an expanded pool of teacher candidates if, with a trustful mind, they acknowledged that other Church programs and certainly participation in liturgy do teach some things; at the least they move the heart and spirit to which formal theology can be added. Diocesan office personnel should extend an invitation to present school teachers, to teacher educators, to parish and campus ministry teams to identify students who show interest and might be interested in teaching in Catholic schools.

Speaking to youth groups, volunteer groups, RCIA candidates about the possibility might plant a seed soon enough so some students would consider choosing Catholic schools as a priority and as a vocation.

Otherwise, preparation, particularly in theology, must be completed when the teacher has begun work through an in-service program. And while not ideal, this may be ultimately where effort and resources will be most effectively used.

Catholic colleges – often blamed for the lack of a fully prepared corps of young teachers – might be more available if considered partners. Educating members explicitly for the ordained and unordained ministries of the Church is not the story of Catholic higher education. Catholic colleges with the exception of a very few have not seen the responsibility or find themselves unable for a myriad of reasons to encourage students to realize a ministry as a Catholic school teacher. Catholic colleges which have education departments and invited as partners can pursue different delivery systems and financial arrangements with dioceses. (There is an active association of colleges and universities in the United States – with one Australian member – which has answered the bishops' request to educate school leaders and offers substantive education to those already engaged in the teaching ministry.) Blaming one another for this lack is hardly productive.

Suggestions for Mapping the Journey

As one of the authors of this chapter (KR) and as a veteran teacher educator at a Catholic university, I realize how many anecdotal experiences I have encountered around Catholic school teacher preparation. As a kindergarten–doctoral Catholic-educated person myself, I assumed that I was of course preparing future Catholic teachers. After all, my university service commitment is clearly linked to curriculum consulting, committee work, board membership, graduate course teaching and advising in Catholic schools and with Catholic school teachers. However, one day late in the fall semester of my Foundations course a young woman, a theology–education major, asked if we were ever going to talk about specific requirements for teaching in Catholic schools. She went on to explain that she had learned about salary scales, school politics, teachers' professional organizations, philosophies of education, the history of American education, national education goals, graduation standards, and licensing requirements, *but* other than the number of Catholic schools and their teachers, historically and presently, she had learned very little in my course about her chosen journey. I admit I was astounded. I had fallen under the misconstrued notion that receiving a teaching degree from a Catholic college meant teachers were prepared for teaching in Catholic schools. I had failed to specifically include content aimed at preparing those teachers; I had not offered Catholic schools as a viable option when discussing charter schools, home schools, magnet schools, or single-sex schools. Since that day, three years ago, I have formulated several recommendations for preparing students for their journey to Catholic school teaching. If I can recommend which route to travel toward preparing Catholic school teachers, I offer the following:

- more theology courses – especially those connected to methodology of teaching religion;
- a strong liberal arts education – the entire college must commit to preparing these teachers (It is not the intention here to rewrite strong recommendations which come from previous research about teacher preparation and liberal arts education. For more information and a review of innovative programs see Johnstone (1989).);
- clinical experiences in Catholic schools;
- intentional partnering with Catholic schools;
- connections with the diocesan education centers;
- reflective practice skills and opportunities.

The theology coursework must speak to teachers' needs of building faith communities and understanding the Catholic education ministry in their schools and classrooms. First-year teachers, along with classroom management, parent communication, and academic assessment, are challenged to embrace the additional role of teacher/minister. The most successful new teacher will have strong theological preparation, a wealth of teaching strategies, and a thorough, content-rich, liberal arts background. This teacher will understand the importance of analytical reflection, a by-product of the liberal arts college experience. As supported by McCaughey-Oreszak (1990):

> The responsibility for teacher education, then, does not rest solely with schools and departments of education. It is the responsibility of the entire college. Partnerships with elementary and secondary schools also are called for in preparing future teachers, but the focus here is on campus communication.
>
> (p. 62)

An excellent example of an undergraduate program that incorporates many of these suggestions is at Thomas More College, Crestview Hills, Kentucky. The college students studying teaching methods meet twice a week from 9:00 till 12:00 at Villa Madonna Academy, a grade 1 through 12 school operated by the Sisters of St. Benedict; Blessed Sacrament, and St. Anthony School. The students attend lectures by their college professors, observe classrooms, work with students, and share ideas and work samples with the classroom teachers. The principals and teachers commented on improved morale in their schools when they realized how much they were contributing to the future of education (Harris 1990).

Although many colleges have begun using this type of school-site methods courses for all of their future teachers, Harris pointed out the importance in preparing Catholic school teachers:

> this approach may have special significance in the preparation of Catholic school teachers. The golden thread of Catholic values connects the total formal education experience. Such continuity holds great promise for the student teacher, strengthening the development of her/his whole person through the many facets of professional life. The teacher education program becomes more than the mastery of requisite professional skills.
>
> (1990: 8)

The diocese must make a conscious effort to connect with area colleges (Catholic or public) in preparation and recruitment of new teachers for their schools. This should not be a piecemeal attempt centered in each school. If the diocesan office were to provide orientation and information sessions for pre-service teachers they could engage these teachers before they leave the college classrooms. At the University of St. Thomas, we invite the director of schools to speak to the student teachers during their weekly, on-campus seminar. The director brings the paperwork for opening a file in the arch-diocesan office, applications for substitute positions, and an enthusiasm for the Catholic system and the work in its schools. We also always invite Catholic school principals to take part in the mock-interview sessions with the student teachers. This allows our students to hear about the ministry of Catholic education and observe the professionalism of the Catholic school leaders; it also gives the principals a chance to connect and, in some cases, hire our soon-to-be graduates.

Finally, pre-service teachers must become reflective about their practice. They can learn this in their college courses through journaling, taking part in reflective practice groups during their clinical experiences, and in student-teaching seminars. In their jobs, new Catholic school teachers require the myriad of skills all new teachers require – classroom management strategies, help dealing with stress, a plan for developing relationships with parents, knowledge about assessing and developing curriculum and instruction content and strategies – but, in addition, new teachers acknowledged their need for "an overview of the church's teachings on the importance of Catholic education, and its mission, philosophy and goals. They recognized a need for this frame of reference to provide the necessary direction and focus" (Brock 1990: 55). In a survey of fifty-five first-year teachers in Omaha Catholic schools, Brock found that they were expected to prepare children's liturgies, teach religion, model and integrate religious values, and prepare their students for the sacraments. It is for this endeavor that the schools must provide mentors to assist in the processing and reflecting on the teaching strategies, successes, and failures. They need time for their own faith journey to continue; the power of prayer and mentor support are invaluable at that point.

Catholic schools might recruit more teachers if they stressed the benefits of teaching in Catholic schools and offered additional perks for their teachers. The benefits include the school as a faith community and family extension, the parent support and involvement, the smaller class sizes, the minimal discipline. One of the incentives could be a partnering with Catholic colleges to provide workshops, leadership development in-service, graduate course-work, and degrees at discounted rates or tuition free. One such program is the Murray Institute at the University of St. Thomas in St. Paul, Minnesota. The Murray Institute, a collaborative venture among the School of Education, the School of Divinity, and the archdiocese, has provided tuition-free, graduate degrees (masters and educational specialists) to over 200 teachers, religious educators, and youth ministers since its inception in 1990.

Ensuring a Successful Journey: Recommendations for All

Future teachers for either the public or Catholic school and all thoughtful teacher preparation programs would benefit from developing what Thomas Groome (1998) calls "a philosophy of life toward people" (pp. 118–67) and "a spiritual vision" (pp. 425–44). Diocesan office personnel, as well, who have the opportunity to work with future teachers can contribute to the formation of both of these ideals.

Groome reminds educators that their own philosophy or more simply their outlook on life and the world, their world view, "make[s] a great differ-ence in their teaching and especially by way of the outlook they encourage in learners" (p. 150). Deeply held beliefs about the inherent goodness of people, the ability of all children to be successful learners, seeing education as a joyful experience, shape the way any teacher approaches the persons in the classroom, their parents, and the act of teaching. Predisposed to see only the half-empty glass, a prejudice about the inability of some to learn, a belief that education is a punitive activity, leads to a woefully depressing educative environment. In other words, what the teacher really thinks about humankind "is a foundation of their vocation as educators ... and how they really look at the world – has great educational import, too" (p. 120). Groome challenges educators to consider a sacramental cosmology – "an attitude that the world is gracious, meaningful, and worthwhile" (p. 130) based on the understanding that everything that God has made is essentially good and that "God mediates Godself to humankind, and we encounter and respond to God's grace and desire for us through the ordinary life ... through everything and anything of our world" (p. 125). Groome suggests this philosophical stance means:

Much depends on our attitude, and, in spite of suffering and evil,
we can afford a positive one.
We can see life and the world as essentially 'good' for us.
We can approach life as gift.
It is always possible to find "the more."
We can approach the world as meaningful.
We can find life worthwhile.
Life is no bed of roses – but we can plant some.
Life invites us to generativity
To live well requires an act of faith.

(1998: 148–50)

In the practical sense, Groome recommends accepting the sacramental cosmology as a philosophic basis for teaching which will enable the teacher – no matter what subject is being taught – to

Turn people to look at and express their lives in the world – what is "there," what they are up to, and what is going on around them, and get people to reflect on their life in the world – to contemplate it, interpret it, question it, imagine new possibilities for it, and even to probe their own reflections on it all, discerning why they think or feel or perceive the way they do.

(p. 161)

This invitation seems at its heart to express the meaning of learning for all educators.

Another ideal suggested by Groome is the necessity for a spiritual vision, which "reflects spiritual commitments that find echo across a broad spectrum of religious traditions and could be embraced by or at least might inspire the work of any educator, regardless of religious identity" (p. 427). A spiritual vision means "allowing the philosophical convictions ... to become operative convictions that seep into one's soul and then permeate how, what, why, and where on teachers – the whole curriculum" (p. 427). School systems rarely get high marks for encouraging creativity and new ideas; new ways to teach a subject and inspire students. Robin Williams' character in *Dead Poet's Society*, who leads the lads marching around a quadrangle instead of sitting in a classroom and who instructs students to tear out a text page because it explains a method for measuring the enjoyment of poetry, is seen as an eccentric gad-fly about to lose his teaching position. In actuality, he provides an example of a teacher who follows convictions about learning – that enjoyment cannot be measured scientifically. Ann Sullivan, the teacher of Helen Keller, believed her student could learn. Her philosophical beliefs became operative convictions guiding her teaching and allowing Helen to learn. A reflective teacher with a well-formed spiritual vision agrees with Ayers:

A life in teaching is a stitched-together affair, a crazy quilt of odd pieces and scrounged materials; equal parts invention and imposition. To make a life in teaching is largely to find your own way, to follow this or that thread, to work until your fingers ache, your mind feels as if it will unravel, and your eyes give out, and to make mistakes and then rework large pieces. It is sometime tedious and demanding, confusing and uncertain, and yet it is as often creative and dazzling; surprising splashes of color can suddenly appear at its center; unexpected patterns can emerge and lend the whole affair a sense of grace and purpose and possibility.

(1993: 1)

It is these kinds of people who should teach in Catholic schools – those who will work with a sense of grace, purpose, and possibility. The Sisters, Brothers and priests of religious orders who some current school leaders long for do not exist in large numbers in the United States. They are a treasure which cannot be replaced. But their counterparts do exist; they are today's service-minded college students. And like their religious-order predecessors, who were not fully formed when they began their teaching careers, this youth is open to the continuous learning necessary of any excellent educator. We believe there are generous, spirit-filled young people who would accept the invitation to teach in Catholic schools – a rich, spiritual journey of fulfillment – if but asked and encouraged by the present generation of school leaders.

References

Ayers, William (1993) *To teach: The journey of a teacher*, New York: Teachers College Press.

Baum, W. (1989) "Christian education of the young," *Origins*, 18, 708–11.

Brock, Barbara L. (1990) "Profile of the beginning teacher," *Momentum*, 21 (4), November, 54–57.

Congregation for Catholic Education (1988) *The religious dimension of education in a Catholic school* (Publication No. 231–4), Washington, DC: United States Catholic Conference.

Galetto, Paul (1996) "Building the foundations of faith. The religious knowledge, beliefs, and practices of Catholic elementary school teachers of religion," Washington, DC: National Catholic Educational Association. (ERIC Document Reproduction Service No. ED 400 246).

Groome, Thomas (1998) *Education for life*, Allen, TX: Thomas Moore.

Harris, Judy (1990) "Closing the gap," *Momentum*, November.

Johnstone, J.S. (1989) *Those who can*, Washington, DC: Association of American Colleges.

McCaughey-Oreszak, Leona (1990) "Arriving where we started," *Momentum*, November.

National Catholic Educational Association (1997) *United States Catholic elementary and secondary schools 1996–97: The annual statistical report on schools, enrollment and staffing,* Washington, DC.

Reif, Margaret (1997) "Service commitments of University of St. Thomas teacher education students," unpublished data.

Schuttloffel, Merylann (1998) "The Catholic elementary school curriculum: Elements of coherence," *Catholic Education: A Journal of Inquiry and Practice*, I, 295–305.

11 Preparation of Teachers for the Catholic Schools

Sister Mary Peter Traviss

Historically the primary purpose for the American Catholic schools has been the protection of the Roman Catholic religion of the Church's children and youth. Colonial schools were Protestant in orientation and the Protestant religion was taught as part of the daily curriculum. After the public schools shed their overt Protestant influences, they often retained anti-Catholic sentiments which Catholic parents understandably felt were injurious to the development of their children. Moreover, throughout the nineteenth century Catholic schools were often associated with specific ethnic groups which helped preserved both the languages and the customs of the dominant group by instructing the children in both. The historian Philip Gleason claimed that the part Catholic schools founded by ethnic groups played in the gradual assimilation of the young into the mainstream American culture cannot be overestimated. "The [Catholic] schools," he wrote, established by ethnic groups, "performed the functions, in addition to intellectual and religious training, of transmitting the ancestral language, orienting the young to the national symbols of the group through successive generations." [1]

Over the past 200 years the purpose of Catholic schools, the protection of the faith, has not altered even though both its expression and the principal threat to the life of faith have changed. Today the goal of the Catholic schools is still the formation of the whole child – religious and moral as well as intellectual and emotional – and the chief determent of faith development is surely the godless secular culture of American society which is preserved and passed on to future generations by the country's public school system. While Catholic schools today are rarely related to a particular ethnic group, a case can be made for the fact that they are counter-cultural; they socialize children into a spiritual community. They foster religious motivation and communication, orient the young to gospel values and virtues, and facilitate an outreach of service to others.

Vital to the purpose of the Catholic school system are those teachers who understand the mind of the Church regarding its schools, provide the post-baptismal formation needed to shape developing Catholics, and are themselves an integral part of the climate of the schools. As role models, ideal Catholic school teachers are considered as one of the most significant elements of the hidden curriculum.

The Church is currently facing a number of questions concerning the teachers in its schools. From where are these teachers recruited? Are these teachers prepared differently than public school teachers? How were the early teachers prepared? Are there aspects of the preparation that should be retained as part of today's teacher training? If so, which aspects? Who is responsible for today's teacher preparation? Who makes financial and educational decisions about the preparation of Catholic school teachers? To gather the data needed to answer these questions, it is necessary to review the 200-year-old role of the Catholic school teacher.

This country's first bishops called upon the vowed religious women from various parts of Europe to help with the formidable task of educating the Catholic children of the new land. Throughout the eighteenth and the early part of the nineteenth century, tens of thousands of teaching Sisters came to the United States to join their counterparts in New York, New Orleans, Louisville, Boston, Philadelphia, New Jersey, San Francisco, Chicago, and St. Louis, as well as in many rural areas. In less than 150 years these valiant women built and staffed one of the most impressive network of schools the world has known – the American Catholic school community – which at its enrollment peak in 1964, the year in which Mary Perkins Ryan wrote her controversial book, *Are Parochial Schools the Answer?*,[2] numbered over 13,000 schools with 6 million plus students and more than 125,000 Sisters and lay teachers.

This unparalleled achievement was one accomplished principally by women. They were women who were regarded by the society of their day as largely powerless and non-influential in the Church to which they had given their lives. The ministerial model they followed was one forged by a young American widow, Elizabeth Ann Bayley Seton,[3] who began the first free parochial school in 1810 with twenty students in Saint Joseph Parish, Emmitsburg, Maryland. Elizabeth Seton was not the first to begin a Catholic school, but she opened her educational institution not as a private school, but one in connection with a parish. Saint Joseph's was the first parochial school established in the United States, a model that was to impact American Catholicism as no other single ministerial effort had done before or since.

The impressive growth of the Catholic schools from 1810 to 1880 also brought about the most divisive issue in American Catholicism of the nine-teenth century. Known as the "School Controversy,"[4] liberal and conservative Churchmen were pitted against each other regarding the future of the Catholic schools. The conservatives insisted that every child be educated in a Catholic school; liberals introduced the notion of compromise and cooperation with the public schools although they agreed that a school be erected *near* every Catholic church. Bishop John Hughes (New York) expressed the opinion of many of the hierarchy when he wrote, "I think the time has come when it will be necessary to build the school house first, and the Church afterwards."[5] As the battle about the schools heated among the male leaders, Bishop Bernard McQuaid (Rochester), the most vocal of the proponents of the Catholic schools, predicted that "the battle of God's Church in this country has to be waged in the school room."[6] Throughout the long and often bitter struggle, the Sisters went quietly about their business of taking in children of all classes, but especially the laboring immigrants, and teaching them. There is no record of their participation in the debate.

There is no record either of the names of hundreds of thousands of women involved in the Catholic school movement. Upon receiving the holy habit of the order, each woman took a saint's name as her own; thus, we have Sister Mary Agnes, Sister Mary Clare, and Sister Mary Patricia. Both baptismal name and surname were left behind in the world. Except for Madeleine Sophie Barat's Madames of the Sacred Heart, Mother Elizabeth Ann Seton, foundress of the Sisters of Charity, was one of the few women in that 150-year-old history whose surname was consistently used. Until the advent of Vatican II, it was typical of religious life that the Sisters (and also the Brothers) did not use surnames, even when publishing their creative work. Major contributions to the educational world in the form of innovative courses of study, teaching aides, nationally used textbooks, and teachers' manuals were often authored by or credited to "A Sister of Notre Dame," or "The Sisters of the Holy Cross." The Sisters who forged the Catholic schools network in the United States did so anonymously.

The resolution of the "School Controversy" was brought to an end by the intervention of Leo XIII in 1893 through his apostolic letter to Cardinal Gibbons of Baltimore. The result was that Catholic parents were not obliged to send their children to Catholic schools. Nevertheless the insistence of the Third Plenary Council of Baltimore on the erection of a Catholic school near every parish, and widespread discussion of *The Parent First* by Rene I. Holaind,[7] influenced the most conspicuous growth of parochial schools in the Church's history. The schools more than doubled between 1890 and 1920. In 1904 the National Catholic Educational Association was founded.[8]

Before Catholic parents began agitating for, and the state requiring, certification of all teachers, i.e., from approximately 1810 to 1950, the Sister–teachers were prepared for the classroom in much the same way that apprentices were nurtured under the tutelage of a master craftsman. Veteran teachers were assigned as "master teachers" for young beginners. The senior teacher had a variety of names depending on the congregation of Sister–teachers; the most common were "buddy," "mentor," "grade partner," or "sponsor." The last term often referred to the older Sister who had counseled the younger Sister into entering religious life and she remained her mentor during her early ministry.

The practice of mentoring, or the craft system, has been criticized by several Catholic school historians, including Timothy Walch,[9] as a poor preparation for the classroom, but recent studies calling upon the reform of teacher education acknowledge the worth of such practices, and have, in fact, suggested their inclusion in the reform movement.[10] Experienced teachers report that mentoring experiences have been as rich and useful as the formal courses they studied; indeed many times they claimed the mentoring was more helpful.[11] There is evidence to suggest that the mentoring is richest when combined with the study of theory and practice.[12]

In 1992 Keating and Traviss,[13] fearful that Sister–teachers were rapidly disappearing as part of the Catholic school scene, interviewed sixty Sister–teachers from thirty different communities in an attempt to preserve the story of how they became teachers, i.e., what was the process of their preparation? The Sister–teachers interviewed for this study came to the convents in the 1920s, 1930s, and 1940s as teenagers, the majority from the lower middle classes. The majority of their grandparents were uneducated, and more likely than not, were immigrants or came from immigrant families. When they addressed the subject of preparation, they spoke of Saturday classes, late-night study, and summer courses, but the quality of their voices changed and became nostalgic and affectionate when they described being taught by the veteran Sister–teachers.

One 80-year-old Sister summarized the craft system when she described her own experiences:

> In those days we learned from our elders. There were traditions, customs, a culture if you will, that had to be learned from those who had done it all before us. There was also a reverence and respect for who and what preceded us.[14]

A Sister from the same congregation, fifteen years her junior, agreed:

> We learned teaching skills as part of a culture handed down from generation to generation. There was an explicit way we planned our lessons. In the library at the Motherhouse we had lesson plan books of some of the older Sisters and they used the same format we were taught. Heaven help us if we left out a step. ... We were taught how to hold a piece of chalk and how to hand it to a child.[15]

The Sisters of the generations between 1810 and 1960 not only learned from one another within groups, but teaching congregations generously shared successes with one another. One Sister who had earned $1.50 a week as a substitute teacher for the Sisters before joining them remembered with a twinkle in her eye that:

The Sisters of Charity were considered very good teachers and other Sisters, especially the Dominicans, would copy what we did.[16]

We borrowed techniques from everyone. The Notre Dame Sisters were very strong in music and one of them gave us a music class every Saturday for about six Saturdays. We followed the Holy Cross method in spelling.[17]

The mentoring system was, of course, a natural part of community life. It was the way the novices learned about religious life, and since almost every member of the community was involved in the school, the mentoring practice was easily used for learning about the classroom. The Keating and Traviss study emphasized the close connection of the community life of the Sister–teachers and their schools and elaborated their findings with some memorable quotations. Of the sixty Sister–teachers interviewed, almost all commented on the connection between the common life of the convent and life with the children within the schoolroom. "The communities were organized around the life of the school," commented one of the interviewees. Our honorarium matched that of the school.[18] A former diocesan supervisor said:

I don't believe there was any doubt that the schoolhouse was an extension of the convent. School routines were extensions of religious life practices. There is a certain serenity in routine and order and I believe that we, in fact, all Sisters had routine, order, and a security in knowing what to do. There was very little ambiguity before Vatican II. That certainty about life, about faith, and that we were all destined for eternal life, all this taught as much as our lessons.[19]

In large measure, the schedule of the school likewise matched that of the convent. Holy days were holidays; visitation from the Mother Superior usually meant an inspection of the school and a free day for the students; school doors were locked at the beginning of afternoon prayers. In fact, several of the Sisters spoke of teaching as an extension of their common life.

One of the greatest contributions [we] made to Catholic schools was the integration of [our] community life into the life of the school. The school was the community's common work. It was the responsibility of each and every Sister assigned to it. We stayed after school to help with the work of the school. We integrated community into our teaching. Just as we made a commitment to helping our Sisters and assuming what they did benefited the entire community, and what I did also benefits the community and each Sister, so we were committed to each child succeeding.[20]

Similar points were made by several Sisters. One Sister–teacher claimed that:

> We learned a lot about teaching from community life. We learned virtues such as patience and tolerance, and the value for each person. We also learned organization, and for those for whom neatness and order do not come naturally, we certainly learned that in religious life organization was very important.[21]

Another Sister–teacher who had taught for over fifty years asserted that:

> Because the Catholic school was such an important extension of the Sisters' community living, as community life changed, so did the school, but I think for the best. In fact, I would say that Catholic schools of today are better than they were ... [they] are more formational, more gentle and loving.[22]

Important as community life with all its supports was to the Sister-staffed schools, it was not considered by the public to be a sufficient preparation to teach. Demands for more formalized training and a better quality of teacher education increased. On April 1, 1948, the National Catholic Educational Association officially set up a section on teacher education at its annual meeting in San Francisco. The first presentation sponsored by this section occurred at the annual convention in Philadelphia the following April; it took the form of a symposium on the theories and practices for the education and training of the young religious teacher. The panelists were some of the most highly regarded Catholic educators of the day: Sister Madeleva Wolff, CSC, the renowned poetess–nun who served as president of Saint Mary's in the shadow of the University of Notre Dame; Mother M. Eucharista, CSJ, the forward-thinking provincial of the Sisters of Saint Joseph in Saint Paul, Minnesota; Father Clarence E. Elwell, who made his mark nationally as superintendent of schools for the Diocese of Cleveland, Ohio; Mother M. Dorothea, OSU, designer of the Ursuline plan and president of the College of New Rochelle, New York; Sister M. Augustine, OSF, president of Alverno College, Milwaukee, Wisconsin; and Brother Emilian, FSC, provincial of the Brothers of the Christian Schools in Beltsville, Maryland.

Published under the title *The Education of Sister Lucy*,[23] the proceedings of the panel written by Sister Madeleva shared various models for the education of the non-existent Sister Lucy, the young Sister–teacher to be. The designs ranged from academic programs at diocesan colleges to simpler precursors of the Sister formation colleges of the mid and late 1950s. The models reflected the requirements for the BA degree of the day, and had the common purpose of graduating the Sister–teacher before she was assigned to minister in the classroom. Commenting on the detailed sequence of the panel's plans, Sister Madeleva wrote,

> On the day of her final profession her religious superiors and her community can receive her as a sister completely prepared by her religious training, her vows, her academic education, to begin at once to carry on the work to which she is dedicated. ... I need not tell you that Sister Lucy does not exist. But I know that we should insist that she shall exist. We are here in part to bring her into existence. Sister Lucy is our 1949 model of the religious teacher of the future, her education and her training.[24]

This panel was one of those watershed points in the growing awareness of the need for a more formalized and professional preparation of the Sister–teacher. Sensitive to criticism of Catholic schools which had been multiplying in an amazing growth throughout the 1940s, and concerned with their less-than-favorable comparison with public schools from even Catholic circles, American Church leaders had been urging an upgrading of teacher training throughout the 1940s, and finally in 1951 Pius XII wrote these galvanizing words to the First International Convention of Teaching Sisters:

> Many of your schools are being described and praised to us as being very good. But not all. It is our fervent wish that all endeavors become excellent. This presupposes that your young teaching Sisters are masters of their subjects they expound. See to it, therefore, that they are well trained and that their education corresponds in quality and academic degrees to that demanded by the State.[25]

The word "state" became the focal word and Sister formation was born. Pope Pius XII did not *suggest* that the young Sister–teachers be "well trained and that their education correspond [s] in quality and academic degrees to that demanded by the state," he ordered that the teacher preparation of Catholic school teachers be improved. "See to it ...,"[26] he said, that this be done. The model for preparation of teachers created by "the state" culminating in a credential was considered the best available. The "credential" became a near-magic piece of paper that indicated not only that one had completed a prescribed course of studies, but that one was a bona fide teacher. The assumption, that without a credential one was not quite yet a teacher, was an attitude that took hold in the 1960s and prevailed throughout the remainder of the twentieth century.

After the advent of the Sister Formation movement in the 1950s, increasing numbers of the Sister–teachers completed their degrees and credentials before they were assigned to classrooms. The Sister Formation movement called for the establishment of "Formation Colleges," often serving several communities, in order to realize the ideal of reconciling the pursuit of the intellectual life, or at least the preparation thought appropriate for the classroom, with the culture of ministry. During the years immediately following Vatican II, as the Sisters pursued other ministries than teaching and nursing and the number of Sister–teachers declined dramatically, the "Formation Colleges" closed and the ideal of integrating academic training with theological and apostolic preparation flickered and died.

Hundreds of Sisters left the convent in the aftermath of Vatican II and became laicized.[27] The schools were cut back, i.e., thirty-two-room schools became sixteen-room ones, and twelve-room schools became nine-room ones. Many schools closed, others merged, or became lay staffed. A great number of the former religious entered the ranks of the existing Catholic schools and the crisis of identity and viability was temporarily averted. The dress changed but not the spirit, the preparation, nor the apostolic purpose. As the former religious reached retirement age in the 1990s and the lack of specialized preparation for the laity became more critical, the questions of identity and viability emerged again, and are a part of the Catholic school problem today.

In a 1980 pastoral letter to the Catholic higher education community, the American bishops appealed to the colleges and universities to help prepare the growing number of lay educators for the Catholic schools "who are evangelizers by call and convenant and mission."[28] Two years later in 1982 a committee composed of the departments of the National Catholic Educational Association (NCEA), The Association of Catholic Colleges and Universities (ACCU), and the Chief Administrators of Catholic Education (CACE) collaborated on a plan for teacher education. First, it issued a call to Catholic colleges and universities to assume the responsibility for providing the education. Second, it defined qualities necessary in persons who would be Catholic school teachers – faith qualities, relational qualities, and professional qualities. Third, it outlined components for any program preparing teachers:

Academic: *Theology/Religious Studies*

- Scripture, God's Word calling for response in faith, covenant, kingdom
- Christology (incarnation, redemption, resurrection)
- Ecclesiology
- Sacramental theology and liturgy
- Moral theology
- Catholic social teaching
- Church history

Foundation of Catholic Education

- History and governance of Catholic schools in the United States
- Philosophy of Catholic education
- Theories of faith and moral development
- Catechesis
- Methods of communicating values[29]

Faith Development

The committee suggested a variety of activities such as retreats, discussion groups, prayer groups, communal liturgy celebrations, and the like, to function in complementary ways. "Regardless of the form these experiences take, their ultimate goal is clear: the strengthening and deepening of religious convictions, attitudes, values and patterns of living."[30]

Field Experiences and Teacher Education

It is at this juncture that the committee wanted the young teacher to get in touch with the Catholic school culture by observation of classroom teaching and other learning activities such as visits to "an Archdiocesan Office of Education, A Catholic Educational Resource Center, a Catholic Television or Communications Center."[31]

To date nothing has come of either call. The reasons are varied. The principal ones seem to be that no single entity has taken responsibility for setting standards for Catholic school teachers other than the state. The bishops of each diocese (and through their delegates, the superintendents of schools) are the only authority that can set minimum qualifications but so far they have not insisted on any special pre-service training aside from state certification. Catholic colleges and universities claim that they do not have the demand needed to support an undergraduate preparation program. They have, however, included in varying degrees graduate courses for Catholic school administrators, and in a few instances some isolated courses for Catholic school teachers. The NCEA sees itself as a service organization without the authority to dictate standards, and the individual diocesan offices of education are understaffed without the educational resources to provide for the kind of training required. The obvious response would be for these agencies to work together, but this approach has not been widely pursued.

One institution of higher education that has partially responded to the need is the University of San Francisco. This Jesuit university inaugurated the Institute for Catholic Educational Leadership (ICEL) in 1976 in collaboration with diocesan educators based on a national needs assessment. The original needs assessment in the mid 1970s surveyed 96% of the Catholic school principals in the United States in addition to over 69% of the superintendents of Catholic schools. Some of the country's foremost scholars in Catholic education designed an MA program for Catholic school administrators. Four years later a doctoral degree for school leaders and an MA in Catholic school teaching was added to the program. ICEL has not yet incorporated a pre-service program for teachers, but that particular component is part of its complete program as is an office of research which will, in time, take on the task of systematic research needed to advance Catholic education. ICEL's doctoral students currently produce more research on the Catholic school community than any other college or university in the United States. ICEL also manages an ERIC-like web site for the use of the nation's Catholic school personnel.

While ICEL is the smallest unit of the six departments comprising the University of San Francisco's School of Education, ICEL attracts adjunct professors from all over the country. It not only hires professors with a scholarly background in their area of instruction, but each professor must also have had Catholic school experience, K–12. The institute conducts an annual needs assessment in order to make adjustments to its core offerings and elective courses so that its graduates are exposed to a rigorous educational program that meets state requirements as well as the current felt needs of working professionals in Catholic schools, and a carefully crafted formation program which helps shape Christ-like ministers of the gospel.

ICEL has not yet realized every aspect of its visionary program, but it works continually on researching what an ideal Catholic educator's program should include, not only to advance the conversation about what is the best preparation for Catholic school personnel, but also to add rationale to the program changes it makes. What are some of these components which ICEL claims are key to the preparation of Catholic school educators – principals and teachers, librarians, coaches, secretaries, bus drivers, crossing guards, and teacher aides?

The basic design has a community component, the kind of community experience described in another pastoral letter, *To Teach As Jesus Did*.[32] In that document the bishops refer to community as "at the heart of Christian education, not simply a concept to be taught, but a reality to be lived."[33] The bishops insist that educators are formed by experience, and in order to teach the concept they must live the reality. An academic program that emphasizes community helps its members grow in personal relationships, trust, love, and hope. It stresses an integral social life which the pastoral maintains is necessary for any personal growth in grace and the spiritual life.

Integrated into the learning community are rigorous course offerings which are designed to form today's Catholic educator, i.e., courses in leadership, personnel administration, law, moral development, curriculum design, foundations of Catholic school history, philosophy and theology, finance, justice education, counseling techniques, assessment, media, and technology. There are also courses in methodology and curriculum, educational theory, research and practice, child and adolescent psychology. There must also be courses of theology, philosophy, and spirituality. The bishops insist that only "those teachers who have been formed theologically and spiritually can respond adequately to the call of professional ministry in Christian education according to the vision of Jesus Christ and His Church."[34] Doctoral students study a wide range of research methodologies, statistics, advanced foundational courses, proposal writing, and in-depth work in chosen focus related to Catholic school interests; candidates are closely mentored in the actual research and writing of the dissertation.

Mentoring plays a major part in ICEL's pre-service programs. The Sister–teachers interviewed for the Keating and Traviss study recommended that a mentor, at least for the first two years of a new teacher's ministry, be appointed from the school's experienced staff members. They commented that coursework was different from on-the-job experience. "Demonstration lessons were obligatory," said one Sister–teacher. "They helped a lot. I remember thinking as I watched the best teachers in our Congregation teach, 'Oh, I can do that.' "[35]

The help afforded by demonstration schools was mentioned frequently, especially by the Sisters on the east coast. The Archdiocese of Philadelphia, particularly, used them to show teachers how to teach. It is interesting to note that at the very time that John Dewey was *persona non grata* in Catholic institutions of high education, in-service models were employing his "learning by doing" techniques. Typically the Sister–teachers would go on Saturdays to observe outstanding teachers with classes of students, demonstrating various kinds of lessons.

> I wish that teachers today had the advantages of Demonstration Schools. It was so helpful to see how "expert" teachers taught a lesson. We returned from observing these marvelous teachers with all kinds of ideas. I copied the lessons from what I observed.[36]

ICEL has great faith in various levels of mentorship, especially the mentorship of the community. Of equal importance for the Catholic school teacher is the ability to create an ecclesial climate in the classroom. This was again a natural thing for the Sister–teacher in the early Catholic schools. Unwavering adherence to the "Rules" of the 1800s and the first half of the 1900s, the common life, and a focused and shared vision, contributed to the building of a strong culture, a way of "doing things." This community culture affected the work of the group, and especially did it affect the Catholic schools, since what the Sisters learned to do, they taught their students. Sergiovanni writes that leaders of organizations which have distinct, identifiable cultures are "legacy builders which governs what is of worth for this group and how members should think, feel, and behave." Their organizations develop and display a system of symbols "over time."[37] Frequently, adults who are strangers to one another are able to surmise that they share a Catholic school experience with one another by their handwriting, the way they answer a telephone or make a genuflection in Church, their vocabulary and phraseology, or their mutual appreciation of small things. While incomprehensible to the uninitiated, this common background, this shared culture, provided the humor in such productions as "Nunsense" and "Patent Leather Shoes."

This responsibility of passing on the Catholic school culture, the Congregation of Catholic Education writes, "rests with teachers, as individuals and as a community."[38] Learning to do this comes from a full awareness of the Catholic schools as a pastoral instrument; "its specific pastoral service consists in mediating between faith and culture: being faithful to the newness of the Gospel while at the same time respecting the autonomy and the methods proper to human knowledge."[39] Whether this knowledge is internalized by a course on the Church documents regarding its schools, by the community passing this awareness on to its members through social activities, community customs, practices, and traditions, or by way of cooperation with diocesan in-service can be determined by each program, but there must be provision for future teachers to acquire a sense of the school as a pastoral instrument as well as effective skills in promoting total human formation.

Those involved in the preparation program for Catholic school teachers become a learning community, similar to the one proposed by Gabelnick et al.[40] It is characterized by a common shared vision of the Catholic school based on an educational philosophy in which faith, culture, and life are brought into harmony (see Figure 11.1). This cannot be provided by public university teacher education programs, nor by Catholic universities and colleges which do not design programs for the Catholic schools. The American bishops have clearly stated that they believe "teacher education programs which are adequate for public schools are inadequate for teachers in Catholic schools."[41] Because of varied backgrounds, motivations, and perspectives of the prospective teachers, it is suggested that any program contain a wide range of electives with some specific core courses. The program may provide refresher courses for veteran teachers and thus foster the interaction of experienced teachers with beginning teachers. Invitations for observation opportunities may even reinstate some of the most valuable aspects of the demonstration schools.

For over 150 years the cost of training personnel for ministry in the Catholic schools was absorbed by the religious communities themselves. Schools of education associated with Catholic colleges and universities welcomed Sister–teachers from across the country every summer, extending reduced tuition rates in recognition of the low stipends paid by the parishes. In addition, many of the sisters attended classes on Saturdays, and in some cases in the evenings. Lay teachers continue to make sacrifices to acquire a professional education for their work in Catholic schools, but the salaries afforded Catholic school teachers make that a challenge, particularly when additional courses continuously have to be added to state certification.

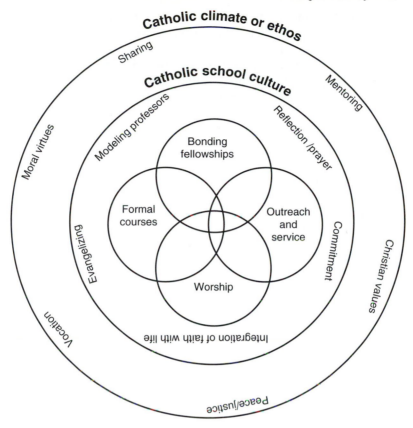

Figure 11.1 Learning community/preparation program for Catholic school teachers

Today, thoughtful Catholic school educators and leaders are challenging the assumption that state credentials are the best means of guaranteeing the preparation of teachers. They want to know how the school and its teachers develop critical thinkers, self-actualizing young people who can internalize their faith life against the hostile environment of an amoral society. In this time of teacher education reform, they are asking what is the best preparation for the Catholic school teacher as the Church faces educating its young for the new millennium. The answer is not the teaching credential as determined by the state.

The answer for Catholic educators is immersion in the culture of the Catholic schools which places value on common prayer and faith sharing, cooperative learning integrating Christian belief and secular knowledge, a life of ministry in the service of others, the practice of virtue, and activities which emanate from the truth that all peoples are sisters and brothers and that God is their father. It is this religious learning experience that must be

153

analyzed, updated, and the best aspects of it linked to the academic programs that have as their aim the preparation of personnel for the Catholic schools. Retaining the religious order charisms in the schools, such as the Dominicans, Jesuits, Franciscans, may no longer be realistic, nor even appropriate after a school has changed into an all-lay-staffed school, but there is a Catholic school charism to be transmitted. It is this charism that must be identified, operationalized, and integrated into traditions, practices, customs, and eventually into a new culture.

Notes

1 Philip Gleason, "Immigration and the American Catholic Intellectual Life," *Review of Politics*, 26 (April 1964): 147–73.

2 Mary Perkins Ryan, *Are Parochial Schools the Answer?* (New York: Holt, Rinehart, and Winston, 1964). This book stunned the Catholic world in the United States when it was published.

3 Elizabeth Ann Bayley Seton became a convert to Catholicism as a young widow and at the suggestion of the Reverend William DuBourg of Baltimore opened a boarding school for young ladies, as a first step to founding a religious institute dedicated to teaching. In June 1809 Mrs. Seton made her vows, a habit was selected, and a rule adopted and the Sisters of Charity of Saint Vincent de Paul came into being. The first parochial school was opened February 22, 1810.

4 The School Controversy raged for three decades toward the end of the nineteenth century between the conservative and liberal churchmen. The point of contention was the purpose, structure, and content of the Catholic schools. Archbishop John Ireland (Saint Paul) wanted to Americanize the Catholics of the United States and felt that in many cases the public school was the best approach. Archbishop Michael Corrigan (New York) held the view that every parish should have a school and that every Catholic child should be educated in a Catholic school.

5 Henry A. Brann, *Most Reverend John Hughes, First Archbishop of New York* (New York: Benziger Brothers, 1982), p. 72.

6 Quoted in John Tracy Ellis, *American Catholicism* (Chicago: The University of Chicago Press, 1955), p. 75.

7 *The Parent First* by Rene Holaind, SJ, Professor of Ethics at Woodstock College, was a response to *Education: To Whom Does it Belong?* by Reverend Thomas Bouquillon, DD, Professor of Moral Theology at the Catholic University of America. The latter brochure challenged the Church's traditional stance that the Church's right to educate was greater than that of the state. Bouquillon asserted that the state had far greater rights over education than the Church had previously declared. Holaind claimed that education belonged to the Church and to the parents. The ensuing debate among the Church's decision-makers over who was more correct can hardly be overstated.

8 The Catholic Educational Association (1904) was an amalgamation of three organizations: The Educational Conference of Seminary Faculties (1897), the Association of Catholic Colleges (1898) and the Parish School Conference (1902). In 1927 the joint organization changed its name to the National Catholic Educational Association (NCEA).

9 See Timothy Walch, *Parish School* (New York: Crossroads Herder, 1996), especially Chapter 9, "The Making of Sister–teachers;" and Sister Bertrande Meyers, *The Education of Sisters* (New York: Sheed and Ward, 1941); Richard Jacobs,

OSA, "U.S. Catholic Schools and the Religious Who Served Them: Contributions of the 18th and 19th Century," in *Catholic Education: A Journal of Inquiry and Practice*, 1, 4 (June 1998): 364–83.

10 Carnegie Foundation, *A Nation Prepared: Teachers for the 21st Century* (New York: Report of the Task Force on Teaching, 1989); Holmes Group, *Tomorrow's Teachers: A Report of the Holmes Group* (East Lansing, MI, 1986).

11 Kevina Keating, CCVI, and Mary Peter Traviss, OP, *Characteristics of Leaders, Pioneer Mentoring in Teacher Preparation: From the Voices of Religious*, in press (St. Cloud, MN: North Star Press of St. Cloud). Parts of this chapter have appeared in the above-mentioned book. As this book goes to press another crisis for the Catholic schools is already being felt. The hundreds of ex-nuns who went into the Catholic schools as administrators at the time the vowed religious left them, have already retired or will soon be retiring. Taking their places will be hundreds of teachers whose training, background, understandings are unknown.

12 Carnegie Foundation, Holmes Group.

13 Keating and Traviss, *Characteristics of Leaders, Pioneer Mentoring in Teacher Preparation: From the Voices of Religious*.

14 Ibid., Interview #59

15 Ibid., Interview #57.

16 Ibid., Interview #42.

17 Ibid., Interview #60.

18 Ibid., Interview #33.

19 Ibid., Interview #47.

20 Ibid., Interview #52.

21 Ibid., Interview #48.

22 Ibid., Interview #44.

23 Madeleva Wolff, CSC, *The Education of Sister Lucy* (Notre Dame, IN: Saint Mary's College, 1949).

24 Ibid., p. 7.

25 Pius XII, Apostolic Exhortation to the First International Convention of Teaching Sisters, September 13, 1951.

26 Ibid.

27 The term "laicized" does not, strictly speaking, apply to Sisters because they are not of the clerical state, but is frequently used to describe their return to secular life.

28 National Conference of Catholic Bishops, *Catholic Higher Education and the Pastoral Mission of the Church* (Washington, DC: NCCB, 1980), p. 6.

29 National Catholic Educational Association, *The Pre-Service Formation of Teachers for Catholic Schools: In Search of Patterns for the Future* (Washington, DC: NCEA, 1982), p. 8.

30 Ibid, p. 9.

31 Ibid.

32 National Conference of Catholic Bishops, *To Teach As Jesus Did*.

33 Ibid., #23.

34 National Conference of Catholic Bishops, *Catholic Higher Education and the Pastoral Mission of the Church* (Washington, DC: NCCB, 1980), p. 6.

35 Keating and Traviss, Interview #35.

36 Ibid., Interview #33.

37 Thomas Sergiovanni, *The Principalship* (New York: Allyn and Bacon, 1987), pp. 58–59.

38 Congregation of Catholic Education, *The Religious Dimension of Education in a Catholic School* (Boston: St. Paul's Books and Media, 1988), #26.

39 Ibid., #31.

40 Robert Barr and John Tagg, "From Teaching to Learning: A New Paradigm for Undergraduate Education," *Change* (November/December 1995); Faith Gabelnick, Jean MacGregor, Roberta S. Matthews, and Barbara Leigh Smith, *Learning Communities: Creating Connections Among Students, Faculty, and Disciplines* (San Francisco: Jossey Bass, 1990); P. Holly and G. Southworth, *The Developing School* (Lewes, United Kingdom: Falmer Press, 1989); Ernest Boyer, "The Basic School: A Community for Learning: A New Beginning," Address delivered to the National Association of Elementary School Principals annual convention, April 11, 1995, San Diego, California.
41 United States Catholic Conference, *Catholic Higher Education and the Pastoral Mission of the Church* (Washington, DC, 1980), p. 6.

12 Ongoing Staff Development in Catholic Schools

Joseph F. Rogus and Colleen A. Wildenhaus

Schools are instituted to serve their communities as havens for learning, not as microcosms of the marketplace. Here students are apprenticed to life in its ideal form, life that is:

> – devoted to inquiry,
> – touched by beauty,
> – informed by justice,
> – guided by reason,
> – guided by simplicity,
> – graced by elegance, and
> – sanctified by caring.

This statement hangs on the front wall of a New England teacher development center, and its message strikes with great clarity. Faculty are unlikely to provide the opportunity for students to fully develop their academic and life skills unless teachers themselves are personally supported in the development of these same abilities. Teachers cannot, for example, help learners develop the competence to inquire without personally being engaged in inquiry, nor are they likely to develop a deep sense of caring for others unless they are personally cared for. Simply put, offering quality programs for students requires that comparable energy first be placed on the provision of ongoing staff development programming for teachers.

Providing ongoing staff development may be the principal's single most formidable challenge. This challenge is formidable, not simply because of the linkage of student program effectiveness and faculty staff development activity, but because the field of staff development has recently experienced several paradigm shifts which have seriously impacted principal behavior.

In the first of these shifts, staff development has come to be defined as what individuals and groups within the organization do in order to pursue their growth. The redefined concept embodies the notions of self-determination, self-assessment, and personalized planning. It connotes that each person and each unit in the organization (department, grade level, and/or cluster) has responsibility for his/her/its own development. This definition represents a dramatic departure from the historically embedded, other-directed definition, familiar to most veteran teachers: that staff development is whatever the organization does to individuals and groups to bring them to a desired level of competence.

In the second paradigm shift, the concept of staff development has also expanded in meaning to encompass both individual and organizational dimensions. Historically, the prevailing paradigm emphasized individual growth only. With the onset of school effectiveness research, however, planners came to see the importance of building a strong organizational dimension to staff development programming. In essence, effective schools have come to be characterized by strong programming on both personal and group dimensions.

The third paradigm shift is likewise fundamental. It calls for evaluators to assess program effectiveness by evaluating the impact of staff development programs upon student learning. This shift is a serious departure from the well-established tendency within the profession to assess program effectiveness simply by asking participants whether they enjoyed the program they experienced.

For the principal, these paradigm shifts pose a demanding threefold challenge: to help faculty assume increasing responsibility for their own growth; to assure that staff development programs encompass both personal growth and organizational development emphases; and to maintain a program assessment perspective that centers on the effects of staff development programs upon student learning. This challenge is further complicated by two "nitty-gritty" factors. First, the shift to staff development by increasing self-direction is easier to talk about than to do. As learners, we tend to do as we have been "done to," and most of our staff development experiences have been largely other directed. Shifting the focus to a self-directed orientation requires careful planning. Second, Catholic school principals have responsibility to enhance not only the professional development of faculty but their spiritual formation as well. Achievement of a program balance is difficult, particularly given the limited staff development time available for faculty use.

The Staff Development Challenge: Building a Comprehensive Staff Development Program

In essence, the challenge to the principal is to assure that faculty are engaged in professional growth and spiritual formation activity that results in improved student learning, and to do so on an ongoing basis. The call is to provide a comprehensive program, one that has an informal and a formal dimension. Honoring this challenge requires that principals carry out the following tasks.

1   View all interactions with faculty as having staff development implications.
2   Make a clear distinction between informal and formal staff development activity.
3   Build a strong, informal staff development program.
4   Set the stage for a strong formal program.
5   Consider specific program priorities: formal staff development and spiritual formation.
6   Identify priorities.
7   Honor basic program implementation guidelines.

Each of these tasks is complex. While the first task rests with the principal alone, all others require the very best thinking of the principal, faculty, and staff.

Task 1: View All Interactions with Faculty as Having Staff Development Implications

Staff development is first and foremost an attitude, a commitment to free people to refine their personal gifts. Where there exists the desire to create a strong and comprehensive staff development program, the principal possesses an orientation to facilitate faculty growth, and faculty and staff know, at least intuitively, that their development is a primary focus of the school's operation. Faculty further understand the linkage between their growth and that of students. Unless faculty are first comfortable with themselves, they are unlikely to provide a growth-inducing environment for youngsters.

Task 2: Make a Clear Distinction Between Informal and Formal Staff Development Activity

Bringing a positive attitude to the staff development charge requires that the principal approach both informal and formal program efforts from an active posture.

Informal staff development relates to what is done on a daily basis within the building to establish a supportive climate for faculty and staff. It relates to what constitutes the culture of the school. Stated another way, the informal program serves as teachers' implicit curriculum, the messages they catch from working in the school. From the daily environment teachers may learn that they are valued as persons, that prayer is an essential part of professional life, that teaching is inquiry, that faculty collaboration is important, and that faculty discussion of the substance of what they teach is normal everyday activity. On the other hand, they may also learn a set of counterproductive messages; they may learn that classroom control is more important than classroom learning, that teaching is isolated activity, that teachers seldom observe and reflect on one another's work, and that staff are too busy to celebrate one another's major life events.

Over time, the messages that teachers internalize as they go about the business of keeping school become a part of their self-concept. In a sense, what teachers experience day in and day out sets the upper limit on the perspective they bring to formal staff development programming.

Formal staff development activity is composed of that set of planned programs designed to bring about changes among faculty and staff. The term formal connotes that a planning group has engaged in a series of steps. The group has: (1) diagnosed the environment and identified a set of staff development needs; (2) established a clear set of program goals and objectives; (3) planned a set of learning strategies to achieve those objectives; and (4) developed approaches for assessing program effectiveness. The planning group then takes steps to assure that the planned program is implemented and assessed, and then proceeds to build more advanced plans.

Task 3: Build a Strong, Informal Staff Development Program

Once the principal has in mind a clear image of the distinction between informal and formal programs, his or her first key challenge is to plan a strong informal staff development program. This implies two major actions:

1   identifying a conceptual framework which can serve to guide the development and implementation of a cultural vision for the school, and this vision will constitute the heart and soul of the informal phase of the staff development program; and
2   working with faculty and staff to identify action steps that might bring this vision to life.

Both steps can bring staff together to strengthen the culture, while serving a valuable program function as well.

Identifying a Conceptual Framework

Saphier and King (1985) examined cultural norms that appear to create a positive impact on school improvement efforts. The cultural characteristics of productive environments that they identified can be helpful in generating a conceptual framework to guide the planning of a strong informal program:

- expressing appreciation for and giving recognition to teachers for the good work they do;
- caring, celebration, and humor;
- experimentation;

- maintaining high expectations;
- providing tangible support for faculty projects;
- prizing the knowledge base of the field;
- protecting the values that are important to faculty;
- maintaining open and honest communications.

(Saphier and King 1985)

In planning for the informal phase of a staff development program, it is not important to adopt any or all of the eight norms; it is significant to focus on a limited number of "guiding concepts" and then develop action steps keyed to these concepts.

Rosenholtz's work (1991), *The teacher's workplace*, can serve as an additional source for stimulating informal programming activity. In her study of "moving schools," she noted several characteristics that make a difference:

- teachers are engaged in developing shared school goals;
- teachers collaborate;
- teachers are actively engaged in their own learning;
- teachers command the knowledge base of the profession and dialogue with one another around that knowledge base;
- teachers are committed to making a difference in the lives of children.

(Rosenholtz 1991)

These characteristics can likewise serve as a starter point in building an informal program and are particularly valuable because their presence is closely correlated with high student achievement. This relationship with academic achievement makes them a highly acceptable set of focal points for both teachers and parents.

In addition to the findings cited from the school effectiveness research, program planners can also look at unique features of Catholic identity and the findings on Catholic school effectiveness to serve as basic values upon which to develop plans for creating the day-to-day school culture. They might consider, for example, the Church's values that Groome (1996) notes, such as Catholicism's sacramentality of life, its communal emphases, its positive anthropology of persons, its appreciation of rationality, or its commitment to tradition. Or they could choose to center on key concepts identified by Bryk (1996) as essential elements of effective Catholic schools such as strong decentralized governance, a strong academic curriculum, communal organization, personalism, and subsidiarity.

To build a positive climate requires that the principal work with faculty to commit to a cluster of values, and to develop action plans to make the vision of that cluster a reality. The most important point to bear in mind while going through this process is that once faculty commit to a core set of values, they will likely grow to view themselves as professionals and then positively respond to formal staff development opportunities that might become available.

Following is an example of how the informal program development process might work. A principal may choose in concert with a faculty planning group to key in on the following values: (a) caring and celebration; (b) appreciation and recognition; (c) prizing the knowledge base; (d) engaging in the goal-setting process; (e) engaging in professional growth; and (f) prizing the dignity of each person. They then could work together in developing action plans designed to bring each of these values to life. These values need not be addressed all at once; each, however, would have to be addressed systematically over the course of a school year. Here is a listing of tactics that might be applied with faculty in addressing the selected values:

Values	*Tactics*
Caring and celebration	Holding birthday parties
	Scheduling a weekly prayer group
	Participating in a coed volleyball league
Appreciation and recognition	Providing public recognition for faculty
	Providing opportunities for faculty and staff to engage in professional meetings
Prizing the knowledge base	Sharing articles/tapes with faculty
	Purchasing prescriptions for faculty
Engaging in the goal-setting process	Writing a vision statement
	Writing a mission statement
Engaging in professional growth	Engaging faculty in personal development
Planning	Supporting faculty in staff development areas
Prizing the dignity of each person	Engaging gently with one another
	Establishing a mentoring program for faculty

Once efforts to create a supportive culture in the building are underway, principals need to focus faculty energy on the formal phase of staff development programming.

Task 4: Set the Stage for a Strong Formal Program

Setting the stage for planning a strong formal program involves two steps: (1) assuring that the prerequisites to developing a strong program are in place; and (2) identifying an organizational emphasis(es) for formal programming. Each of these steps is important; each is ongoing in nature; and each, carried out carefully, has strong potential payoff toward improving the quality of life within the school.

Assuring That Prerequisites to a Strong Program Are in Place

Building a strong formal program requires three basic prerequisite commitments from the principal:

1　Establish a policy with the advisory board that clearly stipulates that involvement with both staff development and religious formation is an expectancy of all members of the faculty.

　　By establishing a clear policy, the board is stating publicly that all employees are expected to pursue both professional growth and religious development. The policy in turn gives to principals who may be less than sure of themselves the support they need to implement planned staff development programs.

2　Establish a separate budget line for staff development and spiritual formation programming.

　　Dollars for staff development, however few they may be, are normally embedded in a personnel line. The result is that the amount that school leaders spend for the professional and spiritual growth of teachers is often masked. Such masking is not healthy for two reasons. First, school personnel do not confront how little they spend on staff development; and second, without accurate baseline data, it is difficult to build the case for increasing the budget. In essence, having a budget line and being precise about what is spent gives the school leadership a solid basis for program planning and for recruiting additional dollars when they find that what they are expending is less than defensible.

3　Commit to engage faculty in the program planning process beginning with the diagnosis of needs and extending through specific program planning, implementation, and evaluation.

　　This commitment is particularly important. The key point is that effective program development is not likely to occur unless those affected by implementation are involved in the planning, implementation, and evaluation processes.

Identifying the Organizational Focus for Formal Programming

The planning group's first task is to identify the level(s) for program implementation. There are three possible centers for focus and each is important:

1   the individual faculty member;
2   the department, grade level, or cluster;
3   the total school.

In essence, if the commitment to professional growth is to permeate the organization, action must be taken at all levels. First, each faculty member must be expected to actively engage in professional/spiritual growth activity. Second, each unit of the organization must be committed to enhancing its growth. Each department or grade cluster, for example, must address the question "What are we doing to strengthen ourselves programmatically so that we are increasingly effective with children?" Finally, there should be an all-school commitment to the staff development emphasis, a commitment to the achievement of a common growth goal.

In a fully functioning program action takes place on all levels, i.e., the individual, the unit, and the school. It is quite understandable to have action going on at only two levels, but the ideal is three. More significantly, it is important that all faculty are engaged in one or more ways in the pursuit of their growth at more than one organizational level.

Task 5: Consider Specific Program Priorities: Formal Staff Development and Spiritual Formation

Once the decision is made to take action on different levels, such as the unit or the school, the challenge is to identify program priorities in the areas of both professional development and spiritual formation. The development of specific program plans then follows.

Before considering the process for identifying program priorities and specific action plans, it is important to differentiate between the two major types of formal program emphases, i.e., staff development and spiritual formation.

Formal Staff Development

Staff development is a broad range of activities designed to promote professional growth. The key phrase in the definition is "broad range," suggesting that a wide range of activity can fall under the definition. The term encompasses committee work, classroom observation, curriculum writing, engagement in inquiry, participation in in-service, and a host of other possibilities. In essence, the forms of formal staff development are limited only by the imagination. If an activity leads to professional growth, if it is long term in orientation, and it involves those who participate in a personal choice, then it is staff development.

Formal Staff Development Models

The following are basic models that warrant consideration in planning:

- individually guided staff development;
- classroom observation – assessment (curriculum revision, problem solving, pedagogical/leadership, program improvement);
- involvement in a development/program improvement plan;
- training;
- inquiry.

These categories of models are broad enough to encompass most types of professional development activity. Each calls for a different implementation strategy (Sparks and Loucks-Horsley 1995).

INDIVIDUALLY GUIDED STAFF DEVELOPMENT

Implementation of the individually guided staff development model involves each participant in the following steps: (1) identification of a personal need; (2) development of a plan to meet the need; (3) participation in a planned learning activity; and (4) assessment of whether the learning meets the identified need. The model enables planners to address the unique needs of teachers of different levels such as kindergarten, sixth grade, and high school following identical procedures. During the implementation process, the principal's major task is to provide for the faculty the support required to facilitate goal achievement.

The individually guided staff development model has enormous power for two reasons: (1) it enables leadership to honor differences in need and interest among faculty; and (2) it places the responsibility for growth on each individual thereby countering what has, in most instances, been an other-directed culture. In the individually guided staff development model, each faculty member is responsible for his or her own growth.

CLASSROOM OBSERVATION–ASSESSMENT

The observation–assessment model assumes that "reflection and analysis are central means of professional growth" (Loucks-Horsley et al. 1987). Observation and assessment provide the teacher with data that can be examined for the straightforward purpose of improving student learning. The model further assumes that observation and assessment of instruction can benefit both involved parties – the teacher being observed and the observer. The final assumption underlying the approach is that teachers are more apt to engage in improvement when they see positive results from their efforts to change.

Peer observation is a form of the observation–assessment model. In peer observation, teachers visit one another's classrooms, gather objective data about teacher or student behaviors, and give feedback in a follow-up conference. The model usually involves a pre-observation conference, observation, analysis of data, and a post-observation conference. From the process of observation, reflection, and sharing, teachers can grow enormously.

INVOLVEMENT IN A DEVELOPMENT/IMPROVEMENT PLAN

Involvement in program improvement efforts constitutes an important third staff development model. Such involvement can take a variety of forms including curriculum development or revision and problem solving. The program improvement model is predicated on three assumptions: (1) that adults learn when they have a need to know; (2) that people closest to the job best understand what is required to improve their performance; and (3) teachers acquire important knowledge and skills through involvement in school improvement processes. While the program improvement model may take a variety of forms, its essential elements are common. The model incorporates the following steps: (1) problem and goal identification; (2) identification of enhancing and constraining forces; (3) delineation of action alternatives; (4) selection of action steps; and (5) making plans for assessing performance. When the problem is curricular in its orientation, it involves the cyclical process of needs assessment, writing curriculum objective statements, pilot testing and evaluation, and implementation.

In any form, the program improvement process involves faculty in reflection, sharing, and helping one another. It is a powerful staff development mechanism.

TRAINING

Training involves in-service programming that is keyed to the improvement of teaching and leadership skills. In essence, in-service is skill-related staff development. Its focus is helping participants learn new behaviors, e.g., to develop conflict management skills, or master the application of new software.

Research has provided us with sound direction on what is necessary to provide effective training. Joyce and Showers (1988) have determined that effective training should include explanation of theory, modeling, practice of a skill under simulated conditions, feedback about performance, and coaching in the workplace. They also cite the importance of discussion and peer observation as training activities (Joyce and Showers 1995).

The training model has extraordinary potential for altering teachers' attitudes, knowledge, and instructional skills.

INQUIRY

Inquiry reflects a belief in teachers' ability to formulate valid questions about their own practice and to pursue objectives aligned to those questions. The overarching assumption of the model is that the most effective avenue for professional development is cooperative study by the teachers themselves of problems and issues arising from their attempts to make their practice consistent with their educational values (Sparks and Loucks-Horsley 1995).

The inquiry model can take many forms, but these forms have a number of elements in common:

- a group of teachers identify a problem of interest;
- they explore ways of collecting data;
- these data are then collected, analyzed, and interpreted by the group; and
- program changes are made and new data are gathered and analyzed to determine the effects of the intervention.

Organizational support and technical assistance may be needed throughout the different phases of the inquiry activity.

The inquiry approach, like the development/program improvement process, can have an extensive payoff for faculty outside the classroom. As faculty and administrators work collaboratively, they can strengthen the day-to-day spirit of collegiality and build a forged informal staff development program in the process.

Throughout the planning process, the principal's challenge is to keep these five models in the forefront as the group reflects on the models that have potential for impact at the individual, unit, and building level.

Spiritual Formation

The diminishing numbers and changing role of religious in schools, the shifting context within the Church, and the expanding responsibility of Catholic schools point to the need for focus on extensive religious formation for all faculty. Keeping Christ at the center of all that faculty do is an important challenge for Catholic school staff, and this challenge requires that planners focus on a set of spiritual development outcomes and action plans to address those outcomes.

Following is a listing of spiritual formation categories and a set of action approaches from which faculty might choose in order to pursue their spiritual formation.

Category	Action approaches
Changes within the Catholic Church	Presentation/discussion of topics of religious interest, e.g., systematic theology, scriptural studies, pastoral theology
	Making available journals, magazines, and books which address topics of interest to Catholics
Personal religious formation	Liturgical events planned and implemented by faculty throughout the year
	Retreat programs
	Spiritual direction
	Prayer groups
	Faculty involvement in student religious activities
Commitment to Catholic education	Participation in school accreditation processes
	Development of school vision and mission statements
	Explanation of the religion program used throughout the building
	Identification of the specifics that define the school's Catholic identity
Religious development of the young	Formal study of how students develop morally, including the stage development theories of Kohlberg and Fowler
	Engaging in case studies of normal and abnormal religious development
	Participation in liturgies, retreats, prayer groups, and discussion with students
Involvement with social justice	Participation in student justice programs
	Integration of social justice issues into the curriculum
	Bringing in speakers to address topics of social justice, hunger, and peace

The principal and planning group must carefully review each category and action alternative and then decide what they might do to best support faculty as they make themselves the most giving teachers they are able.

Task 6: Identify Priorities

An extraordinary challenge to the principal and staff in planning a balanced formal program is coping with the fact that staff development time and resources are limited. One way of addressing this challenge is to decide upon an emphasis(es) under each category (professional development and spiritual formation), one that is likely to have a positive impact upon faculty and students, than to focus on making these emphases come alive.

In essence, in addressing the priority-setting challenge, the planning group needs to keep in mind the following with respect to comprehensive programming:

- Equivalent emphasis must be centered on professional development as well as spiritual formation activity.

    This point may be obvious, but it is very difficult to keep at the center. The day-to-day program demands of science, history, literature, and the writing process can push to the background proper concern for the extent to which faculty are honoring the school's Catholic identity. The principal and the planning group must take great care to assure that this does not occur.
- Not all faculty need to be engaged in the same staff development model during the same time frame.

    Some faculty, e.g., the mathematics department, may be engaged in curriculum revision; the English department may be focused on obser-vation–assessment; and the social studies department may be undergoing computer training. In addition, all faculty may be experi-encing the individually guided staff development model.
- Program effectiveness must be assessed by how well children learn.

    As noted earlier, the bottom line in assessing the efforts of staff development programs is the impact of the program on the learning of students. No matter how intrinsically satisfying the staff development activity may be, planners must continually ask: "Are students better off because of what we as adults are doing for our own growth?"

In identifying program priorities, planners have a choice. They could first look at the needs of learners and determine their staff development programs from those needs; they could look closely at the needs of faculty; or they could consider a combination of the two factors.

Building from Student Program Needs

Following are three examples of student program needs and sample staff development programs that might emerge from those needs.

Student needs	Staff development program
Student performance on the standardized algebra examination administered by the school is one standard deviation below the norm	Members of the mathematics department will receive training in an individualized mathematics program and implement the program with the freshman algebra group
Less than 30% of juniors and seniors enrolled in advance science classes over the past two years	Science department faculty will engage in inquiry on why students are not enrolling in science classes in higher percentages and develop an action plan designed to increase enrollments
Less than 30% of seventh- and eighth-grade students choose to participate in a tutorial program with third- and fourth-graders	Seventh- and eighth-grade faculty will master the *Tutorial Program*, train all seventh- and eighth-grade students in carrying out the program, supervise the program's implementation, and assess its effects

Building from Faculty Needs

A second approach is to engage faculty, individually as well as by unit, in identifying needs or wants they have which, addressed effectively, may result in their being more effective teachers. One single straightforward approach to gathering planning data is asking teachers to identify needs/interests they have under a specific set of categories, such as:

- spiritual formation;
- instructional improvement;
- understanding Church documents;
- personalizing instruction; and
- strengthening classroom observation.

Once data are collected and considered alongside the student program needs identified earlier, priorities for the year can be set.

The most pivotal question in setting those priorities needs to be, "Which program outcomes, effectively addressed, will result in the greatest difference in the quality of life for students and faculty?" Once planners respond with certainty to this question, the planned program will be well on its way.

Task 7: Honor Basic Program Implementation Guidelines

After the decision has been made as to where to place the program emphases for the semester or school year and to what extent to center on professional and spiritual dimensions, principals need to carefully manage the programs they have set in place. Implementation guidelines are relatively easy to state; they warrant particularly careful attention, however, because the busyness of the day often pushes these guidelines into the background. This is why most program problems can be traced to difficulties with implementation as opposed to conceptualization.

Program Guidelines

To assure the presence of a strong staff development program, principals need to honor the following guidelines (Caldwell 1989; Orlich 1989; Wood and Thompson 1980). The principal will:

- participate fully in the school's staff development program. The modeling power of this involvement can in no way be underestimated.
- involve each faculty member in formal staff development activity. Teachers will have choices with respect to their form of involvement, but do not have the choice of whether to be involved.
- predicate the staff development programs on what is known of adult learning. Participants engaged in staff development programming should be actively involved in a variety of learning activities including role play, simulation, observation of one another's classes, and actively helping one another.
- consider one-shot in-service sessions as anathema. They may be held on rare occasions on the direction of a higher authority, such as the diocesan office or the school board, but only when teachers are willing participants.
- provide resource support for faculty.
- schedule staff development programs as close to the actual site of teaching as possible; activities should be held at the school of program participants whenever appropriate.
- do everything possible to assure that staff development activities are perceived as non-threatening and non-judgmental, even informal and relaxing.
- arrange for support teams to offer help to teachers. Such teams might include a veteran colleague, a school principal, a state department specialist, and a clinician from a local university.
- provide time for faculty outside the defined student day in order to participate in staff development activity. In addition, provide monetary reimbursement for them and recognition of their involvement.

• study carefully the correlation between student academic and spiritual growth and faculty staff development activity. It may not be possible to draw a one-to-one correspondence between the factors, but effort must be devoted to finding a relationship between them.

Conclusion

In this chapter we have presented a strategy for developing and maintaining an ongoing staff development program at the building level. In presenting a program planning strategy, emphasis was placed on the following: the importance of the principal's approaching all interactions with faculty from a staff development perspective; building a comprehensive staff develop-ment program; assuring that the basic prerequisites to developing a strong formal program are first in place; specifying where the program's formal organizational focus will be centered; and identifying specific program plans (both professional development and spiritual formation).

The importance of managing the program both effectively and efficiently was then emphasized.

In reflecting on the management of program matters, the authors noted the importance of principals keeping in the forefront the principle that spirit always transcends form. Putting it another way, leaders cannot permit the mechanics of the staff development program to drive the program's purposes to the background.

Principals and others with leadership responsibility must remind them-selves as they supervise the implementation of staff development programs that:

• the primary purpose of staff development is to free teachers to refine their gifts so they are better able to serve students;
• the most basic way in which we free teachers to refine their gifts is by providing for them a strong informal program that results in a supportive day-to-day culture wherein they come to value themselves as strong contributing professionals; and
• once a supportive culture is in place, we provide faculty opportunity to access a variety of professional growth and spiritual formation models, and support them as they participate fully in those models.

We do this so they may grow in their ability to teach as Jesus did, therein helping all youngsters fully develop their academic and spiritual gifts.

References

Bryk, A. (1996) "Lessons from Catholic high schools on renewing our educational institutions," in T. McLaughlin, J. O'Keefe, and B. O'Keefe (eds.), *The contempo-*

rary Catholic school: Context, identity and diversity, pp. 25–41, London: Falmer Press.

Caldwell, S.D. (ed.) (1989) *Staff development: A handbook of effective practices*, Oxford, OH: National Staff Development Council.

Groome, T. (1996) "What makes a school Catholic," in T. McLaughlin, J. O'Keefe, and B. O'Keefe (eds.), *The contemporary Catholic school: Context, identity and diversity*, pp. 107–25), London: Falmer Press.

Joyce, B. and Showers, B. (1988) *Student achievement through staff development*, New York: Longman.

Joyce, B. and Showers, B. (1995) *Student achievement through staff development* (2nd ed.), New York: Longman.

Loucks-Horsley, S., Harding, C., Arbuckle, M., Murray, L., Dubea, C., and Williams, S. (1987) *Continuing to learn: A guidebook for teacher development*, Andover, MD: The Regional Laboratory for Educational Improvement of the Northeast and Islands.

Orlich, D.C. (1989) *Staff development: Enhancing human potential*, Boston: Allyn and Bacon.

Rosenholtz, S. (1991) *The teacher's workplace: The social organization of schools*, New York: Teachers College Press.

Saphier, J. and King, M. (1985) "Good seeds grow in strong cultures." *Educational Leadership*, 42 (6), 67–74.

Sparks, D. and Loucks-Horsley, S. (1995) *Five models of staff development for teachers*, Oxford, OH: National Staff Development Council.

Wood, F. and Thompson, S. (1980) "Guidelines for better staff development," *Educational Leadership*, 37 (5), 374–78.

13 Kaizening[1] into the Future

Distance Education

Sister Angela Ann Zukowski, MHSH

The animated message flashed across my computer screen: "The Internet, or whatever succeeds it in capacity and ability, will simply determine what life-long learning programming looks like in the 21st century." Thus began a month-long Internet conversation with colleagues from around the world searching to define alternative methodologies for our curriculum designs in our diverse distance education practices.

There is no doubt that lifelong learning is a central feature of the Information Age. John Sculley (President of Apple Computers) predicted that "the universities as networks of interdependence" are going to be the center of a new renaissance.[2] Thus, as we engage in the application of the Internet and other telecommunication resources to enhance our teaching and learning, we are fundamentally preparing our students by nurturing life-long learning skills. Two-way or multi-way distance education is no longer a dream but rapidly becoming a reality in more and more Catholic schools at all levels. This chapter both explores a concrete example of how distance education is being integrated into the Department of Religious Studies graduate program in collaboration with Chaminade University (Hawaii) and engages the reader in our insights resulting from continuous research and development in distance education in our attempt to shift our paradigm of teaching and learning at the university graduate level.

Distance Education Is Not a New Concept

The development of the postal service in the nineteenth century jettisoned a new way of learning into American culture. While interest in distance education continues to grow, an effort to define the concept remains inconsistent, and in many cases dated and incomplete. This is particularly true as some educators continue to link distance education chiefly to correspondence study having the following characteristics: (1) physical separation of student and teacher; (2) separated in time from the teacher; and/or (3) learners are independent of contact with the teacher or with other students.[3]

With the passing of time educators have used other methods of instructional delivery besides the traditional correspondence study via the postal service. The telephone, along with other media conduits such as radio and television broadcasting and computers, began to play an important role in teaching and learning. The term correspondence study which was associated with the written and printed word was not perceived as adequately describing distance education utilizing these non-postal modes of delivery. This created a problem for educators attempting to gain acceptance for their new distance education methods. Verduin and Clark indicated that distance educators did not share a large common body of knowledge, theory or philosophy; thus, they borrowed from related fields specifically instructional television and continuing education.

Verduin and Clark[4] imply that the term distance education was popularized in German (*Fernunterricht*) by the German educator Otto Peters in the 1960s and 1970s and was employed as a title for distance teaching institutions in France (*tele-enseignement*). The English term, distance education, was probably reintroduced in North America by Bjorn Holmberg and Michael Moore at a meeting of the International Council for Correspondence Education.[5] The Educational Resources Information Center (ERIC) did not begin to use distance education as a descriptor until 1983.[6]

Today we are beginning to understand that the introduction of telecommunications technology calls for a restructuring of the definition. The term "distance education" is being used according to Barker et al. more frequently by educators and legislators to refer to simultaneous telecommunicated delivery of instruction from a host site or classroom to distant sites, coupled with live audio, and/or video, and/or text interaction between teacher and student(s) – not to correspondence study in the traditional sense. In places like Alaska, Australia, and Montana, where many primary and secondary students are scattered in remote areas, youngsters have for a long time been taught at home via radio and television. Today we face a new reality with the emergence of new information technologies especially like the computer and specifically the Internet. If in a remote rural community or high school, there are one or two students who want to take some course that is not immediately available in their small school or community college, those students can be connected to another remote college/university or high school where such a course is offered through the Internet or other telecommunication technology.

The rapid evolution of the Internet's capabilities has triggered a battery of new questions, concerns, and opportunities yet to be revealed, understood, or, engaged for enhancing the quality of Catholic education on all levels. Turkle[7] suggests that the new technologies, especially the computer, catalyze change not only in what people do, but in how they think. The new information technologies – combining computers, telecommunications, and video technology – represent a whole new generation of learning tools. While some educators perceive these new technologies as being bold, grandiose, and exciting there are others who do not share this vision or enthusiasm. What is required now is to move beyond the claims and the rhetoric, to begin to establish a base of rich experiences with the new technologies within our learning environments.

We have a great need for paradigm pioneers within our Catholic education circles for distance education. Our research in 1998 indicated that Catholic education on all levels is far behind general education in the creation of alternative forms of distance education. This does include Catholic colleges and universities. Catholic educators need to experiment with a variety of approaches to using these technologies, to carefully evaluate the processes and results of their use and report their results. Thus, the conversation about defining distance education has only begun to be explored. It is imperative that we continue to clarify the definition in order to understand the inherent strengths that new technologies bring to our educational environments and to guide related curriculum research and design in the new information age. As Catholic educators continue to understand and experience the value of redefining not only distance education but also creative design and application of it within their learning environments, new opportunities emerge for nurturing lifelong learners.

The last survey[8] taken regarding distance education indicated that a third of our colleges and universities are offering some kind of electronically delivered courses, with another quarter of them getting set to do the same. The report indicated that 23% of the institutions that offered distance education courses in fall 1995 offered degrees that students could complete by taking distance education courses exclusively, and 7% offered certificates that could be completed in this manner.[9]

Another indicator of how big this already has become is the size of the 1998 *Peterson's Guide to Distance Learning Programs*, which has more than 700 very large pages. Numerous two-way, full-motion interactive television projects are operating between cooperating high schools in Minnesota, Wisconsin, Iowa, Illinois, New York, and other states. Considering the expeditious involvement of schools and related educational agencies growing and offering rich course diversity especially on the Internet, these figures continue to rapidly expand. So also do the number of students engaged in the process. The most recent figures, which are three years out of date, tabulated three-quarters of a million students taking distance learning courses.[10]

Fueled by state-sponsored curriculum reform intended to upgrade secondary graduation requirements, the concept of "distance education" has caught the attention of both national and state education officials.[11] As higher education administrators face the challenges of declining enrollments, an aging student population, and reduced levels of state funding they are beginning to demonstrate interest in the alternative possibilities that distance education could offer.

Designing a Prototype for Graduate Religious Studies Distance Education

I am one of the old-time pioneers in distance education. In 1972 I began producing adult religious education, teacher formation, and enrichment courses as well as high school religious education courses on cable TV. Many experts in the field of education informed me that there was no future in cable TV; thus, I should abandon these initiatives for more traditional approaches. Well, we did not take their advice and moved from airing our pre-taped cable TV courses into thirty-five rural communities to eventually in 1984 produce live synchronous video teleconferences/courses on the Catholic Telecommunications Network of America for national distribution. The rich experiences from 1984 to 1993 demonstrated to me the great potential distance education offered to our Catholic educators and interested adults throughout the United States. In 1994 I began exploring how the integration of computers and specifically the Internet could further advance the teaching/learning process. The advent of a new collaborative partnership with the University of Dayton and Chaminade University (1996) to offer graduate courses with the support of telecommunication technologies created another new perspective on teaching and learning. The challenge was to bring to bear on this new experience all our research and experiences in distance education. It was decided that with a combination of innovative distance learning and traditional classroom interaction new opportunities would evolve for both our students and faculties.

We were aware that the learning curve for Internet and distance education teaching/learning was steep, especially for persons with little computer or Internet skills. We believed that the formation of a community of learners is imperative for the socialization process for effective teaching/learning. We knew we would have to design a process that would combine the best of what we had found exhibited in existing distance education courses/programs around the country.

The courses we have been designing[12] evolve through three phases of participation. The first phase is a traditional multimedia classroom experience. Students meet for three- to four-hour sessions for five consecutive days forming a community of learners, being introduced to the basic principles and concepts of the courses' content, and developing the technical and interpersonal communication skills required to participate in the following phases. Each class is multimedia as both Astound computer presentations and videocassettes are woven into the learning experience. The class is interactive as a diversity of interactive communication experiences are created to advance the formation of our community of learners.

The second phase gives the students eight weeks to commence the required readings and engage in individual personal critical reflection relating readings to life experiences. This phase encourages the students to become aware of the importance of quality quiet time or personal reflection on the course content/theme. A study guide enables the students to thoroughly review the material and prepare them to participate in the conversations and case studies to be presented in the third phase of the course.

The third phase engages the students for nine weeks. Every two weeks students participate in a live interactive video class. Both sites are fully equipped with ISDN lines and a PictureTel system that offers camera, microphone, video projection unit, videocassette recorder with sending and taping capabilities, monitors, document camera, and data transmission capabilities. It is a synchronous learning experience. The system, with units in both classrooms, uses a voice-activated camera with a sensor that searches for and automatically zooms in on the professor and/or student speaking. Multidirectional microphones offer complete coverage of each classroom. Each live video class is sixty minutes long. Guest presenters or conversational facilitators are invited to share their area of expertise that is related to the course content and the readings. The primary professor, in this case myself, adds continuity with the course development by guiding the students in connecting the guest presentation with earlier phases of the course and their Internet Discussion Board academic work.

In the weeks between the live video classes students use the Internet to study cases, participate in the course discussion board, e-mail other students and professors about readings, and share insights about working on their final project for the course. Regularly the professor monitors the discussions and keeps in touch with the students affirming, encouraging, and motivating the students to realize the outcomes of the course. Students are encouraged to create special interest groups on given books or themes discussed during the online sessions and live video classes. Thus, even after a particular book is finished and the class has moved to another concept, some students may decide to continue the conversation on a particular theme. This initiative is an opportunity to further support the formation of a concept of a community of learners. The students can preserve the online seminar interactions. Messages can be collected from the threaded conversations, saved on a diskette or in a (PC Internet) file, and become permanent records for future reference. Also, each live video class is taped; thus, students can have access to the previous classes to review the material at their own leisure or post-view the class due to an absence. The taping of each live video class enables the professor to expand video resources for accessibility and integration into future classes on the related subject. This contrasts with the completely ephemeral nature of verbal discussions in seminars in traditional learning environments. There is no doubt in my mind that there is a steep learning curve required to participate in these distance education experiences. This is especially the case with traditional learners and/or older adults who are returning to college with limited experience of telecommunication realities and new learning experiences. Students begin to feel more comfortable as the professor is aware that he or she is required to offer constant and consistent presence and attention to the dynamics operative among the students on the Internet.

Each year we notice a more technically sophisticated student participating in our courses. As this occurs, we are able to experiment and advance a variety of approaches in applying these technologies for supporting our community of learners on their lifelong learning programs and paths.

We are aware that a variety of modes and systems can be used to deliver distance education as mentioned earlier in this chapter. These are audiocassettes, telephone, radio, television broadcast/cable/telecourses, microwave broadcasting compressed video, CDs, VCDs, satellite broadcasting, videocassettes, computers, Internet, and print. Many of these can be combined into multimedia packages that appeal to students with different learning styles.

What We Have Learned as We Move Forward

There is no doubt that print has many advantages as an instructional medium. It is familiar, inexpensive, and portable. Its format allows readers access to any section, in any order, for any length of time. It is the only medium that can be utilized without additional equipment, anytime and anywhere that a source of light is available. Print media still remain the backbone of distance education and are used in combination with other media.

There is something comfortable with the traditional classroom. Depending on how creative or media-savvy a professor is with integrating multimedia into the learning experience, the classroom can be uncomplicated and the content and process well controlled by the professor. It basically appears to be a safe learning environment. Or is it? Our learning environments need to be more than safe. They should be experimental, challenging, invigorating, inviting critical reflective thought and authentic dialogue (which is not monologue) in the searching for new ideas and insights to stimulate the intellectual, social, political, educational, and even religious imagination of our students.

We have designed a threefold kaleidoscopic map (Figure 13.1) to guide us in our design and development of alternative learning experiences through the application of multimedia and/or distance education. The kaleidoscopic map enables us to keep focused on key aspects for enhancing our learning experiences.

The kaleidoscopic map guides us in asking and creatively responding to key questions: what criteria and techniques will we use to determine if, when, and how multimedia or distance education should be integrated into the learning environment? How do we keep the personal, interpersonal, and critical reflective dimension of our educational experiences in focus in the information age? We want to avoid the so-called "tyranny of the either/or"

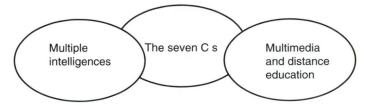

Figure 13.1   The threefold kaleidoscopic map

which states we can *only* teach this or that way! We believe in the evolution of new learning combinations and collaborations that can enhance the quality of our educational environments. The new "Net Generation" is growing up during the dawn of a completely new interactive medium of communication which is already stimulating awesome learning experiences within the lives of our students. Thus, as shown in Figure 13.2, the three circles of the kaleidoscopic map represent the diverse elements we utilize in our conversations about designing our distance education learning experiences.

The kaleidoscopic map in Figure 13.1 indicates (1) that Howard Gardener's theory of multiple intelligences has something significant to offer our process in applying the resources of the new media age; (2) that we consider the

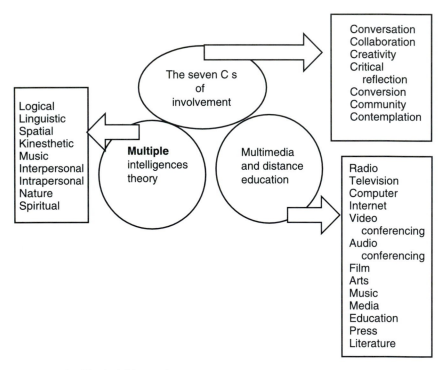

Figure 13.2   The kaleidoscopic map

seven C's of conversation, collaboration, creativity, critical reflection, conversion, community, and contemplation as essential criteria for discerning if, where, and when we apply new technologies to our learning environment; and (3) that serious consideration of all telecommunication/multimedia techniques be continually pondered as offering potentiality to our learning experiences – whether they are synchronous or asynchronous experiences.

The Need for Enriched Communication Skills

The movement of the individual adult learner from one behavioral state to a desired new behavioral state that has personal meaning to the learner is no easy task for distance educators. During the learning experience, the communication lines must be open for interpersonal interaction. Open communication can lead to instructor–learner rapport, which reassures the student of support, encouragement, and process in learning. Critical feedback of progress to the adult learner is necessary to further ensure the success of the learning experience.

Technologies that mediate communication produce social environments different from traditional classrooms, impacting interactions and group dynamics. For example, research has shown that the nature of groups and communication in-groups is changed when interactions are computer mediated.[13] For distance education, computer conferencing is a powerful social constructivist learning tool because of its capability to support interaction and collaboration among diverse and disperse students.[14] Yet, we must be aware of the studies which have found that computer conferencing produced lower amounts of interaction which decreased over time (as opposed to high amounts of interaction that increased over time for face-to-face groups), and low, slightly increasing amounts of off-task (social) communication. From this McDonald and Gibson conclude that text-based communication might hinder the group's ability to maintain group well-being and provide member support, thereby negatively affecting group members' ability to work together effectively.[15]

Communication is critical because in distance education the instructor and the student are physically separated during the majority of instruction. Activities that enhance sharing and cooperation can further develop openness and solidarity within groups. Understanding group processes helps courseware designers create spaces and interactive capabilities even in distance education environments. McDonald and Gibson indicate that learners need to be made aware of the new challenges that surround them in their new distance education environments and develop the techniques and strategies to deal with them in an effective manner.[16] And, as Garrison states,[17] education is a collaborative experience that depends on communication. It is, by definition, the giving and receiving of meaning and at the concrete level is actually the mutual exchange of ideas, needs, perceptions, options, facts, and other items of interest. To be effective, communication should flow multidirectionally (to all people concerned) and should be two way in nature.[18] Communication is also important in conveying other information in addition to instructional information to external students and between the administration, faculty, and staff of the distance education program.

The Value of Inter-institutional Collaboration

The University of Dayton's collaborative experience working with Chaminade University is enhancing our distance education abilities and capabilities. Our institutional sharing is maximizing limited resources, course offerings teaching, learning, and research. As our decision-makers weigh the advantages, disadvantages, costs, and benefits of distance education, they want us to think both inter- and intra-institutionally. As we continue to identify additional potential academic institutional partners, we realize that both our faculty and students will be challenged to advance their teaching, learning, and research in fresh and new ways.

If we truly desire our faculty to commence participating in our creation of a new academic paradigm of distance education, a supportive framework for faculty training, compensation, and faculty teaching rewards must be established to the degree that it is on par with that in traditional programs. Resources must be available to provide for faculty in-service training in a variety of dimensions including new cognitive learning theory, multimedia/ technology skills, instructional design, communication skills, using the institution's technological platform, engaging students in discourse in varied settings, planning for "fall-back" lessons if technological problems appear during interactive classes, meeting students' learning styles in unfamiliar settings, and evaluating teaching and learning in distance education.[19]

Distance Education Instructors Must Be Master Teachers

You can be a sure that a poor teacher in a traditional classroom will be a poor teacher in distance education – and the problems may even be intensified because of the telecommunications or media dimension of the new learning process. Barker indicates that instructors of distance education must understand and model principles from the literature on effective teaching, and know how to best use technology to convey their teaching.[20] The design of distance education courses requires the instructor to engage artistic sensibilities and quality media production skills. The interactive multimedia technologies require that effective techniques, visuals, and appropriate timing be the foundation for the class preparation. In one sense, educators are called to either be the new media producers or work collaboratively with those who are educational media producers. Instructors who are more comfortable simply reading old or new class notes, solo lecturing with no audio-visual complements or interactivity, are at a loss in distance education. If the distance education technology requires the "presence" of the instructor then it is imperative that he or she capitalize on what "presence" means – as in television presence.

Distance education requires that instructors be on top of required interaction between teacher and students, understanding that a slower pace of instruction is required along with very clear logical presentations with the appropriate audio-visual components. We have found that there are a specific series of basic abilities that instructors need to teach students for students to engage in online courses. Instructors should never presume that students have already acquired these skills. Keep in mind that the learning curve for technology-limited students is much steeper than for those who are skilled in computer technology or having previous distance education experience, placing the former students at a disadvantage. Students may need to: (1) access the Internet; (2) engage in online discussions, course conferences, and live chat session: (3) access resources from the World Wide Web; (4) store and maintain files on disk, online, or on hard copy of course materials; (5) submit assignments online, using a word-processing program or e-mail; (6) upload and download files; and (7) work effectively and collaboratively on tasks and exercises with peers in small, online groups. We have found the best way to address and ensure these skills in our students is to either: (a) require all students to participate in an initiation mini course to develop these skills; and/or (b) begin each course with a full session explaining and engaging in praxis with all the technological skills required for the course. This latter approach has been quite successful for us. The process quickened the enhancement of the development of a community of learners as students with these skills assist students within the initiation session.[21]

A Simple, Basic Process for Course Development[22]

There are some basic design guidelines that can help the instructor facilitate the planning process. First, keep in mind that new technologies do not obviate the need for careful planning. Indeed, planning is more crucial, since the instructional environments can be more complex. Distance instruction developments should provide a common framework for organizing development activities, design issues, and assigning tasks and responsibilities. One of the first things one learns when planning for distance education is this: it has to be a team effort. There is no room for 'lone rangers' if one wants a quality program. Thus, the affirmation of talents and gifts, the delegation of roles, and consistent collaboration and discernment with the team can evolve into a quality learning experience.

Consider the instructional context within which the instructors and students will navigate or engage. Who are the learners? Where are they located?

Where will their learning occur? If you plan to integrate new information technology into the distance education experience, does the target learner group have access to it? If not, how will you plan to have them locate it or acquire it?

As indicated earlier there is a distinction between immediate synchronous (real-time) and asynchronous (delayed) interaction in distance education. A distance educator can be immediate or delayed depending on the type of media integrated into the learning experience. Kearsley states that the distinction between delayed or immediate interaction is very significant because it determines the logistics and "feel" of the distance learning experience.[23]

Library support is central to the design, delivery, organization, and administration of quality distance education programs. Kascus[24] indicates that in a recent survey of library school deans and directors, half of the respondents agreed with the statement that the lack of library support is perceived by off-campus students and faculty as a disadvantage for off-campus instructional programs. She states that remote access technology is helping to bridge the gap between the library and the distant learner and has the potential to significantly enhance the quality of distance education.

Use your creative imagination to think of new combinations for teaching and learning through the support of multimedia in your distance education plans. The kaleidoscopic map may be helpful here. Since distance education is relatively new there are hundreds of new approaches waiting to be discovered. Calling forth a community of designers for distance education from within your academic institutions or regional affiliates or partners can assist in stimulating the imagination.

An effective learning environment should ensure that that interface be "transparent" so that learners are less aware of technology as an intervening tool. There are some classrooms that can appear threatening to the student with the massive array of technology tools surrounding them or creating a barrier between themselves and the instructor. Our PictureTel system is quite a transparent system. Students who initially walked into the room and wondered were awed by the simplicity and non-threatening appearance of the system.

Listen carefully to your students. They give you clues to where and when documentation and assistance may be required to be designed to enable them to participate in the distance education learning in a stressless atmosphere.

We have been using an instructional systems design model that integrates knowledge of the learning process and communications theory. There are four phases to the process. Each phase has a series of steps to enable the instructor to research alternative options to ensure an effective quality learning experience. The research phase (I) engages the professor and/or team in defining the course theme or problem, analyzing the learning environment, formulating the tools, objectives, and instructional strategies for the course, reviewing existing materials for their appropriateness (refer to the kaleidoscopic map Figure 13.2). The design phase (II) applies the research information to the design or development of the new instructional materials and distance education processes, secures copyright for materials, identifies the objectives and methods, and determines the precise direction and format of the distance education learning experience. The evaluation plan is also developed within this phase. The implementation phase (III) introduces the new course into the learning experience with a specific group of learners. Careful monitoring and continual interaction among the community of learners is required during this phase. Finally, the evaluation phase (IV) analyzes the results or desired outcomes with students, facilitators, and administrators. Recommendations are presented for further redesign and implementation of the course.

Conclusion: Opportunities and Challenges

The success of classroom-focused distance learning programs is ultimately dependent upon the manner and quality of instruction delivered. From the US Office of Technology Assessment's landmark study, *Linking for Learning: A New Course for Education*, the following are among findings noted as successful practices of ongoing classroom-focused distance education programs:

> *The key to success in distance learning is the teacher*. If the teacher on the system is good, the technology itself can become almost transparent. Conversely, no technology can overcome poor teaching; poor teaching is actually exacerbated in distance education applications. But when skilled teachers are involved, enthusiasm, expertise, and creative use of the media can enrich students beyond the four walls of their home classroom. Outstanding teachers can also serve as "electronic mentors" to other teachers.
>
> *Teachers using distance learning have had to find new ways to structure student–teacher interaction*. Old styles of teaching may not be appropriate or effective. The inherent limitations in distance learning technologies can be catalysts for instructional design and teaching techniques that enhance the learning process.
>
> *Teachers must be trained if they are to use distance learning technologies effectively*. Training opportunities, however, remain limited. Few pre-service and in-service programs focus on how to incorporate technology into instruction, create new opportunities for interactivity, or develop materials and use the media most effectively.

Important conversations continue to unfold beyond wiring, infrastructure, and the latest incarnations of computers around who is providing the transmissions of courses, tapes, CD-ROMs, and/or multimedia packages of content. New types of relationships and/or collaborations between the courseware and software providers and those who apply these to the learning experiences need to be pursued more assertively than in the past. The dilemma we are facing is that some courseware and software developers do not seem to be in sync with teachers. The developers complain that the teachers are not using the existing courseware and software while the teachers indicate that some of the material is irrelevant. There is a growing concern that technology is driving the mission of our schools instead of the schools (mission) driving the design and production of courseware and software. Finding ways to contribute to a collaborative dialogue to address this issue is paramount today.

We believe that distance education is going to reflect continual and rapid growth. As more and more students discover that their needs are not being met by more traditional methods of educational delivery, they will be seeking out courses on the Internet or other telecommunication sources. As businesses continue to require specialization of their employees and engage in actual training of their employees via distance education, distance education will become an essential ingredient in our academic communities as well.

We believe that distance education is a method of managing learning that is by its very nature innovative, and therefore it must innovate continually. Thus, teachers must be skilled in tactics of innovation for the change and uncertainty they will regularly encounter in the new information age.

We believe that distance educators should develop models or frameworks for judging the appropriateness of new technology applications in their field, rather than assuming that use of new distance technology will revolutionize learning. In lieu of this fact, distance educators must strive to an equitable distribution of education benefits, not just for a large quantity of learners. They must use strategies designed to meet the basic needs of disadvantaged peoples who may lack the necessary resources or educational experiences to advance the dignity and development of people in their region or country.

Finally, we believe that distance educators must adopt a global vision and assist in the development of a global learning network based on common technology and accessibility. Such a move can detour the emerging new forms of information of cultural imperialism in the twenty-first century. Distance education can offer a plurality of rich, diverse cultural learning experiences that can build bridges of understanding, peace, and justice for all.

Notes

1 *Kaizen* is a Japanese word that calls for total quality effort in continuous improvement. *Kaizen* is all about the ability to make very small improvements in processes and products every day.
2 Rossman, Parker (1993) *The Emerging Worldwide Electronic University: Information Age Global Higher Education*, New York: Praeger, p. xi.

3 Barker, Bruce, Frisbie, Anthony, and Patrick, Kenneth (1995) "Broadening the Definition of Distance Education in Light of the New Telecommunication Technologies," *Video-Based Telecommunications in Distance Education*, American Center for the Study of Distance Education, No. 4, p. 1.

4 Verduin, John and Clark, Thomas A. (1991) *Distance Education: The Foundations of Effective Practice*, San Francisco: Jossey-Bass, p. 8.

5 Moore, M.G. (1987) "University Distance Education of Adults," *Tech Trends*, 32 (4): 13–18.

6 Verduin, John and Clark, Thomas (1991) *Distance Education: The Foundations of Effective Practice*, p. 9.

7 Turkle, S. (1984) *The Second Self: Computers and the Human Spirit*, New York: Simon & Schuster.

8 This survey was provided by the US Department of Education's National Center for Educational Statistics (NCES) and presented in the report prepared for the Council for Higher Education Accreditation by The Institute for Higher Education Policy entitled *Assuring Quality in Distance Learning*, April 1998.

9 Ibid., p. 7.

10 Hoffman, Nicolas von (1998) "Distance Learning: Earning a Degree on Your Home Computer," *Architectural Digest*, September: 160.

11 Anderson, B. (1986) "Educational problems facing the region," Address delivered at the Shaping Education through Coalitions Conference sponsored by the Southwest Educational Development Laboratory, Austin, TX. Reference in Barker et al., *Video-Based Telecommunications in Distance Education*, p. 8.

12 The two introductory courses for the MAPL (Masters of Arts in Pastoral Leadership) Theology of Leadership and Theology of Communication are the initial courses designed with applying our current research and experiments in distance education of the past ten years. These courses are closed domain and are available only through registration at Chaminade University.

13 McDonald, Jeannette and Gibson, Chere Campbell (1998) "Interpersonal Dynamics and Group Development in Computer Conferencing," *The American Journal of Distance Education*, 12 (1): 7.

14 Bruffee, K. A. (1993) *Collaborative Learning: Higher Education, Interdependence, and the Authority of Knowledge*, Cambridge, MA: Harvard University Press. 1993; Bruner, J. (1960) *The Process of Education*, Cambridge, MA: Harvard University Press; Granger, D. (1990) "Bridging Distances to the Individual Learner," in M. Moore (ed.), *Contemporary Issues in American Distance Education*, London: Pergamon Press, pp. 163–71; Jonassen, D.H. (1994) "Thinking Technology: Toward a constructivism design model," *Educational Technology* 34: 34–37.

15 McDonald, Jeannette and Gibson, Chere Campbell, *Interpersonal Dynamics and Group Development in Computer Conferencing*, p. 9.

16 McDonald and Gibson, ibid., p. 22.

17 Garrison, D.R. (1989) *Understanding Distance Education: A Framework for the Future* Boston: Routledge & Kegan Paul.

18 Verduin and Clark, *Distance Education*, p. 179.

19 Gatliff, Bee and Wendel, Frederick C. (1998) "Inter-institutional Collaboration and Team Teaching," *American Journal of Distance Education*, 12 (1): 26–34.

20 Barker, Bruce O. (1996) "Strategies to Ensure Interaction in Telecommunicated Distance Learning," in Michael F. Beaudoin (ed.), *Distance Education Symposium 3*, ACSDE Research Monograph No. 12, p. 7.

21 McIntosh, B. and Shipman, H. (1996) "The Power of Collaboration: Peer Collaboration – a powerful mechanism for effecting change in science teaching," *Journal of College Science Teaching*, 25 (5): 364–65.

22 Information is gleaned from our University of Dayton ongoing research and expanded insights from Locatis, Craig (1987) "Instructional Design and New Technologies. Technologies for Learning Outside the Classroom," *New Direction for Continuing Education* 34: 89–98.

23 Kearsley, Greg (1996) *The Nature and Value of Interaction in Distance Learning*, ASCDE Research Monograph No.12, p. 84.

24 Kascus, Maria A. (1995) "Library Support for Quality in Distance Education: A Research Agenda," in Michael F. Beaudoin (ed.), *Distance Education Symposium 3*, ACSDE Research Monograph, pp. 72–73.

25 US Congress Office of Technology Assessment (1989) *Linking for Learning: A New Course for Education* (OTA-SET-430), Washington, DC: US Government Printing Office, pp. 87–88.

Part III

Issues in Catholic School Leadership

14 We Are Called

The Principal as Faith Leader in the Catholic School

Theodore J. Wallace

There is a major identity crisis occurring in Catholic schools. The dramatic shift from religious to lay personnel raises the question of whether or not some Catholic schools are becoming private schools with a religious memory but a secular presence. The tension between survival, mission, and market are central to this crisis.

At the heart of this tension is the principal. Ciriello (1994) produced three volumes that extensively delineated the roles and responsibilities of the Catholic school principal. They are captured in the three leadership descriptors: spiritual, managerial, and instructional. These works were designed to assist those who wished to be proactive in preparing the next generation of Catholic school principals. Ciriello (1989) also asked superintendents of Catholic schools in the United States to identify the most distinguishing characteristics of effective Catholic school principals. The most important characteristic, according to the superintendents, was the ability of principals to be faith leaders in their schools. Faith leadership includes a broad spectrum of responsibilities and should hardly be posited as a distinctly separate role.

Cappel (1989) believed that principals in Catholic schools are "called" – that they are in fact spiritual persons who *become* Catholic school principals and not the other way around. How exactly is this calling identified and nurtured? How can this crisis of Catholic identity be confronted? How can any individual responding to this call be an effective faith leader?

The answers lie in several domains. First, in the person of the principal. Second, in the policies and practices of each school. Finally, the school's Catholicity and the ability of the principal to be an effective faith leader depend on how well the mission of the school is defined, owned, and actualized by all who work in the school each day.

The Person of the Principal

Drahmann and Stenger (1989) stipulated that a person who is a Catholic school principal first brings spiritual attributes to the job influenced by one's personal lived faith experience. How does one transmit a single lived faith experience into the ability or integrative power as referred to by Gorman (1989) to build and maintain a faith community comprised of students, teachers, staff, and parents? To do so, the person must *know and model* his or her faith. To know, according to McDermott (1986), Catholic school adminis- trators must be conversant with critical Church issues and teachings in order to challenge teachers to relate these in context of each academic discipline.

The faith leader (Manno 1985; Buetow 1988) must be knowledgeable about the history of Catholic schools and the Church, as well as Church law, documents, and teachings. Wallace (1995) found in a study of lay Catholic high school principals in the United States that nearly three-fourths rated their formal preparation to be faith leaders to have been inadequate. (See Table 14.1.) They cited, primarily, a lack of knowledge of Church and Catholic school history and Church teachings and documents. They did, however, credit their ability to be faith leaders to their own lived faith experience, their personal and professional experiences in Catholic schools, and their mentors, many of whom were vowed religious. But is this enough back- ground with which to be *effective*? These same principals said as much when they responded to another question about whether today's Catholic schools are as successful in transmitting the faith when compared to Catholic schools in the 1950s that were predominately staffed by vowed religious. (See Table 14.2.) They believe that as lay leaders they are more *intentional* about providing faith leadership in order to respond to those who are concerned that Catholic schools have indeed become less "Catholic" due to the decrease in the day-to-day presence of vowed religious.

But just how can these lay leaders *model* their faith if they have, by their own admission, little formal *knowledge* about Church teachings, documents, and history? Caltigrone (1988) described the Catholic school principal using the servant model – that the principal must "re-present Christ." Can this be accomplished by only bringing a positive lived faith experience and good mentors to the job? How many Catholic school principals, superintendents,

Table 14.1　Response to the statement: your formal preparation for the principalship adequately prepared you for the faith leadership role

Response	Frequency	
	N	*% of total*
1 Strongly disagree	89	28
2	86	27
3	46	15
4	33	11
5	38	12
6 Strongly agree	22	7

Note:　Total $N = 314$

Table 14.2   Response to the statement: today's Catholic high schools are not as
successful in delivering the mission because of the decreased presence of
vowed religious when compared with the schools of the 1950s

Response	Frequency	
	N	*% of total*
1 Strongly disagree	78	25
2	89	28
3	50	16
4	52	17
5	30	9
6 Strongly agree	15	5

Note: Total *N* = 314

and teachers for that matter could exhibit proficiency of knowledge of the
Catholic social teachings, of the Bishops' statements on Catholic education,
and of the history of Catholic schools in their own country?

Could it be that many are convinced that they need only a cursory knowledge of such foundations because the culture in which they work emphasizes
managerial abilities (i.e., balanced budget, good discipline, strong enrollments, etc.) when determining a "job well done?" As this torch of leadership
in Catholic schools is passed from vowed religious to lay persons, is it possible
that there is a hesitancy to challenge "good lay people who work hard"
because the entire system of schools was ill-prepared for this transition?
While this may be so, it has not happened in the total absence of persons who
have called for action in preparing our future Catholic school principals.

In 1989, the president of the National Catholic Educational Association,
Catherine McNamee, CSJ, described an urgent need to identify, prepare, and
retain leaders for Catholic schools in the United States. This alarm had been
sounded by others who claim that there was a lack of leadership in Catholic
schools: "mediocre leadership" (Greeley 1992: 234), "leadership void not
frequently mentioned" (Ristau 1991: 5), and "a need for leadership"
(Convey 1992: 168). Calareso referred to the current situation as a "leadership predicament" (1989: 16), asserting that the future of Catholic schools
depends on the willingness to invest in its future leaders.

In their White Papers for the National Congress for Catholic Schools,
both Rogus (1991) and Ristau (1991) called for an increased commitment to
the preparation programs which will better develop those who will lead
Catholic schools. Ristau (1991) further stated that there are insufficient true
Catholic leaders, both in quantity and quality. Buetow (1988) described
Catholic schools as the starting point for full life in the Catholic Church,
and he maintained that schools are a process of "information, formation
and transformation" (p. 7). This could offer an intimidating responsibility

for those aspiring to be principals and those trying to prepare persons to be faith leaders in Catholic schools.

Twenty-five directional statements for Catholic schools were created during the National Congress for Catholic Schools in 1991. While the highest priority was placed on the challenge of the entire Catholic community to make a radical commitment to Catholic schools, the second most important priority focused on the issue of Catholic identity in the schools. This statement guaranteed opportunities for ongoing spiritual formation for Catholic school faculties, staff, and leadership (Executive Summary, 1992). The "faith formation" role of the principal is particularly crucial given the increasingly lay teaching staff. The percentage of lay teachers in grades K–12 in Catholic schools in the United States increased from 47% to 77% from 1965 to 1984. Further, Yeager (1985) predicted that by 1995 many faculties will have become totally lay. Lay persons now comprise more than half of all Catholic high school principalships (Mahar 1998). The combination of increased numbers of lay teachers and principals has created a priority to prepare principals who are capable of "institutionalizing Catholic traditions and doctrinal emphases" (Heft 1991: 5). The National Congress (Executive Summary, 1992), also in its directional statements, stressed the need to allocate time and funds for the professional development of school leaders and to provide for the ongoing spiritual formation of faculties.

How has the Catholic educational community responded to this direction? Indeed, many (arch)diocesan offices have designed and are delivering preparation programs for prospective Catholic school administrators. Some of these programs are affiliated with Catholic colleges and universities. The Association of Catholic Leadership Programs (ACLP), founded in the mid 1980s, has grown from its original six Catholic colleges and universities to its present number of forty-five. These schools are offering part or all of a graduate program designed to assist in the formation of future Catholic school leaders. Regrettably, however, few of these programs are offered *exclusively* for Catholic educators due to the need to be viable in the marketplace by also preparing the multitude of public school educators. In some cases, religious orders continue to offer some form of leadership formation for those interested in ministering in schools that are sponsored by these orders. In total, though, the comprehensive nature of this formation challenge is far from being met by these noted examples.

Many Catholic schools have, in recent years, chosen to hire educators who have taken early retirement from public education and who can now afford to work in Catholic schools. While most of these persons are Catholic, they tend to bring experience as a managerial leader, but little to no formal preparation to be faith leader in a position that calls for them to be, as Buetow (1988: 260) described the Catholic school principal, "like a trusted counselor who facilitates the marriage of God and His people." Are these people being hired in such significant numbers due to the lack of qualified applicants emerging from the ranks of Catholic school faculties?

While only representing one-fourth of the respondents in the Wallace study, those principals who rated their formal preparedness to be faith leaders to have been excellent had one very distinct common denominator. They all had attended a graduate program that was designed specifically for Catholic educators that featured two components: (1) formal coursework that focused on Church documents, history, and such; and (2) a process of personal faith development that challenged each prospective administrator to appraise one's own faith journey and develop a comfort with the key faith leadership role in a Catholic school faith community. Much could be learned by studying how effective these principals have been as faith leaders when compared with those who are underprepared with formal knowledge or training and thus rely mostly on their own faith and professional experiences.

School Policies and Practices

According to Hater (1981), the priorities that the principal sets for the religion curriculum, liturgy, hiring of teachers, and the ongoing religious formation of the faculty and students tell how competent the principal is as faith leader. Additional policies and practices that contribute to the community of faith include student discipline, admission (whom does the school seek to serve?), teacher and staff evaluation, and professional development. Much has been written about effective staff development for Catholic schools and some of this relates to faith development. Nevertheless, it is hypothesized here that a significant opportunity for faith leadership and the development of the collective ability of the faculty to provide faith leadership is not properly focused upon. This opportunity is available through the hiring practices of the school.

Each and every year, many opportunities (sometimes too many) present themselves to Catholic school administrators to search for teachers, administrators, and staff members for their school. How are these opportunities handled? Most are attended to during the summer between school years. Many times one administrator is given the task of doing all of the hiring. This may be due to a small staff and school and/or the fact that administrators are busy trying to fit in the vacation time allotted to them before starting another school year.

How are most candidates for faculty and staff positions assessed? Paper screening of resumes and references usually produce those to be interviewed. Interviews are often conducted in assembly-like fashion, with the pressure of filling the vacancies always looming. Exactly what strategies are employed by the interviewer to assess each candidate's commitment to the school's mission and his or her ability to contribute to the faith life of the school? How often is this even minimized in deference to the need to find someone qualified to teach a particular subject area that may be hard to fill? How often do you hear a principal say "I am looking for a Catholic school teacher who can teach science" as opposed to the more familiar refrain, "I need a science teacher?" What cumulative effect does this type of hurried, market-driven hiring practice have on the ability of the principal and faculty to create and nurture a community of faith and to be an effective faith leader? Most obviously, in too many cases, it means that there are more people added to a staff who are in need of a significant level of faith formation and who, in the meantime, will be unable to contribute much to the principal's need to place a critical mass of adults in front of the students everyday who are well prepared to be faith leaders themselves.

Drahmann and Stenger (1989), Heft (1991), Perri (1989), and others have maintained that the Catholic school principal must be specifically attentive to the faith development of the children entrusted to them. Catholic education must include the experiences that will develop convictions in the students that will affect their decisions, especially regarding others, for their lifetimes. This requires that the principal invest the time necessary to attract new people to the school who are already equipped to personally contribute to the quality of the community of faith in that school.

Another danger that lurks in a Catholic school to hamper the effectiveness of the faith community is the lack of qualification of many who teach religion. In Catholic elementary schools, most teachers are assigned to teach religion. Extensive research would probably yield startling results if the preparation of all Catholic elementary teachers to teach religion was examined. In many cases, the undergraduate courses of study required to be elementary teachers in the United States include little to no formal preparation to be teachers of religion, even if one attends a Catholic college or university. In most cases, (arch)diocesan policies require that all have religion teaching credentials upon the date of hire, but the reality is that is not the case, thus requiring central offices to provide coursework so that teachers can, at *some time* in their careers, acquire the necessary credential. What impact does this practice in many Catholic schools have on the quality of instruction of the Catholic religion?

In Catholic high schools, the teaching of religion is the responsibility of only a few teachers. This makes it difficult for the principal to convince teachers of other subjects that they too have a responsibility to integrate Catholic teachings into their academic disciplines. Most of those hired to teach high school religion courses have been well prepared in the content of the courses but have little to no experience and instruction in the art of teaching. This problem lies primarily in the reality that most religious studies majors in college are not required to take the education courses that generate state certification for teachers of all other academic disciplines. So, in addition to sometimes feeling isolated as teachers of religion in a Catholic high school, religion teachers struggle as beginning teachers because they have not been instructed in classroom management techniques and a variety of teaching methodologies. This, too, places an added burden on the principal to deal with the capacity of those employed by the school to be faith leaders.

Dealing with student discipline issues causes conflict for the principal as faith leader. Student discipline decisions are a source of daily tension because the principal must be involved in the application of rules and consequences that are not positively received by some of the parents and students involved in each particular incident. Cries of "how can you call yourself a principal of a Catholic school?!" come from some who disagree with discipline judgments. It is difficult for the principal to balance these and other managerial realities of the role with the call to lead the school community in prayer, the desire to attend and participate in retreats for students, and simply to maintain a positive presence at school activities.

One other prominent example of an underutilized faith leadership opportunity for a Catholic school principal is inherent in the evaluation process for teachers, administrators, and staff. How many formal evaluative instruments currently in use in Catholic schools effectively address how well the individual contributes to the Catholic mission of the school?

Emphasis always includes the teacher's preparedness for class with regard to lesson plans, the presence of course objectives, and the fairness of the student assessment process employed by the teacher. Even the teacher's consistency in enforcing such policies as the proper student dress code are often dealt with in depth and seriousness. But what does each person employed by a Catholic school hear being reinforced with respect to what and how they can contribute to the community of faith that is so central to the existence of a Catholic school? Once examples of individual contribution are assessed, how is this integrated into job performance objectives to be developed for enhanced performance for the coming year? What do people hear, if anything, from the principal as faith leader in this regard? If such feedback is not provided, according to Gilroy and Leak (1996), the role of Catholic school teacher is functionary and not, therefore, supportive of the Catholic school culture. Further, what does the principal hear as a result of his or her own evaluation with regard to an assessment of teachers' abilities and contributions to the Catholic culture of the school?

In summary, Catholic school principals are expected to be visionaries as faith leaders while, as Roche (1996: 46) asserted:

> On a daily basis they struggle to deal with a complex constellation of contentious realities. Their unenviable, but vital task is to meet these challenges in a way that contributes to the nature, mission and culture of the school. Catholicity demands that not only the outcomes but the very processes by which they are achieved embody the gospel values. The creation of a genuine Catholic school culture lies in the synthesis of response and result. It is because of the chaotic nature of these times,

rather in spite of them, that Catholic school principals have a wonderful opportunity to exemplify approaches, practices and responses that, by their very nature, contribute to the development of a Catholic school culture.

Clarity and Ownership of Mission

In "The Catholic School on the Threshold of the Third Millennium" (1998) by the Congregation for Catholic Education in Rome, it is asserted that due to the complexity of the modern world, it is "all the more necessary to increase awareness of the ecclesial identity of the Catholic school." Just how well defined and activated are the mission statements in Catholic schools? Are policies and practices influenced by this mission? Is the Catholic nature of each school promoted first and foremost to prospective families and potential financial contributors? Are Catholic school principals truly the visionary leaders so essential to Catholic education as Bernadin (1989) called forth?

Hater (1981) described the faith leadership role of the principal as one that expresses a commitment to the concept of Christian community; is sensitive to the needs of all in the school; and works to bring the school into harmony with the mission of Christ. How well do principals, as Helm (1990) described, promote and integrate a Catholic vision in the daily activities of the school? Buetow (1988) characterized the faith leader as one who has no doubts about the school's exact identity. Assuming the school's exact identity is clear to the principal, how is it then activated in all programs and classrooms in the school?

Definition and activation of the mission of a Catholic school is so vital to the ability of a principal to provide visionary and meaningful faith leadership. This definition must reflect what the Congregation for Catholic Education stated about the very reason for the existence of Catholic schools:

> It is from its Catholic identity that the school derives its original characteristics and its "structure" as a genuine instrument of the Church, a place of real and specific pastoral ministry. The Catholic school participates in the evangelizing mission of the Church and is the privileged environment in which Christian education is carried out. The ecclesial nature of the Catholic school, therefore, is written in the very heart of its identity as a teaching institution. It is a true and proper ecclesial entity by reason of its educational activity. Thus it must strongly be emphasized that this ecclesial dimension is not a mere adjunct, but it is a proper and specific attribute, a distinctive characteristic which penetrates and informs every moment of its educational activity, a fundamental part of its very identity and the focus of its mission.

To this end, the Catholic school principal must convince the complex constituencies of parents, teachers, board members, donors, and graduates to own what is important for this school which must be stated forcefully, but succinctly, in its mission and belief statements. Many "forces" mitigate against this succinct or core mission statement. Anyone who has ever served on a committee to create or rewrite a mission statement for a Catholic school can well attest to the diversity of opinions that contribute to a complex journey to define who we are and whom we wish to serve as a Catholic school.

Grace (1996) claimed that all of these contributing constituencies have a strategic role to play in the maintenance of a distinctive character of Catholic education. He argued further that this is a most difficult task in today's context of the fundamental tension between Catholic values and the influence of market values. The principal has a key role in developing this needed clarity of the mission amongst the competing values represented by the people who comprise each Catholic school community. Grace cautioned that Catholic schools must keep in proper perspective the notion that academic achievement is not an end in itself but an enterprise serving the larger purpose for a Catholic school to exist.

There is evidence that in recent years, more and more families are seeking schools that do an exemplary job of achieving this balance of offering an exceptional academic experience for its students while effectively integrating the religious values and teachings upon which they are founded. The Jewish community in the United States has recently embarked on an effort to create new Jewish schools that will more clearly and consistently pass on their faith to their young people. Christian schools have grown tremendously in recent decades. This success has been primarily due to their ability to clearly articulate their mission as educational entities that are grounded in the fundamental teachings of the Scripture. These schools have attracted families and teachers who are drawn to contribute to the furtherance of their mission. How well do Catholic schools articulate their mission? Is it clear to all who support and work in Catholic schools exactly what the "end product" will be by virtue of having attended a Catholic school?

A Tool for Reflection for Faith Leadership

I have developed and used a set of questions for in-service experiences to assist teachers, administrators, and staff in Catholic schools reflect on their role and contribution to the community of faith that exists in their schools. After a succinct review of the literature to help define faith leadership in Catholic schools, I spend time with each question by using examples from my own teaching and administrative experiences in Catholic schools. The participants are then asked to spend time alone with each set of questions and then share some thoughts with one other person that have been triggered by this reflection time. Each dyad is then asked to share one reflection with the entire group. Finally, after all questions have been discussed, each person is asked to identify, in writing, two very specific strategies that they will use to enhance or improve their abilities as contributors to the faith community in their school.

The questions are divided into the two main categories of modeling the faith and knowledge and integration of the faith, and relate to each person's level of contribution to the school's mission, practices, and policies. The questions in the modeling section are divided further by being postulated from three perspectives: (1) from the eyes of the students; (2) from the eyes of our colleagues; and (3) from our own eyes. This guides each person through a reflection on his or her ability to enrich the faith life of their school not just from their own perspective but to delve deeper by considering how their actions are seen and *felt* by others.

The reflection questions are as follows.

Modeling the Faith

From the eyes of the students:

1 Do you use inappropriate language or sarcasm when interacting with students?
2 Do the students see you participate in school liturgical events and community service projects?
3 Do you take an active role during times of student(s) personal crises?
4 Do you pray with your students? If so, how often and why? If not, why not?
5 Do you squelch student interaction when you are aware of someone being picked on or put down?
6 Would your students say or feel that you genuinely care about them?

From the eyes of your colleagues:

1 What impression or attitude have you given to your peers regarding the religious orientation and practices of the school?
2 How would your peers at the school describe your daily interactions with, or conversations about, the students? The parents of students? Administrators? Fellow staff members?

From your eyes:

1 What are the primary reasons you work at a Catholic school? Do you feel that your work is part of a ministry? If yes, explain further. If no, why not?
2 What is your own level of agreement and commitment to the mission of the Catholic school and the teachings of the Catholic Church?

3   Do you lead school-wide prayer over the public address system? Are you comfortable expressing your faith convictions to your students and colleagues?

Personal Knowledge and Integration

1   How much do you know about the teachings of the Catholic Church on such issues as euthanasia, capital punishment, sexual morality, abortion, and war?
2   Which of these (and other) topics would you like more information about?
3   How do you integrate these teachings in your curriculum units?
4   Are you consistent in enforcing school policies?
5   Are you familiar with the mission statement of your school? What does it mean to you? How do your daily actions influence the successful realization of this mission?
6   Do you believe that your effectiveness as a faith leader should be considered each year in your formal evaluation and as a condition for (re)employment? If so, how do you suggest this be measured? If not, why not?

Conclusion

Catholic schools face a critical juncture in their history as important instruments of the Church. Developing effective faith leaders who will serve as visionaries for each Catholic school is a daunting task for all who wish to see Catholic education flourish into the third millennium. In recent years, due to an extensive transition of leadership and a changing educational marketplace, Catholic educators, in many cases, seem better able (or more comfortable) to promote excellence in their schools in more academic terms than for their ecclesial purpose.

According to Orsa and Orsa (1997), the viability of Catholic schools as defined by their ability and success with religious goals leaves little room for complacency on the part of Catholic educators. They believe that there are few models to help us define how to make the transition to lay leadership in Catholic schools, but that the "rules are changing" nevertheless. Further, they believe that the accountability of the Catholic school to be Catholic is going to be much higher and more problematic when lay people make demands on other lay people.

There should be no doubt that the principal, especially as faith leader, is the key to this growing accountability for schools to be demonstrably Catholic. This will require a comprehensive identification, education, and nurturing of persons to serve in this capacity. Knowledge of and personal experience in the Catholic faith are essential attributes of those spiritual persons who will be called to become Catholic school principals.

References

Bernardin, J. (1989) "Catholic schools: Opportunities and challenges," *Chicago Studies* 28 (3).

Buetow, H.A. (1988) *The Catholic school: Its roots, identity, and future*, New York: Crossroad.

Calareso, J.P. (1989) "A gift in a gauntlet," *Momentum*, 20 (2), 16.

Caltigrone, C.L. (1988) "Principal concerns: Part VI, a servant model," *Today's Catholic Teacher*, pp. 82–84, Dayton, OH.

Cappel, C. (1989) "A reflection on the spirituality of the principal," *Reflections on the role of the Catholic school principal*, Washington, DC: National Catholic Educational Association, pp. 17–27.

Ciriello, M.J. (1989) "Leadership in Catholic education: From the catbird seat," *Momentum* 20 (2), 18.

Ciriello, M.J. (1994) *The principal as spiritual leader*, Washington, DC: Department of Education, United States Catholic Conference.

Congregation for Catholic Education (1998) *The Catholic school on the threshold of the third millennium*, December 28, 1997.

Convey, J. (1992) *Catholic schools make a difference: Twenty-five years of research*, Washington, DC: National Catholic Educational Association.

Drahmann, T. and Stenger, A. (1989) *The Catholic school principal: An outline for action*, Washington, DC: National Catholic Educational Association.

Gilroy, N. and Leak, L. (1996) "The principal's role in personnel management," *Expectations for the Catholic school principal*, Washington, DC: United States Catholic Conference, p. 80.

Gorman, M. (1989) "The spirituality of the Catholic school principal," *Reflections on the role of the Catholic school principal*, Washington, DC: National Catholic Educational Association, pp. 29–33.

Grace, G. (1996) "Leadership in Catholic schools," *The contemporary Catholic school: Context, identity and diversity,* London: Falmer Press.

Greeley, A.M. (1992) "A modest proposal for the reform of Catholic schools," *America*, 166 (10), 234–38.

Hater, R. J. (1981) *Ministry in the Catholic high school*, Los Angeles: Sadlier.

Heft, J L. (1991) "Catholic identity and the future of Catholic school," *Catholic identity and the Catholic schools*, Washington, DC: National Catholic Educational Association, pp. 5–20.

Helm, C.M. (1990) "Cultural and symbolic leadership in Catholic elementary schools: An ethnographic study," (Doctoral Dissertation, The Catholic University of America, 1989), *Dissertation Abstracts International*, 50, 1156A.

Mahar, M. (1998) *Catholic schools in America*, Montrose, CO: Fisher.

Manno, B.M. (1985) *Those who would be Catholic school principals*, Washington, DC: National Catholic Educational Association.

McDermott, E.J. (1986) *Distinctive qualities of the Catholic school*, Washington, DC: National Catholic Educational Association.

National Conference of Catholic Bishops (1972) *To teach as Jesus did: A pastoral message on Catholic education*, Washington, DC: United States Catholic Conference.

Orsa, J. and Orsa, T. (1997) "Reimagining Catholic school leadership for the third millennium," *Quality Catholic schools*, Archdiocese of Brisbane.

Perri, S. (1989) "The principal as teacher of teachers," *Reflections on the role of the Catholic school principal*, Washington, DC: National Catholic Educational Association, pp. 64–74.

Ristau, K.M. (1991) "The challenge: To provide leadership within Catholic schools," *Leadership of and on behalf of Catholic schools*, Washington, DC: National Catholic Educational Association, pp. 19–39.

Roche, K. (1996) "Creative insubordination," *Catholic school studies – A Journal of education for Australian and New Zealand Catholic schools*, 9 (2), October, 45–46.

Rogus, J.F. (1991) "Strengthening preparation and support for leadership in Catholic schools," *Leadership of and on behalf of Catholic schools*, Washington, DC: National Catholic Educational Association, pp. 19 39.

Wallace, T.J. (1995) *Assessment of the preparedness of lay Catholic high school principals to be faith leaders*, unpublished Doctoral dissertation, University of Dayton.

Yeager, R.J. (1985) *The Catholic high school: A national portrait*, Washington, DC: National Catholic Educational Association.

15 Truths and Half-truths About Leadership

Ancient and Contemporary Sources

Father James Heft, SM

I have recently completed fourteen years of academic administration, and have moved into a university professor position that allows me maximum freedom for teaching and scholarship and working more closely with other faculty in faculty seminars.[1] I have also been named chancellor of the university, which extends a privilege I enjoyed formerly as provost, of representing the university to various external publics.

When I began to think about the topic of leadership, I found myself recalling vividly my feelings after completing my first year as chair of a large and rambunctious department. I then told a friend:

> I no longer have the luxury of belonging to a clique; I can't pass on gossip about certain members of the department; I have to find ways to be helpful to individuals whom I don't particularly like; and I have to keep a certain distance from all the members of the department, even my close friends, so as to remain equally accessible and fair to everyone.

I paused and then added, with a smile, "I hate this job; it is forcing me to be virtuous!" Indeed, positions of administrative leadership carry within them a very demanding asceticism, as do the roles of teacher and parent. Administrative leadership in an educational institution demands a capacity to work with many different types of persons; in fact, it constitutes a sort of liberal education – in getting quite diverse sorts of people committed to a common vision and task.

During the years that I held such positions, all in a Catholic university, I found some of those challenges particularly demanding. For example, how should I articulate the Catholic tradition without reminding various members of the faculty of the bad experiences they have had with that tradition? How could I emphasize the value of the tradition without seeming to impose from the past ideas that appear irrelevant to the present? And if I don't draw on that tradition, how would I help prevent the strategic planning of the university from becoming an exercise that would be virtually the same as that in a secular university?

Another challenge was that of persuading individuals of the importance and value of changes that could be made in academic programs. For example, since the late 1970s, the university had been involved in developing a more integrated general education program. Our first efforts left much to be improved; in particular, the courses approved for general education needed greater integration. A smaller, more highly integrated, core curriculum program already thriving within the university became the compelling example for greater integration. Few factors support more an argument for change than successful visible examples of the proposed change. Even if they are just small pilot projects, they make change much more likely, especially if they are directed by persons the rest of the faculty respect. Credible examples persuade more effectively than exhortations.

Fourteen years in administration also convinced me that leadership takes many different forms, that any type of leadership moves some people and not others, and that no form of leadership moves everybody. To compensate for inevitable blind spots in leaders, mentors play a key role. Leaders tend to live a lonely existence – all the more reason for leaders to have a few confidants with whom they can share their hopes and doubts, and from whom they can receive advice.

Choosing between what might work well at the moment and what is right but inconvenient constitutes one of the more difficult decisions in leadership. Money for the university's endowment offered by a corporation whose products are immoral might be very attractive, but in principle unacceptable. Financial aid offered only to prospective students who can pay more of the cost of tuition than qualified students from poorer families may improve the university's bottom line, but not meet its moral obligations. Pressure from alumni to fire a certain professor or demands by rich donors to discontinue certain courses, or fear of bad publicity because of a controversy – all such occasions test an administrator's convictions about the freedom of the university to conduct its own business in the way the university determines is best.

Finally, I came to realize that people are more fragile than I had thought, and that words of encouragement and appreciation contribute more to morale than merely articulating high standards. The fragility of some people manifested itself in grievances that they had allowed to build up in themselves over a span of years against previous administrators, but then when I or a new administrator arrived, the grievances continued to be expressed, even if their original causes were long gone. I also learned that publicly criticizing people with grievances against the administration rarely "sets the record straight;" patient endurance, accompanied by a restatement of the mission, seems the better response. Personal criticism needs to be given in private to the person.

Personal experiences of trying to lead have not been my only source of understanding leadership. Those experiences have been informed by two other sources. First, and most important, has been my Christian tradition, which in its own way has continued to shed light on the meaning of community, the role and responsibility of leaders within communities, and the actual situation of ordinary human beings. Second, over the years, I have read a number of books on leadership – a few very good, and most not so good. In this chapter, I will explore five themes in the Christian tradition that have been valuable to me, and strike me as particularly important today. Since the popular literature on leadership rarely draws explicitly from biblical sources and the Christian tradition, a straightforward exposition of ideas rooted in the Christian tradition and relevant to leadership will be helpful. After developing five such ideas, I will then examine, in the light of them, suggestions for leaders found in some current popular literature, pointing out both strengths and weaknesses. Some of the most popular authors have written so positively about leadership, about "win/win" outcomes and creating oneself and one's own future, that I have found it difficult seeing in such ideas any resemblance to my own daily experience of administration. In contrast, when I turn to the Christian tradition, I have found a palpable realism.

Christian Leadership: Avoiding Distortions

Not all writing about leadership by Christian authors possesses this palpable realism. A continuing tension exists between the conviction that Jesus speaks to every age and the realization that we frequently hear only what we want to hear. When we listen selectively, we usually end up expressing what we already think is important. We have filtered out everything else. Unfortunately, a sizeable number of Christian authors writing about leadership paint portraits of Jesus that make him out to be an entrepreneur, a capitalist, an urban reformer, and the world's most successful ad man.

Some recent examples of this genre of Christian books are Laurie Beth Jones' *Jesus CEO* (Hyperion, 1996), and Mike Murdock's *The Leadership Secrets of Jesus* (Honor Books, 1996) and *God's Little Devotional Book for Leaders* (Honor Books, 1997). The latter, one in a series of such books written also for couples, men, mom, students, and so on, begins each short chapter (two pages) with a biblical passage and then adds an inspirational commentary that can be read in a minute. The message remains the same: Jesus was a great leader who knew how to influence people and get them to follow him.

The temptation to reshape the image of Jesus to fit our own immediate needs, of shaping the contours of his image to coincide with our projections, seems to affect everyone. Ultimately, such distortions root themselves in an inability to transcend oneself, to open oneself to a point of view other than one's own. According to the Bible, those who worshiped what they made with their own hands committed the sin of idolatry. To avoid this danger of distortion, people should form their picture of Jesus in conversation with others who are different from themselves, and with those who lived in earlier ages and faced different challenges. Such conversations help people develop an understanding of Jesus that is not merely a projection. In other words, those who work within the Christian tradition, which is a 2,000-year-old conversation, have a better chance of avoiding grossly distorted portraits of Jesus. Why? Because a tradition such as Catholicism represents the collective thought of literally millions of people over the centuries. The more deeply a person interiorizes the multifaceted Catholic tradition, the more that person transcends being merely contemporary. Indeed, a person immersed deeply in a religious tradition can bring the wisdom of that tradition to bear on the present.[2]

Two examples, one from earlier in this century and the other more recent, will illustrate the balance a tradition provides. In 1924, Bruce Barton published *The Man Nobody Knows*, which sold over a half-million hardback copies and recently has been returned to print. Barton saw himself as returning to the real Jesus of Scripture, who had been emasculated by liberal Protestantism. Emphasizing Jesus' vigor and gregariousness was Barton's way of convincing people that Jesus could speak to the modern era. In the process, Barton overemphasizes Jesus' humanity at the expense of his divinity, presenting him as an advertising genius whose every contact and whose every word and gesture offer sales managers today all they need to know to be successful. The tone for the book was set by the opening quotation, "Wist ye not that I must be about my father's *business*?"[3] In 1988, Martin Scorsese's film, *The Last Temptation of Christ*, provided another example of an imbalance – again, an overstatement of Jesus' humanity – which Scorsese was in part moved to produce in order to counter the exaggerated divinity of Jesus that characterizes so many of the sermons of fundamentalist and occasional Catholic preachers.[4] Unfortunately, as the history of Christology so vividly demonstrates, it is much easier to stress one nature of Jesus over the other than it is to keep the mysterious balance. The great Christian tradition, preserved in the teaching of the creeds and the councils, hands on a longer and deeper wisdom about Jesus, one that affirms both his divinity and humanity.

Drawing upon that tradition, I will highlight five themes that have stood the test of time, avoid various exaggerations, and remind us of insights that today are all too often overlooked.

Five Christian Themes Relevant for Leaders

Anyone who wishes to write about leadership is not starting from scratch. In fact, in the last few years, a number of theories about leadership in the secular world have come and gone. An article that appeared in the *Administrative Science Quarterly* reviews this rapidly changing parade of ideas about leadership:

As we survey the path leadership theory has taken, we spot the wreckage of "trait theory," the "great man" theory, the "situationist" critique, leadership styles, functional leadership, and finally, leaderless leadership, to say nothing of bureaucratic leadership, charismatic leadership, group-centered leadership, reality-centered leadership, leadership by objective, and so on. The dialectic and reversals of emphases in this area very nearly rival the tortuous twists and turns of child-rearing practices, and one can paraphrase Gertrude Stein by saying, "a leader is a follower is a leader."[5]

In view of this rapidly changing body of literature, will reflections on "Christian leadership" simply add another theory to the wreckage pile? The answer is no, since the five themes I will develop are deeply rooted in a 2,000-year-old tradition, and therefore are not likely to be superceded in the next decade by new themes. What then are some of the palpably realistic themes that can be drawn from that tradition and be of assistance to those who lead educational institutions?

The first theme emphasizes the individual person's need to remember they are part of a larger community. Rather than be led into thinking that persons create themselves, the Christian tradition recognizes fully that each person is a part of a larger family, larger indeed than an individual's biological family. Families, especially large families that trace their history back two millennia, repeat stories and perform rituals. Membership in the family requires not just hearing the stories of the family that have made it what it is, but telling them to others. Membership also carries with it the expectation that individuals join with others in rituals that act out those stories. In other words, membership in the Christian community requires persons to recognize that they are shaped by the stories it repeats, and formed by the rituals it celebrates.

Some contemporary writers on leadership, by contrast, see tradition as an obstacle to leadership. As a result, they present "spirituality" as a positive force, and "religion" as a restrictive imposition. They seem to think that extracting spirituality from the rigid framework of religion promises maximum flexibility to the individual. No dogmas, no required practices, indeed, no obligations to a community. Separated from these burdens, individuals tailor spiritualities to fit their particular needs. One of the most striking recent examples of the "spirituality without religion" approaches to leadership may be found in Peter Vaill's book, *Managing as a Performing Art*. He writes:

> The real premise here is that our tendency to equate discussions of spirit with discussions of religion is a significant part of our problem as a society and as a profession of managers. ... Religion has rendered the question of spirituality almost undiscussible [*sic*] except within a framework of

doctrine and language that sound stilted and artificial to many in the world of work.[6]

It is not a bad thing that writers on leadership and management take spirituality seriously; however, leaders of Christian institutions are better served if they recognize that the Christian tradition with its various practices fosters a rich and multifaceted spirituality, one that is both personal and communal at the same time. Once, while being pressed to answer a reporter's question about her "style as a leader," Dorothy Day, the founder of the Catholic Worker movement, finally responded: "Leadership isn't only something in you, in a person – your personality. Leadership depends on where you are as much as who you are, and it depends on the company you're keeping." Every time the reporter returned to the question of her personal authority and style, she "came back at him with a plea that he realize how much of our actions depend on the people we're here to learn from: we take our cues from them."[7] Day underscores the importance Christian tradition gives to community, and does so when she points out the critical importance of community for leadership.

Identifying oneself as a part of a religious community that lives from its tradition with its stories and practices need not lead to stilted gestures and indoctrination. As Jaraslov Pelikan, echoing Chesterton, notes, "tradition is the living faith of the dead and traditionalism is the dead faith of the living."[8] When leaders understand that spirituality ought to be embedded in a tradition, they will more easily recognize that people are not just individuals but members of communities that engage in practices that form the whole persons.

Because it realizes that people are best understood as members of communities and enriched by tradition, the Christian tradition also emphasizes that moral and intellectual forms of learning are intimately related, the second theme that I want to emphasize. In recent years, public schools have promoted "character education" in order to ensure a greater degree of civility, decency, and respect among students. Leaders of the movement separate an ethic of responsibility and fairness from any particular religious tradition, and argue therefore that such an ethic may rightly be part of public education. In the setting of a public school, leaders of this movement must operate under pluralistic and secular assumptions. Leaders of Catholic schools are in this sense more free to draw on the resources of their own educational tradition and acknowledge the inherently religious roots of morality.[9]

Our second theme affirms the importance of both the intellectual and moral dimensions of life. Knowledge, the intellectual dimension of learning, does not always translate into virtuous behavior, the moral dimension; the brightest are not always the best. Writing about the contribution of the recently deceased Catholic philosopher Josef Pieper, Gilbert Meilaender spells out the close relationship between learning and virtue, suggesting that the more persons mature morally, the more likely it is that they will be able to learn what is true:

> We have, [Pieper] writes on one occasion, "lost the awareness of the close bond that links the knowing of truth to the condition of purity." That is, in order to know the truth we must become persons of a certain sort. The full transformation of character that we need will, in fact, finally require the virtues of faith, hope and love.[10]

In other words, in the Catholic vision of things, to see deeply into reality, one must be religiously transformed – or more accurately, embrace the life-long process of religious transformation. Just as the practices of the community's traditions supply the context for that religious transformation – our first theme – so the intimate relationship between intellectual and moral education – our second theme – elucidates the two principal goals of Catholic education: intellectual development and formation in the faith.

A third theme from the Christian tradition broadens people's minds as to the many forms leadership takes. I have chosen to emphasize the multiple forms of leadership as my third theme precisely because so much contemporary literature on leadership, as we shall see later, emphasizes primarily the charismatic personality; it does not recognize the many different forms leadership does take. In contrast, persons with "catholic tastes" have a certain breadth of interests and appreciate a wide variety of things; they are said to be cosmopolitan. Catholicism characteristically emphasizes the wisdom of a both/and rather than an either/or approach. The great Swiss Catholic theologian, Hans Urs von Balthasar, describes four types of discipleship, singling out the New Testament figures of Mary, Peter, Paul, and John.[11] The canonized saints of the Catholic church are hardly clones: Thomas Aquinas and Thérèse of Lisieux (the Little Flower), Francis of Assisi and Augustine, Elizabeth Ann Seton and Edith Stein.

A number of these striking figures of holiness sang the praises of lesser known persons whom they believed made it possible for them to be the persons they were. In our own time, Dorothy Day, a striking embodiment of the virtue of justice and love for the poor, claimed that were it not for the less well-known Peter Maurin, an eccentric and chronically unorganized individual, she would have accomplished little. According to her, he was the "needler," the one who kept pointing out what God "wanted doing." She disdained any attribution of leadership to herself, although people today readily identify her as the person who has inspired several generations of people to live simply and act justly.[12]

Despite her many disclaimers, Dorothy Day had a certain charismatic impact. A very different form of leadership was exercised by John Henry Newman. He was anything but charismatic, yet he also has exercised considerable influence. In his one attempt in his life to exert academic leadership, he failed miserably. Invited by the Irish hierarchy in 1853 to found a university in Ireland, he ultimately returned to England after several wearisome years of fruitless effort. But during that time, he gave several lectures about the nature of university education and the relationship that exists among the various branches of knowledge. Later collected into a book entitled *The Idea of a University*, these lectures, which he gave to support and help define a project that failed, have continued to influence generation after generation of leaders of higher education, both public and private, religiously affiliated and not. Was the quiet, shy, and temperamental Newman not a leader in a very real sense? Are there not many ways to exercise significant leadership? As we shall see, he would never have qualified for leadership in most contemporary books on the topic.

I have stressed the importance of the community and tradition, the intimate connection between intellectual and moral education, and the multiple forms in which leadership can be exercised. Two more themes from the Christian tradition shed further light on the meaning of leadership. As I develop both of these themes, a few more of the half-truths so typical of some of the popular leadership literature we will next examine will become apparent.

The fourth theme focuses on justice. Leaders of Christian educational institutions inherit a tradition, reaching back all the way back to Hosea, Isaiah, and Jeremiah, that asserts that everyone, especially the poor and the marginalized, are God's children, that people should be compensated fairly for their work, that kings and princes and appointed officials need to be accountable for their actions, and that the fruit of working for justice is peace. Throughout the nineteenth and the first half of this century, Catholic schools helped many generations of immigrants acquire educations that made it possible for them both to learn about their faith and to participate fully in the larger society, which in many ways wanted to exclude them from benefits to which they were entitled.

In our own day, the challenge remains much the same in the inner cities, to the extent that the Church has retained its educational institutions there. Today, however, rather than Catholic immigrants, many of those living in the inner city are African–American, Haitian, Asian, and many are Protestant or non-Christians. But like the earlier immigrants, they too are poor and marginalized and continue to suffer discrimination. By contrast, the challenge in our suburbs, where most Catholics can now be described not as the "have nots" but as the "haves," is quite different. For these well-to-do suburban Catholics, many of whom are now Republicans, the social teachings of the bishops sound like "the Democratic Party at prayer!" At their June 1998 meeting, the American bishops issued a statement in which they acknowledged that "our social doctrine is not shared or taught in a consistent and comprehensive way in too many of our schools, seminaries, religious education programs, colleges and universities."[13] Among the themes highlighted in the letter from the bishops are the call to family, community, and participation; human rights and responsibilities; the option for the poor and the vulnerable; the dignity and right of workers; and care of God's creation. The bishops ask that the leaders of Catholic schools help the faculty to learn more about the social teachings of the Church and to integrate them into their curricula.

Two obvious consequences flow directly from a serious personal appropriation by Catholic educators of the social teachings of the Church. First, our schools should never be havens for the well-to-do who want their children to get a bigger piece of the financial pie while not losing their faith. That the leaders of some Catholic high schools tout more than anything else the academic scholarships their seniors win from prestigious universities indicates that the social teachings of the Church occupy a very small place in their consciousness. Indeed, the graduates of Catholic schools should succeed, but the definition of success has to include the concepts both of discipleship and of citizenship.[14]

Ultimately, the leaders of Catholic schools, colleges, and universities should never desire that their graduates simply "fit into" society but rather that they should help transform it.

The second consequence underscores perhaps the main reason why it is so difficult to promote the social teachings of the Church: those who accept and act on these are required to undertake the difficult and complex work of social analysis. Dom Helder Camara, the now retired bishop of Recife in northeastern Brazil, one of the poorest dioceses in the country, once remarked, "when I give food to the poor, they think I am a saint; when I ask why the poor do not have bread, they think I am a communist." Social analysis goes beyond service and being kind. It requires individuals to study the causes of poverty, to work for more equitable and just treatment of people – especially the poor – and to risk their own status and standing for the sake of those less fortunate. Jesus was crucified because he spoke truth to power, and he calls those who wish to be Christians to do the same.

Nearly all management and leadership literature presents as one of the desired qualities of the leader "effectiveness," understood as, for example, turning around a failing company, or, on a more personal level, knowing how to realize one's own potential. Leaders of Catholic schools must be sure to ask deeper questions than those of effectiveness (though in certain spheres, such questions have their value); they also need to ask whether certain goals are in fact worth striving to attain. The criterion of "effectiveness alone" does not suffice. Suppose, for example, that the results of a social analysis made it clear that to avoid negative social consequences, a company would have to cut by half its profit margin, or close down its potentially most lucrative product line – because that product had been shown to harm many poor people or to create unsolvable ecological problems. Social analysis, in the Christian tradition, would require that monetary profit always be weighed against issues like the common good, the impact on the poor, and the effect on the environment.

One of the most ironic recent examples of praise for a Machiavellian preoccupation with means ("effectiveness") and not ends may be found in a March/April 1998 article in the *Harvard Business Review*, "The Discipline of Building Character." The author, Joseph Badaracco Jr., illustrates his thesis with three examples of individuals who forged their character at "defining moments when a manager must choose between right and right." The article employs throughout the language of "values" and "principles." His third example, the most striking for our purposes, tells the story of Eduoard Sakiz, the CEO of Roussel Uclaf, a French pharmaceutical company, who wanted to introduce into the international market the abortifacient pill RU-486. In his conclusion, Badaracco praises Sakiz who "not only stayed closely connected to his personal values and those of his organization but also predicted what his opponents and allies outside the company would do. The result was the introduction of a drug that shook the world."[15] Though Badaracco seems to think that he is writing about values and morality and principles, his discussion of Sakiz's character-building "defining moment" completely avoids coming to grips with the morality of abortion or any of the other moral issues that the RU-486 pill itself raises. Sakiz, Badaracco concludes, was masterfully effective, and, in that very effectiveness, has made it possible, I would argue, for millions of people to commit a great evil with greater ease and privacy than ever before.

Facing the moral questions that go beyond mere "effectiveness" requires not only careful thought, but also courage.[16] For leaders of Christian educational institutions, an emphasis on justice will require that ends and not just means be examined and that students learn how to analyze the structures of society and how to oppose those that perpetuate various forms of discrimination. Leaders of Christian educational institutions form graduates who believe they have an obligation to transform society.

Finally, the Christian tradition recognizes the fragility that marks the human condition. People are broken and in need of healing. Our fifth theme, then, is the Christian doctrine of original sin. The Christian vision of life assumes that people sin and fail.[17] The doctrine of original sin – that we are all broken and in need of healing – invites leaders to be more compassionate than if they presumed everyone, if only they tried hard enough, could be perfect. Leaders also learn greater patience than if they believed that the road to the goal was short, and that everyone who reports to them could get the job done quickly. They come to realize that people need not only to be led, but also to be nourished.

Not long ago, I came across an article in a religious magazine entitled, "Who Feeds the Shepherds?" Indeed, how many teachers and administrators recognize and provide for their own nourishment? How many carve out time for refreshment and renewal? Stephen Covey, about whose widely read book, *The Seven Habits of Highly Effective People*, I will have more to say later, tells the story of someone who comes upon an individual in the woods trying to saw down a tree. The individual looks exhausted and when asked how long he had been at the task, responds "for hours." When the visitor suggests that he take a moment to sharpen the saw, the individual tells him he doesn't have time to do that since he is so busy sawing.[18]

Frank Rhodes, the very successful president emeritus of Cornell University, pinpoints several reasons why leaders of educational institutions fail in doing their task well. The first is exhaustion: "Lack of sleep, no time for exercise, shortened vacations, and repeated involvement in crises are the warning signs on the road to personal exhaustion."[19] Leaders need to sustain themselves not only with time for reading, but with responsible work habits that will allow them not only to read, but to keep clear their priorities, keep close to their families and loved ones, and, as I have tried to emphasize, draw upon the insights of the Christian tradition. Ordinary people often expect leaders to be extraordinary; they forget that everyone, including leaders, are only human.

Workshops on leadership rarely feature what this fifth theme clarifies: that people are fragile and insecure. Being this "realistic" seems to many people like fostering immaturity or even depression. Most workshop leaders instead focus on positive thinking, on being whatever one wants to be, on learning how to get what one wants for oneself or from others. But if popular leadership gurus avoid dealing with this aspect of the human condition, a few major writers and even some popular singers still address it clearly. Walker Percy, the Catholic novelist, once asked: "Is it too much to say that the novelist ... is one of the few remaining witnesses to the doctrine of original sin, the imminence of catastrophe in paradise?"[20] The songwriter Bruce Springsteen explains, in a remarkable interview, the power that Flannery O'Connor's stories have had on his craft:

> The really important reading that I did began in my late twenties, with authors like Flannery O'Connor. There was something in those stories of hers that I felt captured a certain part of the American character that I was interested in writing about. They were a big, big revelation. ... There was some dark thing – a component of spirituality – that I sensed in her stories, and that set me off exploring characters of my own. She knew original sin – knew how to give it the flesh of a story.[21]

If indeed people are fragile, if they are burdened with a "dark thing" that can be spoken of only with the deeper language of religion, then leaders need to realize that people will need time and understanding and support to change. Leaders will realize that defense mechanisms must be dealt with carefully to avoid needless threat in an already threatening existence.

Leaders will rather gradually help others to open themselves to the work that is at hand.

In summary, the Christian tradition offers valuable wisdom for leaders of Christian educational institutions. It reminds them that besides being their own person, they need also to be members of a community committed to both intellectual and moral learning, aware and appreciative of the many forms that leadership takes, guided by the social responsibilities that flow from the gospel, and, finally, sensitive to the fragility of everyone, especially themselves and those with whom they work and teach. If, as Dorothy Day said so simply, leadership has also to do with the people who surround leaders and from whom leaders must naturally learn, then leaders will do everything they can to attract to their institutions the kind of people who will readily join in on the common effort.[22]

Some Current Leadership Literature

Having examined five themes from the Christian tradition that shed light on certain aspects of leadership, I now turn to a number of recent books, some very popular, on leadership. I intend to highlight some of the valuable insights offered by the authors of these books as well as to argue that some of their suggestions, evaluated in the light of the Christian tradition, are either deficient or just plain wrong. I wish to focus my attention on two works, one in which I find a great deal of merit, and in the other much less.

One of the best books on leadership in my opinion is Ronald Heifetz's *Leadership Without Easy Answers*.[23] Two concerns make Heifetz's approach especially valuable. First, he recognizes that each of the four theories teaches us something about the meaning and shape of leadership. He learns from all of them and illustrates each with well-developed examples from history. In this way, Heifetz affirms my Christian theme that explains that leadership can take many different forms.

Second, he attempts to go beyond the typical "value-free" approach of the social scientists who dominate this field of literature. After all, he asks, if leadership is the moving of masses of people to act, then both Hitler and Ghandi were leaders. Fundamental questions such as "leadership for what?" and "to whose benefit?" must be asked to correct the flawed neutral approach. In an article cited earlier, I described how the author praised a clever business leader who manipulated several groups to get an abortion pill on the market. That author presented the business leader as someone whose character had been deepened by this "defining moment." Apparently, that definition lacked moral analysis.

Questions about the moral dimensions of leadership force us to recognize that simply because leadership is official, i.e., possesses authority bestowed through a set of procedures followed by the many, it may not for that reason alone be moral. Moreover, when official authority defines moral authority, then it excludes many thoughtful people from exercising moral leadership: Martin Luther King Jr., Lech Walesa, Vaclav Havel, and Mother Teresa. Indeed, reliance only on official authority excludes the entire prophetic tradition in Judaism and Christianity. Leaders should realize that other people in their organization exercise leadership, and sometimes prophetic forms of leadership. In fact, strong leaders do not dismiss their critics, but give them a fair hearing, and even protect them from those who, because of an exaggerated sense of loyalty to them as leaders, might try to marginalize and even destroy such critics. Strong leaders thereby broaden their circle of influence and take initiatives that more often than not are moral.

The situations that leaders of institutions face are complex. Heifetz recognizes this complexity and distinguishes three types of situations: (1) the problem and the solution are clear; (2) the problem is clear but the solution requires learning; and (3) neither the problem nor the solution is clear. A leak in the cafeteria ceiling provides a clear definition of the problem with an obvious solution. Rapid turnover of faculty poses a clear problem, but the solution requires learning to ascertain the actual causes. But suppose it is asked how the sciences and the social sciences should be understood and taught at a Catholic school precisely because it is Catholic. How many teachers and principals would have a clear sense of the problem, much less an understanding of how to solve it? While it may be clear to many in a Catholic school that it ought to be truly and distinctively a Catholic school, little consensus exists on what that would mean concretely in terms of curriculum other than, perhaps, the teaching of religion. And suppose further that the problem to be solved was not limited to the curriculum, but also included the moral formation of the students. In such a case, both principals and faculty must work hard to think these issues through together, initiating and evaluating changes designed to impart a distinctive educational experience, in terms both of curriculum and of moral formation.[24]

Heifetz in particular shows an awareness of the time that people need to embrace change, and of the skills that leaders need to acquire to help individuals and communities to undertake the difficult process of change.[25] He understands the fragility of human beings. And, as we have also seen, he does not limit effective leadership only to magic impact of charismatic personalities. Rather, he emphasizes those forms of leadership that guide processes which direct people's attention to real problems, sift information for reliability, frame issues, make room for conflict, and clarify ways to make decisions.[26] Such leaders do not need to appear to have all the answers; rather, they need to know how to help a group arrive at solutions together. Heifetz describes those who avoid the hard work of change as engaging in "work avoidance" behavior. The reasons for such behavior are many, including fear of change, refusal to assume any responsibility for the problem, unrealistic expectations of what the leader should be able to do on his or her own, and simply refusing to admit that there is a problem.[27]

When things are very difficult, the pressure on the leader to solve the problem as soon as possible is great. In difficult situations, good leaders often choose to keep a certain pressure on others, not an overwhelming pressure, but one that makes it more likely that an appropriate urgency will be sustained until a resolution can be found as a community. But sustaining pressure is not enough. Leaders assist the community by framing the issues, and perhaps even orchestrating some conflict while working carefully at the same time to contain disorder.[28]

Heifetz views leadership as a service. Understood as service, leadership then can be given and taken away from a person in an official position, depending on whether the leader provides the service that is expected.[29] He also makes the distinction between formal and informal authority. Formal authority is instant. One day a person is not the principal of a high school; the next day the person is. By contrast, informal authority is earned over a long period of time.

Formal authorization brings with it the powers of an office, but informal authorization brings with it the subtle yet substantial power to extend one's reach way beyond the limits of the job description. Formal authority changes in quantum jumps at discrete moments in time when formal mandates for action are given: at swearing-in, hiring, firing, signing of legislation, issuance of a license. In contrast, informal authority changes constantly as one's popularity and professional reputation rise and fall.[30]

The great value of Heifetz's book is that it deals with real complex leadership situations for which there are no simple answers. He focuses on dealing with groups and leading institutions, and recognizes that leadership necessarily takes many forms given different situations. He does not romanticize the challenges of leadership, nor ignore its difficulties. He understands that institutional change takes time, needs to be carefully brought along, and that ultimately effective change is not imposed, but embraced by all the members of an institution through a process of hard work. Heifetz is one of the few "leadership authors" whose views strike me not only as credible, but also as insightful. His views strike me as realistic.

As a contrast to Heifetz's book, I wish to discuss briefly a book that has sold much more widely than Heifetz's, Stephen Covey's *The 7 Habits of Highly Effective People.*[31] Not only does Covey currently advise eight out of ten of the top Fortune 100 leaders, but he also influences many leaders in Catholic schools throughout the country. Workshops for principals have been designed along the lines of the seven habits, and workshop materials for "effective schools" have been distributed at many diocesan leadership programs. And indeed Covey has some valuable things to say. Noteworthy are his desire to develop "principled leadership" and character (the subtitle of his book is: "Restoring the Character Ethic") as opposed to mere personality. He realizes that leaders need to do "inner work," and that "spirituality" contributes in an essential way to a leader's vision. He makes recommendations that are as helpful as they are simply a matter of common sense: be proactive, distinguish between the important and the urgent, learn to listen and understand, and take time to renew yourself – or, sharpen your saw.

On the other hand, there are serious deficiencies in Covey's version of things, particularly if one is seeking advice as how to lead an institution. Covey offers advice to individual persons, which to him seems to be persons who do not lead institutions; they are simply individuals faced with the challenge of self-realization. The persons for whom Covey writes are supposedly not shaped by any particular religious tradition.[32] The readers, Covey assures them, can find within themselves all the principles needed for leadership. But to be preoccupied with effectiveness, with what works, people are forced to forego, as we have already seen, serious reflection on the criteria that they need if they are to assess whether something that was effective was also right. To promote "win/win" strategies they rely on compromises; people can avoid ever saying, for example, "on this issue there is no compromise" or "a decision has to be made and someone will have to lose." Covey, like the army, tries to persuade his readers that they can be just about anybody they set their minds to be. People are to exercise "mastery" over themselves; in fact, the very first step is "self mastery."[33] This is not surprising, for the self and, more specifically, the inner consciousness of the self, is, Covey insists, where a person's source of power is found. At the beginning of the chapter devoted to explicating the second habit, "Begin with the End in Mind," he cites Oliver Wendell Holmes: "What lies behind us and what lies before us are tiny matters compared to what lies within us." He emphasizes the critical importance of creating oneself, of writing one's own script.[34] The individualism that is so characteristic of our society not only goes unchallenged by Covey's understanding of what it takes to be a highly effective person, but also is highly supported by it.

Covey not only promotes individualism, he also favors the charismatic leader over the manager. Those who will settle only for charismatic leadership overlook many other effective forms of leadership. A given school, at its particular point in history, might need a leader with strong management skills. Another institution might need a change-agent, and still another someone who can heal hurts and re-establish trust. As Heifetz pointed out, charismatic leaders have no problem getting followers, but seldom succeed in getting people to face their problems.[35]

The charismatic leader is also favored by Warren Bennis, who writes in *On Becoming a Leader* that those leaders who "forge the future" will have certain things in common: a broad education, boundless curiosity and enthusiasm, belief in people and teamwork, a willingness to take risks, devotion to long-term growth rather than short-term profit, commitment to excellence, readiness, virtue, and vision.[36] Bennis thinks of the differences between "leaders and managers as the differences between those who master the context and those who surrender to it. ... Managers wear square hats and learn through training; leaders wear sombreros and opt for education."[37] Covey also makes the distinction, citing Bennis, but seems not quite as enthralled with it since he allots to management an important "follow up" activity: "Management is efficiency in climbing the ladder of success; leadership determines whether the ladder is leaning against the right wall."[38] In most of the literature, the "leader" embodies sets of characteristics that approximate divinity.[39] Some aspiring leaders construct resumes to match such exaggerated expectations.

But, as we have seen, no one is perfect; all humans are flawed. Leadership takes many forms and the community constitutes an integral part of the reality of leadership. Basic Christian insights into leadership would temper messianic expectations and impart a palpable realism to much of the most popular leadership literature.

Conclusion

In summary then, I find the approach to leadership taken by Heifetz much more realistic and helpful than that taken by Covey and Bennis.[40] Heifetz realizes that the issues faced by leaders are complex, requiring the important skills of helping people as a group to face problems that only they as a group can solve. In fact, some problems do not lend themselves to solutions, but rather must be dealt with continuously. The realities of defense mechanisms, family and institutional histories, the fear of change and the difficulties in leading a process of change – these are all dealt with in insightful ways by Heifetz. Covey, on the other hand, focuses so much on the individual that he does not really address the organizational challenges that face leaders of schools, or, for that matter, of any institutions. Heifetz validates multiple types of leaders, while Covey gives primacy to the charismatic leader capable of self-mastery and effecting win/win solutions.

The five themes drawn from the Christian tradition elaborated in the first part of this chapter provide important elements in constructing a sound framework for leadership. That framework first includes attention to the broader community and its tradition, the contexts in which our fragmented selves are healed. For the Christian, moral principles guide people as they face "defining moments." Since the obligatory practice of social analysis exposes injustice, Christian educators must never be satisfied with simply preparing their graduates to be successes and to "fit into" society. Graduates of Christian schools should certainly be effective and competent; but more importantly, they should also be generous, loving, and courageous. Leaders of Christian institutions require more wisdom than can be found in popular leadership books.

Notes

1 Each year I conduct a seminar with about a dozen faculty that lasts a full semester and includes financial support for individual summer research, all focused on their disciplines as they relate to the Catholic intellectual tradition For a description of the first seminar, see "Ethics and Religion in Professional Education: An Interdisciplinary Seminar," in *Current Issues in Catholic Higher Education*, Association of Catholic Colleges and Universities, 18 (2) (Spring 1998): 21–50.

2 See T.S. Eliot's "Tradition and the Individual Talent," in *The Sacred Wood* (London: Methuen University Paperbacks, 1969), pp. 47–59. For Eliot, the poet learns what is to be done only when "he lives in what is not merely present, but the present moment of the past," and when "he is conscious, not of what is dead, but of what is already living" (p. 59). See also Aidan Nichols, "T.S. Eliot and Yves Congar on the Nature of Tradition," in *Angelicum*, 61 (1984): 473–85.

3 See Patrick Allit's "The American Christ," in *American Heritage* (November, 1988): 128–41, at p. 139. Not only entrepreneurs distort the image of Jesus, but also academics. C.S. Lewis's fictional character, Screwtape, an experienced and retired devil, acts as a consultant for his nephew Wormword, just beginning his career as a professional tempter, and suggests to him that devils need to wean their temptees from sincere devotion and participation in the sacramental life. Gradually then, God becomes remote and shadowy: "Instead of the Creator adored by its creature, you soon have merely a leader acclaimed by a partisan, and finally a distinguished character approved by a judicious historian," in *Screwtape Letters* (New York: Macmillan Paperbacks Edition, 1970), p. 107.

4 See my article, "The Perennial Temptation of Christians and 'The Last Temptation of Christ,'" in *Catechist* (March, 1989): 12–15.

5 Warren Bennis, *On Becoming a Leader* (Reading, MA: Addison-Wesley, 1994), p. 39.

6 (San Francisco: Jossey-Bass, 1989), pp. 212–13. For Vaill, spirituality starts within the self, focuses one's own spiritual development, and characterizes all true leadership (p. 223). See, however, Eamon Duffy, reader in church history in the University of Cambridge, who recently wrote: "What worries me about the whole 'spirituality' industry ... is the support it gives to the notion that growth in faith, hope and love is a matter of cultivating what you might call our holy bits – which rarely include the brain." And again, "I distrust the implication that the spiritual is something which starts when you close your eyes and retreat inwards, that it is about your *soul*, which in our culture is a notion almost invariably associated with subjective feeling." *Priests and People* (November, 1997): 452.

7 Robert Coles, "On Moral Leadership: Dorothy Day and Peter Maurin in Tandem," in *America* (June 6, 1998): 10. According to the Memorial Library Newsletter (Marquette University) (May, 1994): 1, "The Dorothy Day Catholic Worker Collection," Day was "widely regarded as the most influential lay person in the history of American Catholicism for her steadfast living of the Gospel message."

8 See his *Vindication of Tradition: The 1983 Jefferson Lecture in the Humanities* (New Haven, CT: Yale University Press, 1984). At the beginning of this series of lectures, Pelikan quotes Goethe's *Faust*: "What you have as a heritage, take now as task; for thus you will make it your own."

9 "Ethics" is a term that has its roots in the Protestant tradition, and has been taken over by professional communities who adhere to various ethical codes; for example, the ethical codes of engineers or medical doctors, regardless of their religious tradition. Catholicism prefers to speak of "morality," by which it understands a set of behaviors that flow from certain religious beliefs carefully

reflected upon by the community over time. In the Catholic tradition, "moral theology" is a faith-based systematic reflection on the lives of disciples of Jesus. For the integral relationship between the religious and the ethical, see my article "Can Character be Taught?," *Journal for a Just and Caring Education*, 1 (4) (October, 1995): 389–402.

10 Gilbert Meilaender, "A Philosopher of Virtue," in *First Things*, No. 82 (April, 1998): 17.

11 See for example his *The Office of Peter and the Structure of the Church*, trans. by Andree Emery (San Francisco: Ignatius Press, 1986), pp. 204–87; also *Church and World*, trans. by A.V. Littledale (New York: Hereder and Hereder, 1967), pp. 44–111; and "Theologies of Religious Life and Priesthood," by David N. Power, OMI, in *A Concert of Charisms: Ordained Ministry in Religious Life*, ed. Paul Hennessy (New York: Paulist Press, 1997), pp. 82–83, where Power notes that Von Balthasar respects the various "callings" in the Church, allows none to be placed above the other, and emphasizes their interdependence.

12 Robert Coles, art. cit. Maurin also warned Day that "if you're going to teach people, you'd better be clear about what you want to come of it, because a teacher is a leader and if a teacher doesn't know that, there's trouble to pay" (p. 9).

13 "Sharing Catholic Social Teaching: Challenges and Directions," in *Origins*, 28 (7) (July 2, 1998): 102–106.

14 See the writings of John Coleman, SJ, especially "Discipleship and Citizenship," in Mary Boys (ed.), *Education for Discipleship and Citizenship* (New York: Pilgrim Press, 1988); "Discipleship and Citizenship: From Consensus to Culture Wars," in *Louvain Studies*, 17 (4) (Winter 1992); and "Under the Cross and the Flag," *America* (May 11, 1996).

15 Joseph L. Badaracco, Jr., "The Discipline of Building Character," in *Harvard Business Review* (March–April, 1998): 124. The idea of character being shaped by "defining moments" as the time when people must decide between two alternatives, both of which seem right, has merit. My argument, however, is that the author focuses on the defining *moment*, and not on the moral dimensions of the choices that need to be evaluated before being made.

16 One is reminded of the old ditty, "Mr. Business went to Church, he never missed a Sunday; But Mr. Business went to hell, for what he did on Monday."

17 Typical of much of the "New Age" spirituality is a vision of happiness and fulfillment that escapes tragic choices or loss. In an otherwise wonderful recent CD by Barbra Streisand, "Higher Ground," one of the songs, "Lessons to be Learned," assures us that there are "no mistakes, only lessons to be learned." Surely in this imaginary universe, no hell but only various forms of heaven bless everyone, regardless of behavior.

18 Stephen R. Covey, *The 7 Habits of Highly Effective People* (New York: Simon & Schuster, 1989), p. 287.

19 Frank Rhodes, "The Art of the Presidency," *The Presidency*, 1 (1) (Spring 1998): 17.

20 Cited by Robert Ellsberg, *All Saints* (New York: Crossroad, 1997), p. 235.

21 "Rock and Read: Will Percy Interviews Bruce Springsteen," from *Double Take*, published by the Duke University Center for Documentary Studies, Issue 12 (Spring 1998): 2. Springsteen described his work as "food for thought," addressing "how we live ... and how we ought to live in the world" (p. 4), an effort to "establish a commonality by revealing our inner common humanity, by telling good stories about a lot of different kinds of people" (p. 5), and sustained by "companionship which means breaking bread with your brothers and sisters, your fellow human beings" (p. 9). Springsteen reflects the Catholic imagination.

22 Max De Pree, the chairman emeritus of the Herman Miller Company, wisely observes:

> Major college coaches recruit carefully and diligently because they know their success as coaches depends on their recruits' potential. They know the high school coaches who turn out the best-prepared players. Coaches reach their own potential by combining the natural gifts of the young people they recruit and the context in which those gifts have been shaped.
>
> *Leading Without Power: Finding Hope in Serving Community*
> (San Francisco: Jossey-Bass, 1997), p. 87

Leaders of educational institutions should be as careful about the teachers and personnel they hire as their collaborators, and work with them to form a community.

23 (New Haven, CT: The Belknap Press of Harvard University Press, 1994). Heifetz surveys the theories of leadership, reducing them ultimately to four (pp. 16–23). He singles out the following four theories: (1) the "great men;" (2) the "situationist;" (3) the "contingent;" and (4) the "transactionist."

24 Heifetz, see pp. 69–76.

25 Heifetz, p. 76ff. See especially his description of how a physician might handle a patient who must deal with the reality of terminal cancer.

26 Heifetz, p. 113ff.

27 Heifetz illustrates "work avoidance" on the level of national leadership by discussing the SDI (Strategic Defense Initiative) that President Reagan attempted to effect. Instead of learning how to deal with the new world reality – the necessity of international interdependence and cooperation – Reagan avoided that hard task and proposed instead a "technical fix" which in the opinion of many respected scientists was impossible to create in the first place. See pp. 40–48.

28 Heifetz puts it this way:

> the cook regulates the pressure of the holding environment [a term that Heifetz uses to describe when one person can hold the attention of another in order to help that person change] by turning the heat up or down, while the relief valve lets off steam to keep the pressure within a safe limit. If the pressure goes beyond the carrying capacity of the vessel, the pressure cooker can blow up. On the other hand, with no heat nothing cooks.
>
> (p. 106)

29 Heifetz, p. 57.

30 Heifetz, p. 102. Later in his book he writes:

> Authority figures become repositories of hope by virtue of taking office. ... But they also become repositories of frustration to those whose expectations they have failed. In relatively stable periods of time, these failures may not be of much significance and passion, and an authority figure can survive without too much wear and tear. Humming along on routine problems, people can operate according to well-understood procedures without much disappointment. In unstable times, however, when norms and procedures break down, adaptive pressures are high, and disequilibrium is rising, the expectations and frustrations with authority build as well.
>
> (p. 237)

31 (New York: Simon & Schuster, 1989). It has sold over 10 million copies and has been translated into twenty-eight languages. Covey taught at Brigham Young until 1985 when he resigned his teaching position to found the Covey Leadership

Center, which later was called the Franklin Covey Company, because it merged with the company that makes the Franklin Planner. For an especially incisive critique of the entire Covey mystique, and in particular of the weaknesses of the "effectiveness" approach, see Alan Wolfe's "White Magic in America: Capitalism, Mormonism, and the doctrines of Stephen Covey," in *The New Republic* (February 23, 1998): 26–34.

32 Wolfe discusses the extent to which Covey's Mormonism actually shapes his vision of leadership and the seven habits. In Mormonism, there is no hell, no original sin, and no sense of salvation as a gift – one earns salvation through good deeds and problem solving. Wolfe writes: "Mormonism was an engineer's religion, a doctrine for the pragmatic, no-nonsense kind of person who practiced a kind of white magic on the material world, demanding that it yield its secrets for the cause of human betterment" (p. 29). In Wolfe's view, Covey's seven habits are practices that flow from a thinly disguised Mormon vision of things, a vision of life that is highly authoritarian and sexist. Wolfe, I believe, is basically right in this criticism.

33 In the chapter in which he talks about self-mastery, "Principles of Personal Vision," he opens the chapter with a quotation from Henry David Thoreau: "I know of no more encouraging fact than the unquestionable ability of man to elevate his life by conscious endeavor" (p. 66).

34 Covey, p. 103.

35 Heifetz, pp. 13–14. Later, he writes:

> When the stress is severe, we seem especially willing to grant extraordinary power and give away our freedom. In a historical study of thirty-five dictatorships, all of them emerged during times of social distress. Unhinged from their habits, people look with greater intensity to authority figures for remedies.
>
> (p. 65)

36 Bennis, pp. 201–202. If this list were not daunting enough, Bennis adds:

> And as they (these leaders of the twenty-first century) express themselves, they will make new movies, new industries, and perhaps a new world. If that sounds like an impossible dream to you, consider this: it's much easier to express yourself than to deny yourself. And much more rewarding, too.

In the last analysis, leadership is reduced to creative and aggressive self-expression, which Bennis describes as "the most basic human drive" (p. 123); " 'letting the self emerge' is the essential task for leaders" (p. 113).

37 Bennis, pp. 44–45. He apparently means that managers are linear and unimaginative in their thinking, while leaders are creative and multifaceted in their thinking.

38 Covey, p. 101. But Covey is still insistent, "leadership is not management," loc. cit.

39 Evidence of this tendency to inflate the desirable qualities of a leader precedes our own century. A member of the Board of Trustees at Yale in the nineteenth century described the characteristics of the person they were seeking to fill the position of president:

> He had to be a good leader, a magnificent speaker, a great writer, a good public relations man, a man of iron health and stamina, married to a

paragon of virtue. His wife, in fact, had to be a mixture of Queen Victoria, Florence Nightingale and the best dressed woman of the year. We saw our choice as having to be a man of the world, but an individual with great spiritual qualities; an experienced administrator, but able to delegate; a Yale man, and a great scholar; a social philosopher, who though he had the solutions to the world's problems, had still not lost the common touch. After lengthy deliberation, we concluded that there was only one such person. But then a dark thought crossed our minds. We had to ask – is God a Yale man?

(Cited by Frank Rhodes, art. cit.)

Ironically, Rhodes goes on in the article to spell out his view of a president's responsibilities that, while a little less ideal than those listed for the Yale presidency, nonetheless would, in my view, still remain very difficult, even for a gifted mortal, to fulfill.

40 Lest I seem to be negative about most books on leadership and management, allow me to mention a few other books that I have found to be quite thoughtful: Peter Senge's *The Fifth Discipline* (New York: Doubleday, 1990); Jon Katzenbach and Douglas Smith's *The Wisdom of Teams* (New York: Harper Business, 1993); and Max De Pree's books, especially his *Leadership is an Art* (New York: Dell, 1989) and *Leadership Jazz* (New York: Dell, 1993).

16 Leadership in Urban Catholic Elementary Schools

The Reality and the Challenge

Joseph M. O'Keefe, SJ

This chapter offers insights into the role of the principal in contemporary Catholic urban elementary schools in the United States. After a review of salient published literature, the author presents and discusses findings related to the principalship from a national sample of 398 such schools. Then, based on interviews with ten principals from across the nation, he discusses the following topics: contours of the principalship, desolations, and consolations. Finally, he offers reflections on the future of leadership in these institutions.

Literature Review: The Urban Context

It is arguable that in its urban elementary schools the Catholic Church provides its greatest service to the common good of the nation. Emerging from an era of retrenchment and closure (O'Keefe 1996), these schools are a vital presence in deprived areas. Before a review of studies of Catholic school principals in particular, it is important to discuss the broader urban context.

When asked to reflect on the crime rate in their locale over the past five years, 52% of the principals in the current study reported an increase and 31% no change. Moreover, when asked to describe their neighborhoods, principals repeatedly described high levels of poverty, inadequate housing, persistent unemployment or underemployment, all disproportionately affecting ethnic minorities. The perception of Catholic elementary principals is matched by the broader national perspective. Juvenile gun deaths tripled between 1984 and 1994, one-third of the nation's children are without health insurance, the number of children reported abused or neglected as well as the number of children with verified reports of abuse rose between 1985 and 1995, the rate of children in poverty has grown, and the use of illicit drugs has increased (Haney 1998). Dysfunctional families, child abuse, and chemical addiction are as much a problem among affluent suburbanites as those in core cities, and in some ways the bonds of care, community, and affection are greater among the poor than the wealthy. Nevertheless, the urban poor suffer disproportionally from unjust social structures and, as a result, are often unable to deal effectively with the pathologies that plague the contemporary United States. Along these lines, Bill Bradley, former senator from New Jersey, has warned about an impending national crisis that he labels "encirclement."

> Encirclement means that people in cities will live in enclaves. The racial and ethnic walls will go higher, the class lines will be reinforced by ever increasing security forces, and communal life will disappear. What will replace a sense of community will be deepening divisions, with politicians splitting up the shrinking economic pie into ever smaller ethnic, racial and religious slices. There will be a kind of clockwork-orange society in which the rich will pay for their security, the middle class will continue to flee as they confront violence, and the poor will be preyed upon at will or join the army of violent predators. What will be lost for everyone will be freedom, civility, and the chance to build a common future.
>
> (Bradley 1998: 267)

The school, an institution singularly charged with building a common future, is by no means immune from the effects of encirclement. Representatives for the National Network for Collaboration recently explained:

> Today's schools are facing an ever-increasing number of complex social problems that impact their ability to meet the educational, social, emotional and physical needs of their students. Schools are often faced with tired, hungry, homeless and frightened children who are growing up in communities that seem to have forgotten them.
>
> (Perkins et al. 1998: 85)

Prompted by increasing burdens on the school, the role of the principal has changed considerably, from "campus administrator to integrator of school and community services" (Miller 1994: 11), from "myopic manager" to "boundary spanner" (Lieberman 1992: 154). In meeting the diverse needs of children, external relations are primary.

> With more permeable boundaries between the dynamic school and the environment, the principal deals with more and different groups of parents, business representatives, and community agencies. The principal is usually the first contact point with the external environment but will most likely spend more energy with these constituencies than traditional principals who focus most of their efforts internally.
>
> (Goldring and Rallis 1993: 141)

For effective urban principals in the Catholic or public sector, the number of stakeholders in educational planning and implementation has expanded greatly; the principal must be a "top-level catalyst, champion, convener and facilitator ... someone who recognizes and acknowledges that the current delivery of education, health, and human services is not meeting the needs of at least some of the target population" (Zetlin 1995: 423).

Literature Review: The Catholic Context

The empirical fact is that Catholic elementary principals face the same challenges as their colleagues in other sectors. Moreover, because of its gospel mission, the Catholic community is irrevocably committed to those in greatest need. This perspective has been reaffirmed in the Church's most recent articulation of its educational mission:

> In its ecclesial dimension another characteristic of the Catholic school has its root: it is a school for all, with special attention to those who are weakest ... those who have lost all sense of meaning in life and lack any type of inspiring ideal, those to whom no values are proposed and who do not know the beauty of faith, who come from families which are broken and incapable of love, often living in situations of material and spiritual poverty, slaves to new idols of society which, not infrequently, promises only a future of unemployment and marginalization. To these new poor the Catholic school turns in a spirit of love.
>
> (Congregation for Catholic Education 1998: 18)

In turning to the poor, the spirit of love must be matched by effective structures and competent leadership. For the Catholic community as for the secular world, traditional ways of meeting children's needs are often insufficient to the task.

> Catholic schools are challenged by the increasing number of needs which stress the village's capacity to take care of its members. In the days when the parish community was comprised of one or a few major ethnic or cultural groups, the villagers or parishioners created a natural network of caring for one another – answering many of the needs before they ever become obvious at the school. Now many urban parishes encompass a number of different ethnic and cultural groups. While this diversity has strengthened and enriched parish life, the consequent cultural and linguistic barriers have made it more difficult for the parishioners to care for one another. Parishioners are less able to respond informally to the needs of their neighbors, thus increasing the burden on the school.
>
> (Walsh et al. 1998: 77–78)

Based on her personal experience, a former elementary principal and superintendent concurred when she wrote that

> I saw the role of school administrator changing. In the 1970's and 1980's the number of hours that school administrators had to spend doing what they were trained to do grew fewer and fewer. Less time was available for principals to be instructional leader and manager. More time was taken up with meeting students' non-academic needs.
>
> (Haney 1998: 13)

The past ten years have not seen a published study with a particular focus on the urban Catholic elementary principalship. Other studies offer important insights, however. Similar to a two-year-old study of elementary teachers (Kushner and Helbling 1995), the most recent and comprehensive study of the Catholic elementary principalship appeared five years ago (Harkins 1993). Using data from surveys conducted with 783 principals (42% in inner city or urban settings), the researcher presented a wide range of demographic and attitudinal information. The School and Staffing survey conducted by the US Department of Education (McLaughlin and Broughman 1997) has also provided rich demographic information. Annual data collection at the National Catholic Educational Association (Metzler 1998) provides yet another source. In reporting about the current survey, these studies are used whenever possible to provide helpful comparisons.

Other publications about the principalship provide helpful information for practitioners. Most notable is the recent three-volume work by Ciriello (1996). Three similar works have appeared during the past decade (Kealey 1989; Drahmann and Stenger 1989; Walsh and Feistritzer 1991).

Presentation of Survey Data

The current survey sample ($n = 398$) grew out of the 1995–96 census of Catholic elementary and secondary schools, conducted jointly by the National Catholic Educational Association and the market research firm Market Data Retrieval. Data were used to identify urban elementary schools that served low-income students through Title I funding, which eventually numbered just over 1,000 schools. Introductory letters describing the focus of the study were issued to dioceses' superintendents followed by the distribution of the survey to identified school principals. Expansive in both breadth and depth, survey items collect data from the following general areas: school characteristics, student body demographics, teacher and principal characteristics, student family information, schools' community involvement, curriculum and instruction, school finances and development, school religious identity, and five-year trends. Data were primarily collected during the 1996–97 academic year.

The 398 elementary schools are found in thirty-five states, representing all sections of the nation (see Table 16.1).

It is important to note that the response rate from schools in several metropolitan areas – St. Louis and Cleveland – was especially low (see Table 16.2).

The most relevant studies to the one described here were conducted in 1990. McLaughlin and Broughman (1997) used data from the federal government's School and Staffing survey in 1993–94 to report characteristics about private schools. Schools Harkins studied (1993), just under half of which were in

Table 16.1   Location of schools in sample and all Catholic schools

	Sample	All
New England (CT, ME, MA, NH, RI, VT)	4.8%	6.7%
Mideast (DE, DC, MD, NJ, NY, PA)	32.1%	27.2%
Great Lakes (IL, IN, MI, OH, WI)	21.6%	25.1%
Great Plains (IA, KS, MN, MO, NE, ND, SD)	6.4%	11.4%
Southeast (AL, AK, FL, GA, KY, LA, MS, NC, SC, TN, VA, WV)	12.3%	12.0%
West (AK, AZ, CA, CO, HI, ID, MT, NM, OK, OR, TX, UT, WA, WY)	22.3%	17.5%

Source: Data from Metzler (1998)

Table 16.2   Survey responses from twelve largest dioceses

Dioceses with largest enrollments	*Represented in sample*
1 Chicago	29
2 Philadelphia	16
3 New York	24
4 Los Angeles	22
5 Brooklyn	17
6 Cleveland	5
7 Newark	9
8 St. Louis	0
9 Cincinnati	7
10 Detroit	14
11 Boston	13
12 New Orleans	4

Source: Data from Metzler (1998)

urban settings, had an average enrollment of 239. The schools in the present study average 275, with a median enrollment of 249. The schools in the present study are also more heavily diocesan than schools in the Harkins study or the larger population of all Catholic schools (see Table 16.3).

For Harkins, the average tuition fee was $979 per year. For all private schools the figure is $2,157 (McLaughlin and Broughman 1997). The comparable figure of $1,546 (with a median of $1,520) in the present study must be seen in light of the fact that the figure varies in 87.2% of the schools according to the particular circumstances of the child (siblings, in-parish or out-of-parish, Catholic or non-Catholic, family income). In the Harkins study, tuition accounts for 49% of income, 37% from the parish, 10% from school fund raising, and 7% from other sources. Two-thirds of the principals in the current study reported their income figures: 60% of income came from tuition, though 40% of the principals report an increase in non-tuition income and 31% report an increase in grants. The mean income was $551,181 and the median $495,000. Other sources of income, in descending order of amounts, were: parish subsidy (in four-fifths of the schools); "other" (in one-half); annual appeal (in nine-tenths); diocesan subsidy (in three-quarters); grants (in two-thirds); and individual gifts (in two-thirds). Also, 41% report a gift of equipment, mostly computer hardware. On the expenditure side, the mean was $596,925 and the median $500,000.

For Harkins, nearly three-fourths of the students came from two-parent families (73.4%), as opposed to two-thirds in this study. The schools in the current study are much more ethnically diverse than those in the Harkins study or the larger population of all US Catholic schools (see Table 16.4).

In Harkins' schools, 86% of the students were Catholic. In the current study, that figure is 74.2%, the rest being Baptist (12%), other Protestants (9.2%) and others (5.6%), including marginal numbers of Hindus, Buddhists, Moslems, and Jews. Among the Catholics, 71.4% attend the local parish, 20% another parish, and 8.5% no parish.

Harkins' principals resemble those in the present study: they are highly educated white Catholic women, half of whom are members of religious communities (see Table 16.5).

Compared to all private school principals (McLaughlin and Broughman 1997) there are fewer doctorates (14% v. 1.7% and 5%) but more with

Table 16.3 Type of elementary school

	Parish	Interparish	Diocesan	Private
Harkins	71.0%	19.1%	7.5%	2.4%
O'Keefe	61.6%	11.8%	18.3%	3.1%
All RC el.*	81.1%	11.5%	3.0%	4.5%

* Taken from Metzler (1998)

graduate degrees generally (66% v. 85.7% and 93.8%). In the current study, the mean salary from principals is $29,343 and the median is $30,125 (see Table 16.6).

Both studies asked principals to reflect on how they spend their time. In general the principals in the Harkins study spent more time on campus issues of curriculum and instruction than those in the current study.

The current study gathered information without parallel in the Harkins study on staffing and providing for the diverse needs of children and families. Of the teachers in the urban schools, 10% are members of religious communities, 75% are white, 15% are black, 8.4% Hispanic and 2.2% Asian. Nearly 85% are Catholic and 99% are Christian. One-third of them attended Catholic elementary school, one-fourth a Catholic high school, and only one-fifth a Catholic college or university. One-fifth are new teachers (three or fewer years of experience), 36.5% have between three and ten years of experience, and 43.7% are veterans, with over ten years. The staff are less

Table 16.4 Ethnicity of elementary students

	White	*Black*	*Hispanic*	*Asian*	*Nat. Am.*
Harkins	78.2%	10.6%	11.1%	3.6%	1.2%
O'Keefe	36.9%	31.5%	23.9%	5.4%	2.3%
All RC[1]	75.5%	8.2%	10.5%	4.2%	0.4%
All priv.[2]	77.9%	9.3%	8.0%	4.1%	0.6%
All publ.[2]	67.3%	16.3%	11.9%	3.4%	1.1%

Notes:
[1] Taken from Metzler (1998)
[2] Taken from McLaughlin and Broughman (1997)

Table 16.5 Characteristics of the principal

	Female	*White*	*RC*	*Relig.*	*Masters*	*M.+30*	*Dr.*
Harkins	82.3%	96.0%	98.8%	49.8%	73.4%	10.6%	1.7%
O'Keefe	80.4%	84.7%	95.5%	47.5%	67.3%	21.5%	5.0%

Table 16.6 Principals' salaries ($000)

	<20	*20–30*	*30–40*	*>40*
O'Keefe	32%	23%	25%	20%
All priv.*	31%	22%	23%	24%

* Taken from McLaughlin and Broughman (1997)

experienced than those in the larger universe of private schools where 14% are new teachers, 34% have between three and ten years experience, and 52% have ten or more years (McLaughlin and Broughman 1997). Turnover is significant – 27.2% have been at the school less than three years, 43.4% between three and ten years, and 29.2% over ten years; 30% have been at the one school for their entire career. Eighty percent of the teachers are certified and one-third have a master's degree or higher. Other professionals support the educational effort: in 144 schools (36.2% of total) an assistant principal assists in administrative tasks; in one-quarter ($n = 101$) of the schools a part-time paid nurse looks after health care; seventy-three schools (18.3%) employ a speech therapist; in fifty-nine schools (14.8% of total) a paid development officer assists in institutional advancement (twenty are full time, twenty-five work between twenty and thirty-nine hours); psychologists provide services in fifty-four schools and social workers in thirty-seven (9.5% of the total). Forty schools have full-time volunteer teachers and 208 have part-time adult volunteers. Two-thirds of the schools have a board composed of parents (in 247), local clergy (in 200), alumni (in 199), local business people (in 99), teachers (in 79) and grandparents (in 59). Just under half of the boards ($n = 130$) are elected.

In counterpoint to the accusation of elitism leveled against them, it is important to note that in one-half ($n = 201$) of these schools 31,000 children (one-third of the total) are eligible for free lunch, a reliable indicator of poverty status; in forty-one schools over 200 children have this status. Principals report that 12% have no health care and that 10% live in government housing.

In response to children's needs, one-third of the principals report an increase in inclusion of special needs children and 43.2% report an increase in links to social service providers over the last five years (39.3% report no change, 2.1% report a decrease, and 15.4% used the "not applicable" category). When asked if they had ongoing and regular affiliation with service providers outside the schools, the 398 principals mentioned, in decreasing order, high schools (284 Catholic; 91 public), public libraries (249), other elementary schools (233 Catholic, 165 public), police (218), local merchants (209), fire station (199), social service (156 Catholic, 72 non-Catholic), hospitals (93 Catholic, 65 non-Catholic), colleges/universities (90 Catholic, 74 non-Catholic), non-Catholic churches (56), and public housing authorities (43).

Discussion of Survey Data

The survey data paint a helpful picture of the setting in which urban principals work. Several key areas deserve further discussion: financial constraints, increased organizational complexity, racial diversity, religious pluralism, and staffing challenges.

Financial Constraints

The centrality of financial concerns in US urban Catholic elementary schools becomes more evident when one looks at similar institutions in other settings. Within the nation, other Catholic educational institutions – early childhood programs and colleges/universities – receive government assistance. In addition, other Catholic human service providers – hospitals and social service agencies – would not exist without public resources. Outside of the United States, most nations finance religiously affiliated schools as a matter of course. While US Catholic secondary schools face the same prohibition of governmental funding, principals often have at their disposal the staff and population to provide significant non-tuition income. A recent study of 510 high schools nationwide, conducted by this researcher as a complement to the elementary study, found that 86% of the schools had a full-time paid development officer. At one time, financing parochial elementary schools was the responsibility of the pastor. Today urban schools rely more heavily on the principal because more of them are diocesan and because many of the parishes with which they are associated are themselves insolvent. Heavy dependence on tuition is not desirable because it creates a barrier for those most in need of a Catholic education. During the time of decline – from the mid 1960s to the mid 1990s – increasing tuition lead to decreasing enrollment and net decrease in annual income. Beyond annual operating income, significant capital expenditures loom. Half of the schools in the current study were built before 1947 and only ten of the 398 were built after 1970. For urban principals, an ethos of institutional survival must be replaced by an ethos of institutional advancement, an influx of stable financial capital.

Increased Organizational Complexity

For years Catholic schools have provided for their diverse needs through human as well as financial capital. Increasingly, principals will be called upon to oversee varied personnel from different professional organizations, each with its own codes, ethos, bureaucracy, and funding stream. Gone are the days when the principal's administrative responsibilities were limited only to classroom teachers. In addition, volunteerism is a key to the future of these schools. Unpaid professionals can offer medical, psychological, legal, spiritual, financial, and educational expertise. Small but growing numbers of young Catholics are giving full-time service in the classroom in teacher corps that are cropping up nationwide. Part-time volunteers can offer assistance in the classroom as aides and in a number of auxiliary services. As the process of encirclement continues in the inner cities, principals will need to spend more time forming creative alliances to meet the diverse needs of students and their families. On the one hand, the urban setting presents potent challenges, but, on the other, it offers a range of institutions within a small distance. For example, when asked to report on institutions within a one-mile radius, 93% of the 398 principals reported the presence of a public elementary school, 81% a non-Catholic church, 74% a public library, 58% a public high school, 47% another Catholic elementary school, 46% a non-Catholic hospital, and 41% a social service provider. As indicated above, some Catholic principals have been successful neighborhood builders. They can serve as models for principals in the older paradigm of isolated schools offering solely academic services. Today's principals must be creative leaders who manage complex and varied human and financial resources within the school itself and in linkages with other institutions in the community.

Racial Diversity

In June 1992, members of the Black Clergy Caucus wrote about racism, "Catholic social teachings have been bold and uncompromising." The sad problem, it added, is that these teachings "are all too often unknown, unpreached, untaught, and unbelieved" (Gibson 1996: 8). In the current sample of schools only 37% of the students are non-Hispanic whites, but this group constitutes 75% of the teachers and 85% of the principals. Along with fostering multicultural awareness, urban principals need to confront the issue of racism in an ecclesial and cultural milieu that often denies its existence. They need to work with their predominantly white staff to surface issues of prejudice and power. In their particular settings, Catholic principals should bring to the local scene the multiethnic diversity of a world church, arguably the most multicultural organization in the world.

Religious Pluralism

As opposed to an earlier era in which parochial schools were literally that – schools associated with a parish – today's schools serve a more diverse population. According to survey results, fewer than 50% of the children in the school come from the local parish. At one time the principal dealt with educational issues and the pastor with religion. Today principals increasingly find themselves acting in a pastoral role for children and families from a wide variety of settings. Often the principal is the only face of organized religion for children and parents.

Staffing Challenges

Survey data indicate that the faculty in urban Catholic schools tend to be less experienced as teachers and, given the percentage uncertified, not as extensively trained as their counterparts in public schools. This places a significant professional development burden on principals. Moreover, principals are responsible for the spiritual and theological formation of faculty, 15% of whom are non-Catholic. Even among the Catholics, only a small minority attended a Catholic school or university. Finally, the impending teacher shortage in US public schools will pose formidable problems of attraction and retention of faculty. Many people of strong faith and goodwill are likely to find irresistible the significant financial incentive to move to a public school. It will become especially difficult to attract talented people of color.

Discussion of Interview Data

During the 1997–98 academic year, the author conducted semi-structured interviews with ten urban Catholic elementary principals in a pattern generally reflective of areas with a high concentration of such schools: three in greater New York, two each in Chicago, Los Angeles, Philadelphia, and one in Washington, DC. Mirroring the larger population, four were sisters, four were lay women and two were lay men. They were asked about the contours of their job, where they found desolation in the work, how they experienced consolation in their vocation, and what best prepared them for their position.

Contours of the Principalship

In one way or another, all of those interviewed noted the emergence of a multifaceted and complex principalship. One principal from Chicago explained the reasons for a shift from instructional leader to advocate for children and families on a broad range of issues:

> You're dealing with a population that needs an awful lot more than the ABC's and the 123's and so you need to know that you're going to be torn in a million different directions and that your biggest job is to organize the family. It's almost like a parenting thing. And you run the risk: How much do I get into one role without neglecting the others? We shouldn't have to do all of this, but if we don't do it, who's going to do it?

In describing how they spend their day principals often used images traditionally associated with other professions: nurse, social worker, pastor, and financier.

As indicated in the survey data, very few schools have a full-time nurse. Principals and their secretaries often distribute prescribed medication and provide first aid. More significantly, they try to monitor the well-being of each student. For those without insurance and for those with minimal coverage, the clinic or the emergency room is the only venue for health care. As a result, many children do not have a primary physician and preventive care (nutrition, exercise, etc.) is lacking. Often principals are the only trusted professional in a family's life.

Principals report that mental health needs surpass the physical. Sometimes the needs surface in the context of the neighborhood: death, imprisonment of care givers, and violent eruptions. Often inappropriate behavior in school is the indicator: violent acting out, inability to focus, and withdrawal. In a few exemplary schools, on-staff psychologists and social workers provide services within the school community context, working closely with teachers and the principal, engaging in group work as well as individual therapy. In some schools, Catholic charities provide individual therapy in a pull-out fashion. In every school, principals spend large amounts of time meeting with students, teachers, parents, and guardians in a counseling mode. Among the problems principals address are: disruption of family life through divorce and other relational dysfunctions, child abuse, incest, chemical abuse in the home, witnessing violence in the streets, and mourning the death of loved ones.

As religious people, principals understand people's spiritual needs as well as the physical and psychological. In many ways, principals are *de facto* pastors of religiously diverse communities. A New York principal reported that, for Catholics and non-Catholics alike, "sometimes school is the only church the kids know." For many students, church affiliation is Protestant. Principals talk about balancing pluralism with a deep grounding in the particularism of the Catholic faith. The principal of an African–American school in Philadelphia has parents sign an agreement that their children will participate in all aspects of school life because

> sometimes parents come and complain about the Catholicism of the school, especially the whole Mary thing. Last week a mother objected to her son having to learn the rosary. I appreciate her beliefs, but I told her that that's who we are. I went to the file and took out the agreement she had signed. I told her, "We're not trying to convert your son, but we're going to be who we are."

A clear sense of Catholic mission must be balanced by sensitivity. A principal in Washington, newly appointed to the inner city, described his surprise when parents were shocked by fund-raising activities that involved gambling. While this presents no problem for Catholics, it can easily offend some Protestant sensibilities. Overall, principals report that the issue of denominational differences pales in comparison to non-practice across denominations. Principals' attitudes match those expressed in the latest Vatican document on education:

[the Catholic school] has not come into being as a private initiative, but as an expression of the reality of the church, having by its very nature a public character. It fulfills a service of public usefulness and, although clearly and decidedly configured in the perspective of Catholic faith, is not reserved to Catholics only, but is open to all those who appreciate and share its qualified educational project.

(Congregation for Catholic Education 1998: 20)

In these religiously diverse schools, principals need to have an extensive knowledge of the complex Catholic tradition, an understanding of pastoral counseling, an ability to lead public prayer effectively, and credibility as an authentic person of faith. Moreover, they are called upon to build a faith community among adults in the school who will witness to God's presence in everyday interactions with students and each other.

Principals corroborated the survey finding that financial management takes up a very significant amount of their time and energy, especially if one hopes to decrease dependency on tuition as the primary source of income. Paperwork for federal entitlement programs, finding possible foundation and corporate sources, the actual writing of grants, and management of a complex budget are very time intensive.

Desolations

When asked where they find desolation in their work, principals talked about three areas: financing, staffing problems, and personal tragedy. The inability to meet the financial needs of the school community is a source of desolation and discouragement for principals. Inadequate facilities, lack of supplies, and low wages for dedicated staff are among the sad consequences. The situation is most poignant when students must be expelled. In some cases a child's special needs cannot be met by the school; those with disabilities must go to a public school that has the means to provide appropriate programs. In other cases, when all other avenues have been exhausted, a child must leave because his or her family is unable to meet tuition costs. In facing the dilemma of solvency versus service, most of those interviewed echo the comments of a Los Angeles colleague: "People always call me a soft touch, but I figure that when I get to heaven's door, I would rather have erred on the side of being a soft touch than not being compassionate." The latest statement on Catholic education reflects the feelings of the principals:

Finance is a source of further difficulties, which are felt more acutely in those states in which no government aid is provided for non-state schools. This places an almost unbearable burden on families choosing not to send their children to state schools and constitutes a serious threat to the survival of the schools themselves. Moreover, such financial strain not only affects the recruiting and stability of teachers, but can also result in the exclusion from Catholic schools of those who cannot afford to pay, leading to a selection according to means which deprives the Catholic school of one of its distinguishing features, which is to be a school for all.

(Congregation for Catholic Education 1998: 10)

Staffing problems are in several domains. First, principals bemoaned the loss of good teachers because of low salaries. A New York principal remarked, "After they get the experience I want to be able to keep them." Second, infighting among adults in the school is a source of desolation: gossip, grudges, turf wars, and jealousy. This is particularly true when educators have to put up with arrogant and domineering pastors who do not appreciate their work and undo their best efforts. In contrast, several spoke in detail about the progress made in the lives of children when pastor and principal work together. In describing the role of the pastor, one principal put it best: "When they're good, they're very, very good but when they're bad they're horrid."

Finally, principals described the deep sadness that comes from witnessing lives of desperation, seemingly hopeless circumstances marked by emptiness, and despair, addiction, and violence. Several principals recounted tragic stories of young people whose lives are ruined by a criminal record, time in prison, overwhelming addictions, or by an early and senseless death.

Consolations

Some principals spoke justifiably about their demonstrable accomplishments. Most often, however, they spoke about the centrality of human relationships, grace that is found in simple things. Alongside the tragedies of those who live in poverty are stories of remarkable resiliency and goodness, deep faith, and steadfast hope. A New York principal said that she stands in awe of single mothers because of their unflinching dedication and ingenuity in meeting their children's needs. Others spoke of students who overcome steep odds. "Working with inner-city people," said a Philadelphia principal, "it's part of the hundredfold." A principal from New York echoed the sentiment:

> It's a gift that you get. You think you're all this wonderful stuff and then you come in and find out you're like everyone else. I've learned so much about myself, my limitations and who I really am by being here. And that's helped me a lot as a person, it really has. And the kids – accepting you for who you are. And it makes me realize my responsibility for accepting everybody. It's a wonderful life.

Another principal from Philadelphia explained:

> There's something about the kids here. If I had a choice I'd choose inner-city schools. There is a greater receptivity to what we're all about. They don't discount faith, they understand it. People say to me , "Isn't it tough teaching those people?" and I say, "No, it isn't." I'd much rather be here in the inner city rather than in the suburbs. A lot of people there really don't care about anything other than themselves.

A principal from Chicago talked about getting a glimpse of people from a "God's eye view." Where others see failure and ugliness, she prays to be able to see their loveliness. She illustrated her point with a story:

> We want to increase students' verbal skills so we have the speech events. One week it was Michael's turn. He is an unfocused child, totally unfocused. I gave the parent all kinds of things to read about attention deficit disorder. I don't know if he actually has it, but he's got something because he's consistently being punished at home and consistently being punished here. He's hanging on by a thread. I mean, if he weren't part of my inner heart, he probably should have been kicked out. I knew Michael was up, so on Monday I said, "How are you doing?" I told him, "I know you can do this, please try to do it." So he tried and could only do two lines or so. He started and then he would get so distracted. And he kept saying, "They're going to laugh at me, they're going to laugh at me." When the day came he got up and he went through his whole thing. He kept clutching on his pant leg, he was so scared and nervous, but he got through it. Tears were just streaming down my face imagining that he was able to keep that focus. I said to myself, "This week I don't care what happens – Michael got through his speech." I'll ride on those coattails for a long, long time.

The emphasis on relationships is echoed in the Vatican's recent statement on schools:

> During childhood and adolescence a student needs to experience personal relations with outstanding educators, and what is taught has greater influence on the students formation when placed in a context of personal involvement, genuine reciprocity, coherence of attitudes, lifestyles and day-to-day behaviors.
>
> (Congregation for Catholic Education 1998: 22)

Reflections on the Future of Leadership

When principals were asked about the future leadership of urban Catholic schools several remarked, "I just don't know where they'll come from." The coming era in which religious will largely disappear from urban principal-ships will also be a time of administrative shortages in public schools. The average salary in the sample of Catholic schools is $29,343 per year; in public schools it is $54,857 (US Department of Education 1994). Will principals be able to forgo such a powerful financial enticement?

When they were asked about preparing future principals, all agreed that apprenticeship-type experiences are key. Solid teaching experience is a *sine qua non*. One principal explained:

> I had been at four different Los Angeles area elementary schools and had worked with women who had what I would call north, south, east and west styles of leadership. I learned something from them all – things I try to imitate and things I try to avoid.

Most of the principals believe that the university has a constructive role to play, even though they find tuition charges exorbitant. In seeing a place for the university, principals bear out much of what appears in the literature. While they can have recourse to their personal ethical commitments and visionary leadership, they also need new skills beyond their experience.

> The school principal must assume new roles and utilize new skills to implement a school-linked service effort. It is likely that the principal's school leadership training did not emphasize collaborative leadership and shared decision making with other community agencies. Nonetheless, these skills are essential for the establishment of school-linked services.
>
> (Kirst and Kelley 1995: 39)

Mono-professional preparation is a significant liability because "differences in professional training and background result in widely divergent values and priorities, expressed as incommensurable vocabularies" (Eisenberg 1995: 105). Forsyth and Tallerico (1993) argue that proper training can lighten the burden interinstitutional collaboration places on principals. They must function as social architects who "give voice to the moral imperative to address historically nonschooling issues" (Beck and Murphy 1993: 192). Principals cannot be everything, but they need to know something about everything. There is some movement in that direction (Brabeck et al. 1997), but much more needs to be done. Pre-service programs must be supplemented by ongoing education and networking. Selected Programs In Catholic Education, a new initiative co-sponsored by Boston College and the NCEA, is but one example.

One of the crucial areas of interprofessional education is neglected in educational literature: pastoral training. Because of the enhanced religious duties, urban principals should be exposed to the best elements of contemporary seminary training: a thorough grounding in sound theology and spiritual growth and development. They should also engage in ongoing spiritual and theological education. The newly initiated Spiritual Growth Leadership Institute, sponsored by Boston College and the NCEA, is attempting to meet that need.

Conclusion

This chapter is but one attempt to expose the reality and challenges of the urban Catholic elementary principalship to a wide audience. Much more needs to be done: further data collection about the schools themselves, especially the demographics of staff; qualitative studies of principals on site, including interviews that allow their perspectives to be heard; exploration of appropriate models of university preparation that will help principals face a challenging and complex future; and funding that will provide decent wages and professional development opportunities.

At the end of the interviews, the principals were asked to speak directly to those who would read this chapter. Why, they were asked, should the broader community care about their schools? A principal from Los Angeles articulated the sentiments of the group:

> I'd want them to understand how vital our inner-city Catholic schools are in the communities they serve. For these families it's probably the one highlight for so many of them in their lives, one thing they can point to that is positive when so many other things are not. They have to scrape to make a living, they witness all kinds of bad things in the neighborhood, the neighborhoods aren't safe and their kids can't go out at night and play, but the school is really a safe haven for their families and bright minds are going to come out of it. But more than that, good people are going to come out of our inner-city schools. ... I can't think of a more noble work than to be principal of an inner-city school.

References

Beck, L.G. and Murphy, J. (1993) *Understanding the principalship: Metaphorical themes 1920's–1990's*, New York: Teachers College Press.

Brabeck, M., Neisler, O., and Zollers, N. (1997) "Integrating mission into the life of institutions," in R. Haney and J.M. O'Keefe (eds.) *Conversations in excellence: Integrating mission* (pp. 39–56), Washington, DC: National Catholic Educational Association.

Bradley, B. (1998) "Commentary: Race and the American city," in W.F. Katkin, N. Landsman, and A. Tyree (eds.) *Beyond pluralism: The conception of groups and group identities in America* (pp. 261–70), Urbana, IL: University of Illinois Press.

Ciriello, M. (1996) *Formation and development for Catholic school leaders: Expectation in the area of faith development, building Christian community, moral and ethical development, history and philosophy* (2nd ed.), Washington, DC: United States Catholic Conference Department of Education.

Congregation for Catholic Education (1998) *The Catholic school on the threshold of the new millennium*, Strathfield, Australia: St. Paul's Publications.

Drahmann, T. and Stenger, A. (1989) *The Catholic school principal: An outline for action*, Washington, DC: National Catholic Educational Association.

Eisenberg, E.M. (1995) "A communication perspective on inter-organizational cooperation and inner-city education," in L.C. Rigsby, M.C. Reynolds, and M.C. Wang (eds.) *School community connections: Exploring issues for research and practice* (pp. 101–199), San Francisco: Jossey-Bass.

Forsyth, P. and Tallerico, M. (1993) *City schools: Leading the way*, Thousand Oaks, CA: Corwin Press.

Gibson, D. (1996) "Black Catholics in America: A documentation overview," in Committee on African American Catholics of the National Catholic Conference of Bishops (Eds.) *Keep your hand on the plow: The African American presence in the Catholic Church* (pp. 1–8), Washington, DC: United States Catholic Conference.

Goldring, E.B. and Rallis, S.F. (1993) *Principals of dynamic schools: Taking charge of change*, Thousand Oaks, CA: Corwin Press.

Haney, R. (1998) "Conversations in excellence: Creatively meeting the needs of youth and families," in R. Haney and J.M. O'Keefe (eds.) *Conversations in excellence: Providing for the diverse needs of youth and their families* (pp. 13–23), Washington, DC: National Catholic Educational Association.

Harkins, W. (1993) *Introducing the Catholic elementary school principal: What principals say about themelves, their values, their schools*, Washington, DC: National Catholic Educational Association.

Kealey, R. (1989) *Reflections on the role of the Catholic school principal*, Washington, DC: National Catholic Educational Association.

Kirst, M.W. and Kelley, C. (1995) "Collaboration to improve education and children's services," in L.C. Rigsby, M.C. Reynolds, and M.C. Wang (eds.) *School community connections: Exploring issues for research and practice* (pp. 21–44), San Francisco: Jossey-Bass.

Kushner, R. and Helbling, M. (1995) *The people who work there: The report of the Catholic elementary school teacher survey*, Washington, DC: National Catholic Educational Association.

Lieberman, A. (1992) "School/university collaboration: A view from the inside," *Phi Delta Kappan*, pp. 147–56.

McLaughlin, D. and Broughman, S. (1997) *Private schools in the United States: A statistical profile: 1993–1999*, Washington, DC: United States Department of Education, Office of Educational Research and Improvement (NCES 97–459).

Metzler, M.J. (1998) *United States Catholic elementary and secondary schools 1997–1998*, Washington, DC: National Catholic Educational Association.

Miller, N.A. (1994) "Toward a common vision: The change process in practice," in C.M. Reigeluth and R.J. Garfinkle (eds.) *Systemic change in education*, Englewood Cliffs, NJ: Educational Technology Publications.

National Center for Educational Statistics (1994) *Schools and staffing survey*, Washington, DC: United States Department of Education.

O'Keefe, J.M. (1996) "No margin, no mission," in T.H. McLaughlin, J.M. O'Keefe, and B. O'Keefe (eds.) *The contemporary Catholic school: Context, identity and diversity* (pp. 177–97), London and Washington, DC: Falmer Press.

Perkins, D.F., Borden, L., and Hogue, T. (1998) "Standards of practice for community-based educational collaborations," in R. Haney and J.M. O'Keefe (eds.) *Conversations in excellence: Providing for the diverse needs of youth and their families* (pp. 85–105), Washington, DC: National Catholic Educational Association.

Walsh, A. and Feistritzer, P. (eds.) (1991) *Capital wisdom: Papers from the Principals' Academy*, Washington, DC: National Catholic Educational Association.

Walsh, M.E., Buckley, M.A., and Howard, K.A. (1998) "Critical collaborations: School, family and community," in R. Haney and J.M. O'Keefe (eds.) *Conversations in excellence: Providing for the diverse needs of youth and their families* (pp. 63–84), Washington, DC: National Catholic Educational Association.

Zetlin, A. (1995) "Commentary: Lessons learned about integrating services," in L.C. Rigsby, M.C. Reynolds and M.C. Wang (eds.) *School community connections: Exploring issues for research and practice* (pp. 421–26), San Francisco: Jossey-Bass.

17 Dealing with Narcissistic Families

Lessons for Educational Leadership in Parent and Child Guidance

Michael Garanzini, SJ

At a recent meeting of elementary and secondary school principals, the question arose: what is the most difficult aspect of your job as an administrator? Without hesitation, one veteran principal piped up: "For me, the most difficult part of the job is dealing with parents, especially parents in denial, parents who demand that their child be treated as an exception, parents with unrealistic expectations." This principal elaborated that she felt these very parents make excessive demands on her time and on the energy of her colleagues. "They just do not appreciate what we can and cannot do in the school setting." While there are numerous demands placed on educational leaders each day, there may be nothing more frustrating and time consuming than parents whose sense of entitlement can drain us emotionally and physically.

What is a narcissistic home? Why are these families so difficult to deal with? Why do they get under our skin? How do we spot them and how do we manage them when we are confronted by their unrealistic demands?

To place our discussion in context, we begin with an examination of the relational and developmental needs of the child which, when unmet, constitute the definition of the dysfunctional family. Following this, the chapter will examine the features of what is clinically called narcissism and how this adult pathology impacts a family system. Throughout, terms like "narcissism," "entitlement," and "enmeshment" will be used interchangeably to signify the kind of family we experience as excessively demanding, unrealistic in their expectations of the child and the school, and poorly differentiated. This discussion will then take us to an exploration of strategies and suggestions for handling the children of narcissistic families and their parents in the school setting. Lastly, the chapter will explore implications for educational leadership in today's family-sensitive environment. After describing the general characteristics of unhealthy families, and before a more detailed exploration of the narcissistic personality, a case vignette is presented to demonstrate how narcissistic families come to our attention and how toxic these families can become for our school community and for staff cohesion.

Putting the Problem in Perspective: When Is Advocacy for One's Child Unhealthy and a Sign of Dysfunction?

It is important that we not judge every family that advocates for its child as narcissistic or otherwise unhealthy simply because we find ourselves taxed by their demands. The vast majority of parents, quite naturally, want the best for their child. We expect that parents will work diligently to see that their child thrives in school and is treated fairly. Educators, for their part, want to cooperate with parents and see to it that all children under their care are able to make the most of school, to succeed to the fullest extent possible. At the same time, educators, like anyone else in the child's life, can fail to recognize a child's individual needs or even misjudge a child's abilities or intentions. Parents understand this and are often ready to step in to assist in correcting a less than optimal or even unhealthy environment for their child. Over time, as the child develops and grows, healthy parents learn to take a less active role and instead encourage their children to press for their own needs, to acquire their own voice. Healthy parents encourage appropriate autonomy and independence.

However, there are parents who have difficulty separating from their children, who claim to be objective but who have difficulty being so. We experience, from time to time, parents whose advocacy amounts to excessive intrusion. A parent, after all, cannot always be the best judge of a child's academic needs, medical needs, and so on. There are professionals with considerably more experience in areas where a parent cannot be the expert. These professionals, like teachers and doctors, also have a duty to advocate for the child. When concerns arise, healthy parents are able to listen to other authorities in the child's life. Consensus is reached. Divergent opinions contribute to everyone's understanding of the child. One child advocate learns from the other. It is precisely a failure in this rather common give-and-take process that disturbs us and frustrates us when we are confronted by the narcissistic parent.

Before we discuss the particular features of the narcissistic home where parent and child are enmeshed in an unhealthy alliance, it might be helpful to keep in mind that these, like all needy families, have a unique attraction to the Catholic school. Schools that are caring and accommodating are attractive to all families, but are especially attractive to the enmeshed family. Through them, both child and parents gain the attention they crave. Their demands, however, force them to deal with caring adults whose response, hopefully, is to put realistic breaks on their insatiable need to be treated as an exception. Moreover, when properly managed, they learn to accept limitation and appropriate boundaries. As we will see, their demands can be interpreted as an unconscious call for assistance in how to initiate and maintain consistent and healthy relationships with their child and with others, especially those with whom they must learn to collaborate for the good of the child. In short, the healthy educator models appropriate boundaries.

The following case vignette describes one way a narcissistic family might interact with the school personnel. It contains features typical of these situations and dynamics. Role and boundary problems abound. Both parents and child resist demands that are placed by the school system on the child. It also demonstrates a fairly typical constellation of emotional dynamics experienced by those in educational leadership positions.

Case Vignette: Robert and His Parents

Robert is a fifth-grade student in a Catholic elementary school. He is average in height, with a thin build, dark hair, and often sports a baseball cap whenever he can. Robert is a bright student and can manage most subjects without difficulty. He is quick to pick up new material in class. In short, he is capable and, when properly motivated, can do B-level work or better. In sports and at recess, he is often a leader, but is not necessarily the best in any one sport. His teachers consistently rank him in the top third of his class in overall achievement.

Robert was recently the subject of a meeting between the principal and the fifth-grade teacher over his growing tardiness and his tendency to become argumentative when not prepared for his school work, or not paying attention. The conference was necessitated by the fact that his mother works as a teacher's aide in the school and volunteers for cafeteria duty. Her intrusion in matters affecting her fifth-grade son had become annoying and draining for the teacher who felt that Robert's mother was much of his problem. His mother often insisted that Robert was a more gifted student than had been recognized by the school. She once complained to the principal that she felt Robert's teachers had consistently failed to recognize his potential. When told of the teacher's concerns, however, she responded that her son would be more motivated if his teacher's attitude toward him was not so negative.

Robert's father was also involved in parish activities. Robert's older brother attended the school, distinguishing himself as an athlete. Both parents had been known for their involvement in the lives of both sons and were especially strong supporters of the older son. During the previous year, Robert's father had advocated for a program for gifted students with the School Advisory Board, something which became controversial as parish and school insisted that there was no money for a program for the gifted unless parents accepted a cutback in other areas.

After a difficult meeting with Robert's mother, the principal informed Robert's teacher that she was unsuccessful in securing the mother's

---

support. She agreed that Robert's difficulty was complicated by his mother's over-involvement in the school. Together, they discussed ways of dealing directly with Robert and avoiding his mother's entanglement in these efforts. Soon after her meeting with the principal, however, Robert's mother requested a meeting with her husband present. The principal, anticipating that Robert's parents would be defensive, excluded the teacher from the conference and on her own attempted in a gentle way to be supportive of the teacher's concerns that Robert needed to focus more on his work and accept responsibility for his actions.

Robert's father responded first by saying that Robert felt, and so did his parents, that he was being picked on by his teacher. The same issues were rehashed and Robert's behavior soon lost center-stage in the discussions. The mother again stated her position that Robert's teacher was more at fault in this than Robert. The principal attempted to keep the meeting focused on Robert and not the teacher. She tried to return to the issue of Robert's behavior, stating specific incidences of disrespect and laxity. Tensions rose in the meeting to the point that Robert's mother could not contain her anger. She insisted that these descriptions amounted to insinuations that she had failed as a parent, that she knew little about her child, that she was coddling her child. Dumbfounded at these interpretations of the report of the teacher and the principal's assessment of Robert, the principal attempted to soothe the distraught and angry mother but to no avail. At this, Robert's father who had taken a back seat after his opening remark joined his wife in accusing the school of collusion against his son. References to the older brother and how he had turned out were thrown in more than once by Robert's parents. Unable to bring a more positive and conciliatory tone to the meeting, the principal attempted to close the meeting, only to be greeted with: "So, you are throwing us out, too. And this is supposed to be a Catholic school! Perhaps the pastor will listen to our side of the story."

When the conference ended, the principal felt confused and angry. She also dreaded the involvement of the pastor. Despite their good relations, involving the pastor in these matters almost always resulted in compromise. What was there to compromise this time? She realized, too, that this situation might grow out of all proportion to the events and demands created by Robert's behavior. Why were these parents so uncooperative and so touchy? The principal wondered if and when she might hear from the pastor and whether or not she should prepare him for their possible call.

Michael Garanzini, SJ

Some Reflections on the Case of Robert

The brief vignette describes a family we experience as more than ordinarily defensive and protective. With most parents, we expect some effort to appreciate the circumstances surrounding our difficulty with their child. We understand their attempts to minimize our concerns, especially if they themselves are stumped. While not always thrilled to do so, most parents cooperate with us as we search for solutions and may even suggest possible interpretations of their child's behavior. Robert's family and others like his, on the other hand, strike us as overly sensitive to factual explanations of their child's behavior. When families like this become strident in their refusals to cooperate, or when they become demanding, we instinctively feel that something else is at work in the family. Our frustration, confusion, and even, on occasion, anger and resentment which we and our staff feel is one indication that an unhealthy family dynamic is presenting itself to us.

As is often the case, this narcissistic family became threatening when they perceived their child was being "victimized" by a hostile and uncaring community, even though there was little concrete evidence that this was indeed the case. The slightest demands or insistence on conformity, on taking responsibility, were perceived as attacks and threats. Ironically, however, while parents like these seek special treatment or make excuses for their children, we begin to experience them as more concerned about themselves than their children. Reflecting on our dealings with them, we notice that it is hard to focus on the behavior of the child because each encounter seems to revolve more around parents' feelings and perceptions. In some instances, the conference becomes a defense of our behaviors and positions. As was evident in the case of Robert, with amazing speed, the child became lost in a barrage of complaints and counterattacks.

How unhealthy is this response from Robert's family? How threatened should the principal feel by these parents? The answer to questions like these depends on two things: the level and seriousness of the narcissistic wound in the parent, or we might also say the level of neediness in the narcissistic parent, and, second, our reaction and behavior to these demands. With narcissistic families, a strategy for securing help and assistance is wrapped in a sea of complaints and calls for attention and exception from the general norms governing the school community.

As many an experienced administrator knows, these families, if allowed, can be especially good at emotional manipulation and blackmail. For instance, a Catholic school educator might be told that special treatment and attention are the duty and responsibility of someone who proclaims to be acting in the name of Christ and the Church. In other words, these parents are not hesitant to use the school's philosophy and creed to demand exceptional treatment, even when boundaries have been crossed, rules broken, and demands have become unreasonable. Their claim to special treatment, then, becomes a club used to badger those who just might be sensitive to such charges. While such families are more and more common in all schools, they are especially challenging for the Catholic school educator because of the importance placed on the individual child and his or her spiritual development, something easily exploited by unhealthy families.

Defining the Unhealthy Family

While each dysfunctional family is unique, unhealthy homes have some common problems or features. In general, dysfunctional families are those which fail to meet one or more of the critical developmental or relational needs of the child. These two sets of needs arise from the child's innate desire to become a unique person whose talents are fully developed and the child's need to belong, i.e., to be loved. By developmental needs we mean those environmental requirements that help the child live and function in a community, and thus give the child the opportunity to develop as a social being. These include the need for a safe and secure environment, the need for clear schedules, and the need for household rules and responsibilities that, in effect, train the child to take responsibility for behavior and respect the rights and needs of others. In addition to these, a child needs an environment with clear lines of authority and models who demonstrate consistent respect for all the other legitimate authorities in the child's life, i.e., for teachers, police, coaches, and so on. A child growing up in such an environment is secure in the knowledge that the adult world can be trusted, that adults will act in concert and in support of one another. When adults struggle to meet these needs, the child has what Winnicott calls a "good enough" home. Children from such homes are prepared to participate in other communities such as school (Winnicott 1960).

This simple list of needs is not simple to administer or maintain. No parent can be, nor should be, expected to be perfect, but rather, "good enough." All homes become chaotic from time to time. Sometimes things slide. Some children are harder to manage than others. Parents and teachers are well aware of how difficult it is to be consistent and firm when children test the rules, or stretch the boundaries and parameters imposed upon them. Dysfunction does not follow from mistakes and failures. Rather, a home becomes dysfunctional when families cease working or struggling to meet the previously mentioned needs. The same is true for the child's relational needs (see Garanzini 1995).

A child needs more than a "good enough" environment to flourish. A child needs to know he or she is loved and cherished; in short, belongs (Bowlby 1988). Healthy development requires that a child have at least one adult in his or her life who provides that sense of being special and important. This happens when a child is on the receiving end of genuine, selfless care. However, genuine care is work and is available to the child when a sufficiently healthy adult is able to provide, on a consistent basis, several critical elements in the complex process of learning to love and be loved. For instance, the child needs someone who can tolerate his or her demands and failures. The child needs someone to help recognize different emotions and feelings, accept them and manage them, even when they feel dangerous and overpowering. The child needs someone to help assess his or her talents, abilities, and personality traits objectively and honestly. Attachment psychologists speak of the mirroring function of the healthy parent, i.e., the parent who "mirrors" back to the child: you are lovable; you are manageable; these are the positive things about you; and so on. Positive mirroring on the part of a caring adult leads to critical self-knowledge. The child learns: I can manage my feelings; I can correct my faults, and so on. In short, I am a capable and worthy person, even though I am not perfect.

Through this special relationship, a child also comes to accept limitations. In short, a child's own natural, or primal, narcissism becomes tamed. The child becomes increasingly more realistic in the appraisal of his or her worth and value and able to assess the opinions and feedback of others – teachers or peers, for example – with sufficient inner strength to handle their rejection and criticism. Caring adults in the child's life shore up an occasionally bruised ego, patch wounded pride, but also gently point to the validity of the assessments of others, and encourage compromise and conciliation when appropriate. Moreover, it is through management of their own behavior that healthy parents model self-acceptance and self-control. When the child's relational needs are met, then the child not only knows that he or she is capable of being the object of someone's love, but is also capable of returning love, i.e., of forming and maintaining relationships which are mutually satisfying. The extent to which a child receives love and support from a committed adult in his or her life, the child will be able to handle new and emotionally demanding relationships in other settings. It is also the extent to which the child will be able to manage those moments of insecurity that come from experiences of rejection, uncertainty, or even indifference from others.

It is understandable that children who have not been consistently or adequately loved grow up to be adults who have difficulty loving their children. The desire to love one's child does not equate to ability to love in a healthy manner. Individuals without a secure emotional base have a difficult time providing the kind of love and support a child requires for healthy development (Bowlby 1988). These adults experience a child's emotional needs as overwhelming and impossible to satisfy. They may even resent the child's neediness and, unconsciously or consciously, give up on meeting the child's needs for love and support. The critical period during which this drama unfolds, i.e., when emotional bonds are forged and negotiated, is the first three years of the child's life. It is then that the child needs a loving adult who can tolerate the vicissitudes of a child's emotional and affective development. Toleration and proper management of the child's anger and

frustration in the critical third year help the child internalize those mechanisms of self-control and self-acceptance that result in realistic self-love and
self-esteem. It is on this foundation, laid by a home which has struggled to
meet the developmental and relational needs of the child, that the school
hopes to build through advancing the child's mastery of the world of knowledge and through the development of social skill (Winnicott 1960).

What we see in the narcissistic adult, then, is the grown child who may
have been well managed, but who has not received consistent and adequate
care and the mirroring necessary to believe in his or her own capabilities and
worthiness. The problem is a cyclic one. Since the narcissist is ill-equipped to
offer genuine care to his or her own child, children of narcissists suffer the
same fate (Miller 1992). Unable to meet the relational needs of their children, narcissistic parents may substitute vigilance towards the outside world
and excessive attention to appearance for real affection. Unconditional care,
objectivity, and honest handling of emotion and feeling cannot be given by
someone who has not received them. Unhealthy dynamics between needy
child and unhealthy parent evolve during the critical developmental period.
These dynamics become fixed or stabilized over time. They become visible to
us when the demands from the school system threaten to disturb the equilib-
rium that has helped maintain them. These dynamics are brilliantly
portrayed in Judith Guest's *Ordinary People* where a mother's narcissistic
need for the perfect family results in stiff, indirect, and partial communications between herself and her guilt-ridden son (Guest 1982).

The Narcissist's Compensation

It appears, then, that anxiety over the demands of the school, plus the
parents' feelings of inadequacy, propel these parents into unnecessary advocacy for their child. It is as if, by badgering and defending, the parents can
"prove" they are anything but inadequate and uncaring. They badger for
extra attention and exceptional treatment. They become strident especially if
they perceive or interpret treatment of their child by an adult with authority
to be cold and uncaring. In short, they take on a role that helps them replace
feelings of fragility with feelings of heroism and worth. In order to do so,
however, they need to paint others as insensitive and uncaring. It is not
surprising that those who must deal with narcissistic parents end up feeling
put upon, poorly treated, taxed, and the target of unfair criticism. In short,
we feel the same feelings of what the narcissist feels. The inadequacy which
lies at the root of the narcissist's behavior masks, feel some theorists, a
depression and shame which results from their inability to solicit the love
they craved from parents (Sandler and Joffe 1965; Miller 1992; Kernberg
1975). The narcissist's compensation makes sense in light of their unconscious sadness, feelings of emptiness, and deep sense of failure.

The Narcissist's Projection

Like the principal in our vignette, those who must manage such parents find themselves resenting the roles they are forced to play. Our frustrations can become anger and intolerance. We feel not only exhausted from our encounters but come to dread further meetings, even social encounters. Their insinuations grate on us and give rise to "righteous indignation." More accusations and threats can leave us feeling not only resentful but also fragile. We may ask: "What makes these parents think we are here simply to serve them?" And, when they have begun wearing down our teachers, or worse, have decided to attack one of them as incompetent, uncaring, or uncooperative, we have an additional challenge: how to manage the wounded pride, frustration, or resentment of our staff.

It is understandable, then, that parents such as these strike us as needier than their child, as lacking self-control and incapable of taking an objective look at a problem involving their child. This is precisely what we see in the vignette. The school's experience was that Robert's parents were more difficult to manage than Robert was. This tendency to self-referencing and oversensitivity to slights and criticisms are typical features of narcissism. It is essential for the educational leader to step back, in such instances, and recognize that what we feel is a projection, something which is not "our" problem as much as it is an indication of what the narcissist feels. In other words, we feel resentful because they feel angry and put upon. We are being made to feel put upon because this is what the narcissist is feeling as a parent. In effect, then, we are experiencing what it is like to be them, what they felt as a child in the hands of a parent who was overwhelmed and unable to manage their needs.

In sum, it is easy to see why these families are so toxic and difficult in the school system. Parents who are narcissistic view the child's poor performance as a reflection on themselves. They then project their disappointment and rage onto those who are the source of the poor evaluation, i.e., onto the child's teacher, or often enough, the school administrator who thwarts their desire for retaliation or "justice." Anyone who tarnishes their trophy, who dares to treat their child as "average," or who interferes with the parent's sense of entitlement, is seen as personally attacking the integrity, welfare, or the reputation of the family. These parents appear intensely interested in the welfare of the child but are, in effect, too needy to be objective or ultimately helpful to the child. Their unconscious aim when dealing with adult authorities in the child's life is to defend against what they perceive to be callous disregard for the uniqueness of not so much the child as themselves.

What then are the best ways to approach such families? When are their demands legitimate? When should we compromise? When should we stand up and refuse to make exceptions? What kind of access do we allow them to teachers and others who work with their child if these encounters are draining and upsetting to our staff? These are the challenges that we regularly face when a narcissistic family becomes a management issue for us in the school setting. In our efforts, the overarching theme governing our individual strategies is: be gentle but firm.

Managing the Child and Parents in the School Community

There are four important tactics or strategies for handling narcissistic families and their children. Each constitutes a step in the process of modeling appropriate behaviors and instilling realistic expectations. Two preliminary notes are in order. First, it takes some time and effort to put all four into operation. Before one can solicit the necessary collaboration among staff to press a child to take responsibility for his or her behaviors, for example, they must be convinced that the situation is not hopeless. Second, success requires a team approach, i.e., putting all four into operation depends upon the collaboration of teachers and staff, including any other authority which might be used to circumvent our interventions, such as the pastor, school board, or superintendent's office. The elements of an effective strategy can be summed up as follows. (1) We must reinterpret the negative behavior and attitudes of the child and parents in a way that recognizes an unconscious call for help. (2) All responses and behaviors on our part must have as their central purpose modeling appropriate boundaries, roles, and responsibilities. (3) The goal of our interventions must be helping the child take responsibility for his or her own actions and behavior. (4) A by-product of our efforts must be helping the child learn how to defer gratification in order to grow from new unpleasant as well as pleasant experiences. This last point is critical for helping the child expand the definition of who the child is as an autonomous person.

First, reinterpret negative behavior of child and parents as a call for help. The role of the educational leader in the management of difficult families is to serve, first and foremost, as an interpreter of possible underlying issues and dynamics. To bring sanity and understanding to a difficult problem one needs a theory, especially a theory of health. An enmeshed family will enmesh teachers and others involved with the child and family. Confusion over difficult feelings and anger block a teacher's insight and insight is necessary before he or she can be motivated to provide positive and patient responses to the child. By reinterpreting negative behavior as a call for help, we reframe the teacher's experience. These negative experiences are now useful information which serve as a guidepost for appropriate interventions. The student who behaves as if he or she is an exception and is not like all the others may be asking us to help him or her experience how he or she is just like others. This would relieve the student of the burden of being different, something all children desire. Being different is critical only when one is insecure and uncertain. The proper and useful strategy, then, begins with a positive interpretation of the negative material we have been handed.

Irresponsible behavior on the part of a child demands firm and gentle insistence on taking responsibility. Intrusive behavior on the part of parents demands we see this as a call for assistance on healthy boundaries. Why else would these families display their unhealthy attributes to us? Patience, firmness, and consistency require a vision of health and wholeness or they are difficult to maintain.

The educational leader points to the underlying plan for health and wholeness motivating those with problems to repeat their unsuccessful efforts to control their environment. This reinterpretation helps "unhook" those who feel trapped by the unhealthy dynamics of these families. They can ask themselves: why am I feeling as I do? What does this tell me about the child and his parents? Why am I hesitating to take an action? Is it out of fear that I will be attacked and victimized? If so, how realistic is that fear and is giving into this fear in the best interest of the child? Probably not! Helping teachers trust their own instincts, and helping them interpret their feelings and questions, empowers them and solidifies collaboration between school leadership and faculty. In difficult cases, we can ask together: what if this were my child? What would I hope others would do if I was this child's parent?

Second, model appropriate behaviors and boundaries. Treating a narcissistic parent as one would treat any parent is not only helpful for the parents, but also helpful for the child. Therefore, we must be deliberate in all our interactions. How much should we explain regarding our strategies and goals, especially with narcissistic parents? The short answer is: be open and honest. Explain the reasoning behind everything. There is one caveat, however. When we encounter resistance and when our strategies invoke strong reactions from a child or a parent, we should interpret both feelings with caution, if at all. It simply is not wise to say things like: "I know you are upset with me," or, "You are probably disappointed with my decision." Modeling respect and modeling how feelings can be expressed without recrimination, however, are helpful and appropriate. For example, a more direct statement like "Students are not permitted to hit, regardless of the circumstances" is a better response. It states a rule and implies that feelings do not justify one's treatment of others. Indulging in talk of feelings – theirs or ours – may inadvertently send the wrong signal, that feelings give permission for one's actions. Too often, interpreting feelings backfires because these interpretations are resented by someone who is not in control of them.

An important focus of attention in management of the child and parents in the school environment is their poor impulse control. To protect teachers whose own self-esteem or whose patience has been worn thin, a principal can insist that these parents deal only through the principal. Some narcissistic parents disdain those with power and influence over their child, but they disdain even more those with less power. Above all, principals should insist that respect for the child's teacher is essential, no matter the disagreement, unless the teacher's behavior has been problematic.

In circumstances where a teacher has made a mistake or overreacted, there are proper and clear channels for filing complaints and settling such disagreement. Those managing the narcissistic family may even need to spell out the proper procedures and explain the respect a teacher deserves. Firmness and conviction must be evident in the principal's tone as well as in action with these individuals. When the educational leader insists on respect, then the first rule of respect, that it is earned through one's respectful behavior, is placed squarely before this family. The parent who is out of line needs to be told so. The parent who cannot control his or her words or behavior must be told that until such time as this is possible, conferences will be conducted according to very prescribed procedures. Experience has taught us that narcissistic parents with poor impulse control are actually relieved to know that someone is taking charge, that conferences will be managed carefully, and so on. In time, with clarity in who will make the rules and what they will be, anxiety over proper behavior and authority evaporates.

Third, stress the child's need to take responsibility. Because, in narcissistic families, communication is controlled by the narcissistic adult, individuals are not used to having and sharing their genuine feelings or opinions. The adult who serves as the central character for these families validates and sanctions feelings, attitudes and beliefs, and determines the family's stance toward the outside world. It should not be surprising, therefore, that a child or the non-narcissistic parent is not sure what his or her feelings are. Rather, these individuals take their signals from the controlling adult. Moreover, they are not used to making decisions for themselves. This is why modeling respect for the feelings of others and encouraging independent decision making are two things which schools can do to move an enmeshed child toward greater health and individuation. While this will be resisted by the narcissistic parent, school-based activities justify and call for this sort of autonomy. A teacher can rightfully insist on a child making appropriate decisions regarding in-school activity. Making choices in small matters can be legitimate means of awakening the capabilities in a child. It is appropriate, therefore, that we insist that a child experience both the rewards and the consequences for his or her decisions.

Children who have grown up accustomed to having a parent fight battles for them, or have been defended and excused inappropriately, require corrective strategies that stress responsibility and limited options. They require that duties and responsibilities be clearly spelled out. Shift the burden for completing tasks, for improving relationships, for acting more responsibly and respectfully to the child, explaining to the parents why the effort has to be the child's and not theirs. Excuses, if at all relevant, must emanate from the child and not the parent. This can be threatening for some parents, but firmness in dealing with them is essential in this, as in other strategies, or their anxiety and mistrust will overwhelm sound.

Fourth, help the child learn to defer gratification and internalize rewards. Two factors in the dynamics of these families lead to a need to help children of narcissistic parents learn to delay gratification. Because children of narcissists have few interests that they have chosen on their own, most are not able to enjoy an activity for its own sake. They seek to reap from an activity, such as a sport or an artistic activity, what is immediately available to them by way of praise and success. Poorly differentiated from their parents, they harbor values and beliefs that have been sanctioned and promoted by the needy parent and are likely to have carbon copies of the parent's own fantasies. All of us have seen the overly involved parent whose child must be a little league star, and whose behavior with coaches and referees betrays a far greater need for winning than the child's.

An effective strategy for helping the child of narcissistic parents differentiate must include permission for the child to explore new interests and hobbies. Community service projects are one way to "push" the child into new activities and interests. The rewards here are intrinsic to the work. Recognition comes later and sometimes not at all. These parents and their children often have what some therapists call an "all or nothing" approach to the world (Donaldson-Pressman and Pressman 1994). Weaning children of narcissists from this habit requires patient prodding in order that the child might stick with activities that do not produce immediate results, to look for the value to others, to see the "long haul" as worthwhile. In short, activities that require collaboration as opposed to competition are best. Seizing opportunities to introduce a child to community service, even if this might be a consequence of misbehavior, is worthwhile because these activities help forge a re-examination of a narrowly focused self-image.

Implications for Catholic Educational Leadership

It should be obvious by now that it takes skill and self-knowledge to manage these difficult families. Effective leadership comes with experience and commitment but, increasingly, we see the following as important elements promoting and protecting an effective leadership style.

Acquiring Knowledge and Skills

Given the growing number of difficult families coming to our schools, an educational leader must be committed to advancing his or her knowledge of the psychological literature dealing with family dysfunction. More and more, this literature is available to professionals outside the clinical disciplines. Courses in counseling are widely available but a great deal can be learned from consulting with individual therapists from agencies like Catholic

Family Services. Skill development might be especially important for those educational leaders who do not have the luxury of in-house counseling services, or even good referral services in the local community. As we know, even when these services are available, some families resist using them. The educational leader has no choice but to become skilled in management of difficult cases, even if he or she avoids becoming "therapeutic" with these children and families.

Working with Teams

Educational leaders are experienced problem-solvers. Normally, for effi-ciency's sake, they try to involve only those who are "essential" to solving a dilemma or meeting a challenge. This is not a bad philosophy of manage-ment. Too often, however, the nature of the cases we and our teachers must confront and manage requires input and help from other professionals such as social workers and therapists, school counselors, and educational special-ists. Working with a team is not only more efficient and time saving; it is also more likely to result in success. Success within the school setting requires a team approach as well. Compartmentalized strategies and uncoordinated interventions prolong and even advance the ability of dysfunctional families to delay help and improvement. The most toxic families are successful in avoiding change when we are fragmented in our approach to them.

Appraising and Developing Our Resources

Catholic schools offer a great deal to children and to their families, which is why, when they can afford them and when they are available, many Catholic and non-Catholic parents prefer them. But, our schools cannot possibly meet the needs of all children. As we saw, the support and care which students receive in Catholic schools is attractive to certain families and is perhaps more true of those with special needs. The school community, however, must serve all students who are enrolled. The needs of some fami-lies, just like the academic and emotional needs of some students, might be too great for the particular resources of some schools. Leadership requires knowledge of the potentials and the limits of one's school community. Can my faculty handle these issues and can they handle the particular needs of this family or child? If staff and faculty are not equipped to handle difficult families and the families being dealt with are increasingly more difficult, then it is incumbent on the educational leader to look for and sponsor in-service training and development opportunities. One should not forget that school advisory board members and parent–teacher association officers can benefit from being included in development programs.

Committing to Continuous Spiritual and Psychological Growth

As we saw, many families are emotionally challenging and taxing. Some are quite needy and have a way of bringing their own unhealthy dynamics into our school community. The level of support and encouragement which faculty and staff need to carry on in the face of difficult-to-manage children and their parents requires strong and fearless leadership. Many people in the school community look to the educational leader for insight, guidance, decisions, and vision. From what source does the educational leader draw the courage, strength, and wisdom needed to be an effective manager and leader? What supports and sustains the leader of a community whose job it is to inspire and lead? Only the leader who takes his or her own physical, emotional, and spiritual health seriously, who takes the time to feed his or her own soul and psyche, can be an effective advocate for children and families in need, as well as an effective support and guide to staff.

References

Bowlby, J. (1988) *A Secure Base*, New York: Basic Books.

Donaldson-Pressman, S. and Pressman, R. (1994) *The Narcissistic Family: Diagnosis and Treatment*, San Francisco: Jossey-Bass.

Garanzini, M. (1995) *Child-Centered Schools: An Educator's Guide to Family Dysfunction*, Washington, DC: NCEA Press.

Guest, J. (1982) *Ordinary People*, New York: Viking Press.

Kernberg, O. (1975) *Borderline Conditions and Pathological Narcissism*, New York: Jason Aronson.

Miller, A. (1992) *The Drama of the Gifted Child: How Narcissistically Wounded Parents Narcissistically Wound Their Children*, New York: Basic Books.

Sandler, J. and Joffe, W.G. (1965) "Notes on childhood depression," *International Journal of Psycho-Analysis* 46: 88–96.

Winnicott, D.W. (1960) "The theory of the parent–child relationship," in *The Maturational Processes and the Facilitating Environment*, New York: International University Press (1965), pp. 140–52.

18 To Lead as Jesus Led

Father Ronald Nuzzi

Over twenty-five years have passed since the National Conference of Catholic Bishops in the United States issued the pastoral letter *To Teach As Jesus Did*.[1] For many years, this document has inspired Catholic educators to think of teaching as ministry and to model their own behavior after Jesus. That Jesus was a teacher is clear from the many gospel stories told about his large following, his engaging parables, and his use of poignant and relevant examples. Some have even called him the master teacher.[2]

In addition to being a wonderful teacher, Jesus was also a leader. His leadership is seen in the gospels in many ways. As he assembles a small group of his first followers and instructs them in his ways, as he settles disputes among them and helps them to grow, Jesus exercises a leadership role while he is teaching. As the crowds follow him from city to city, Jesus leads them to a comfortable resting place and to new spiritual depths. Even as he faces persecution and death, he leads by example and history has not forgotten the power of his deeds.

As we continue to consider what it means to be a leader in Catholic education, it is not sufficient to teach as Jesus did. We must also lead as Jesus led. One might argue that the situation in the life of the church has changed significantly from biblical times. Such changes are the reason we must continue to model our behavior on that of Christ. More directly, we are called to conform our lives to Christ. Assuming that the example of Scripture is normative for Catholic school leaders, this chapter will discuss the nature of leadership as Jesus exercised it by looking at Scriptural examples from the gospels and the life of the early church. While such an analysis might proceed in a variety of directions, two major emphases are discussed: (1) Jesus' own use of power; and (2) the dynamics of the relationships between his first disciples.

Jesus' Use of Power

The study of and fascination with power, while undoubtedly a modern phenomenon in terms of psychological analysis, is a topic of ancient importance

259

both in the church and in society at large. When one speaks of power in connection with the church, this initiates many associations and recollections, perhaps even emotions. To speak further of power in relationship to Jesus Christ is, then, to open an area of great concern and debate. What kind of power did Jesus have and how did he use it? Is it possible for leaders in today's church to use power as Jesus did?

The gospels give us some access to Jesus' own understanding of his power and authority. After the resurrection, Jesus states, "All authority in heaven and on earth has been given to me. Go therefore and make disciples of all nations."[3] The theological principle that the power and authority of Christ should be understood and derived from this christological vantage point is commonly accepted.[4] The spiritual authority of the apostolic communities that produced the gospels was experienced and accepted as the authority of Jesus Christ. This was a unique and exclusive authority, a power that placed Christ as head of the church and above the church, not as simply the first member of the church. Matthew 23: 8 says: "You have but one teacher, and you are all brothers." Pauline texts repeatedly reference the "Christ raised on high" and given numerous other designations of honor, such as "seated at the right hand of the Father," the "name above every other name," and the simple "Jesus is Lord." It is this recognition of the unique place of Jesus in salvation history that makes a Christian a Christian. Blank summarizes:

> The confession of the kyrios Jesus Christ and His sovereignty is, according to Paul, the *specificum Christianum* which by its nature founds a Church and makes a precise distinction between this Church and both Judaism and all heathen religions as well as the mystery cults. It is the personal confession of all Christians, regardless of the level they occupy and which offices or charisms they possess; in this respect, there is not the slightest difference between ordinary Christians and office bearers.[5]

In a similar fashion, there can be no escape for Christians from this power and sovereignty of Christ, for it is under Christ that salvation and redemption are finally found. In this sense, a hierarchy can be said to exist. God, in Jesus Christ, is over all. All are, therefore, under God and the lordship or sovereignty of Jesus. A church free from this type of power would not be a church at all. As the New Testament Scriptures describe it, we stand under the power of God, fully present in Jesus Christ. The way of life for the Christian is not escape from the predicament, but acknowledgement, acceptance, and submission to it. In essence, Christianity requires the purposeful acceptance of submission to God through Christ. What it means to be a Christian, therefore, is to be subject to Christ.

Jesus' power and authority are often the subject of gospel stories. Throughout the Gospels, Jesus uses his power in a variety of ways. While an exhaustive analysis of Gospel examples is beyond our reach here, three examples of how Jesus uses power can provide a richer understanding of leadership. When Jesus uses his power, it can be interpreted as (1) the freedom and the right to act, decide, and interact as one chooses; (2) the ability to act effectively, as in the potential to cause change; followers of Jesus assume from the force of his teaching that he must have some special authority (cf. Mark 1: 22); (3) authority as absolute power. Mark 1: 22 discusses the initial reaction of the crowds to Jesus' first public appearance in the synagogue at Capernaum: "They were astonished at his teaching, for he taught them as one who had authority, and not as their scribes." Luke 4: 32 affirms that "his word was the authority." In terms of the precise content of the message that would have made this so, the Scriptures are silent. There are no indications as to why his followers might have concluded he had some special power. We only read that Jesus conducted his teaching with an authority that was lacking in the teaching of the scribes of the day. This exclamation or insight by the people is repeated most often following upon miracles, healings, or exorcisms. Upon observing such activities, the people respond: "a new teaching ... with authority."[6] The concept of authority describes Jesus' outstanding ability to act effectively which is clearly seen in all his work and teaching, and for that reason represents a new experience of efficacious power for the people. Finally, Jesus refuses all attempts to explain his purposes or to delve into the origin of his authority and power. He steadfastly resists the call for a sign as a legitimization of his authority.[7] When the chief priests, scribes, and elders ask Jesus about his authority, Jesus answers their question with a question: "Was the baptism of John from heaven or of earth?" The leaders respond: "We do not know." Jesus replies: "Then neither will I tell you by what authority I do these things."[8] Jesus' authority, at least as he perceives it in the gospel, cannot be legitimized or adequately described. There is no way to categorize, measure, or contain it. There is simply no dealing with it. Rather, it turns itself against the challengers who eventually must decide for themselves their own opinion of Jesus. Confronting Jesus' power is, therefore, ultimately a question to oneself about belief in Jesus and that power. Thus, Jesus' power and authority are expressed in his actions and work in such a way that others can experience its saving effect.

In response to such power, leaders in the church today must see themselves as servants, not only of the community, but also of Christ. While those with administrative responsibility commonly speak of "my parish" or "my office" or "my school," the truly Christ-like leaders know that all belongs to God. And it is Christ who is the head of every parish, school, and diocese.

It is difficult to overemphasize this point at a time in history when Catholic schools compete for students, funds, and faculty. The ultimate purpose of the Catholic school is not to perpetuate itself or its style of pedagogy. Its ultimate purpose is to bring its students to life in Christ. All programs and personnel ought to serve that goal.

In portraying Jesus as Lord and as possessive of this efficacious, ultimate authority, it is easy to understand why the early church came to articulate its belief in Jesus as consonant with divinity. "Jesus is Lord" meant that in Jesus Christ the power and presence of God were somehow made real and tangible for people. Quite simply, divinity was the answer for Jesus' awesome power. Jesus was experienced as God incarnate, a visible, earthly, enfleshment of God. Hence, Jesus' power was absolute and ultimate. Whatever kind of power Jesus exercises, be it healing miracles, medical marvels, weather adjustments, or chemical changes, it is clear that his followers believe that his work is far beyond extraordinary. He is Emmanuel: God with us.

If Jesus represents the historical incarnation of God in our human community, and if we accept the biblical notion that the power of God, ultimate and absolute, resides in Jesus, then it will clearly be instructive to ask how Jesus availed himself of that power. In a general way, what kind of attitude did Jesus have about the use of power?

Luke 22: 25–26 says:

> Among the pagans it is kings who lord it over them, and those who have authority over them are given the title Benefactor. This must not happen to you. Rather let the greatest among you be as the youngest, and the leader as the one who serves.

Jesus' admonition suggests that the commonly known leadership paradigms of the day are not adequate for those who would be his followers. Specifically, the secular institutions have leaders that stand over and against their people, using their authority as a weapon against those under them to force their compliance. Jesus' advice turns that model around and suggests that true leadership involves serving the rest, not insisting on one's own way. In this way, Jesus sees his use of authority as diametrically opposed to the accepted styles of leadership in his day.

The gospel of John reaffirms this position in recounting the story of Jesus washing the feet of the disciples. Jesus says:

> Do you understand what I have done to you? You call me "master" and "lord" and rightly; so I am. If I, then, master and lord, have washed your feet, you should wash each other's feet. I have given you an example so that you may do for others what I have done to you.[9]

In this way, Jesus connected the power of his ministry to service for others, a type of power to be used to serve others, not rule over others. To describe what he means, Jesus returns often to words such as *servant* and *slave*. It has been observed by theologians and scholars alike that this preference of Jesus is not due to deficiencies in the language he spoke or in the vocabulary of the Gospel writers. John L. McKenzie, SJ wrote:

> If Jesus had wished to say that those in authority should rule with justice and kindness, there are a dozen ways in which this could have been said. But such words as "rule" are exactly the words which he did not use. The sayings reveal a new conception of society and of authority, which must be formed not on the model of secular government, but on the mission of Jesus himself.[10]

A brief examination of Gospel vocabulary will help to clarify this point. Josef Blank commented on the chosen vocabulary of the gospel in relation to Jesus' exercise of power. Blank observed that "the decisive factor in the New Testament understanding of the concepts 'power, sovereignty', etc., is that all exercise of power in Christ's Church is understood fundamentally as *diakonia* and not as *arche*."[11] The concept of "hierarchy" is not found in the New Testament, nor does the matter as such even arise as a question during the first century of Christianity.[12] *Diakonia* as service tends to be the model of choice, rather than *arche* as hierarchical power.

The words *diakonia* and *diakonos* are relatively new additions to the Scriptures when they appear in New Testament texts. The words only appear a handful of times in the Septuagint, the Greek translation of the Old Testament,[13] whereas the Hebrew *abd* and its cognates are translated throughout by the words *douleuein* and *doulos*, the common Greek words for slavery and slaves, respectively. On the other hand, this designation is never utilized in the New Testament to refer to the relationships of office and ministry within the church, but rather for the relationship of faithful believers and of disciples to God or to Jesus. It is in this light that Paul calls himself "a slave of Christ Jesus, called to be an apostle" (Romans 1: 1). Paul saw himself in a ministering relationship, as a servant towards his master. The emphasis is not on the quality of the relationship as an inferior to a superior, but that of a willingness to meet the needs of the other, to serve the needs of the other, to minister. The choice of the image of slavery is intended, not to create differences between the one served and the minister, but to highlight that the service is offered on a voluntary basis without deriving from this work any status. A fine example of this philosophy of service can be found in the 1999 Academy Award winning film, *Life Is Beautiful*, written and directed by Roberto Benigni. As the protagonist trains to be a waiter in a fancy restaurant, he endures repeated reprimands from his uncle, the head waiter, for the frantic nature of his wait service. But it is when the waiter demonstrates his bow that he receives the sternest reply. "Not so deep, not so deep," chastizes the uncle. "You are a servant of their needs, not a slave to their demands. Both of you will grow in dignity if your service is gracious."

This understanding of *diakonia* is consistent with what we have already seen in the life of Jesus. Ministry of such a nature is much more than an inner disposition or attitude that is altruistic; it is a life choice that is clearly connected to the life and work of Jesus. One does not serve simply inspired by the desire to help others. One serves in response to hearing Christ's command to serve. Recalling again that Jesus was commonly understood to have ultimate power, it is striking to note that his perception on using that power is expressed with the metaphors of "service" and "slavery." Clearly, Jesus sees his power as power for others, to help others, to meet others' needs, and never as power over others to command. This power for others, expressed as "being for others," constitutes the expression of the highest, most perfect love (John 13: 1), a self-sacrifice that brings about salvation, thereby providing the ontological basis for the being of the church and the Christian life.[14]

Two gospel stories relating a dispute among the disciples are noteworthy given this interpretation of Jesus' call to serve. The disputes are questions about rank among the disciples themselves and the debate sheds some light on Jesus' disposition about authority. The first episode appears in all three synoptic gospels (Matthew 20: 20–28; Mark 10: 35–45; and Luke 22: 24–27). The three citations concur that the leaders of nations dominate the people they rule and the greatest among such leaders are those who exercise their authority and make their influence felt. Luke even calls "those who exercise authority" the "benefactors," a royal title of the day. Jesus, on the other hand, says the greatest must be the servant or slave of all. Rather than being royalty, the Christian must be at the service of others. The other debate among the disciples occurs in Matthew 18: 1–5, Mark 9: 33–37, and Luke 9: 46–48. Jesus makes the point that the disciples should be open to welcoming little children, and he concludes by admonishing the disciples that whoever would be the greatest among them must be like a young child.

The images of children, servants, and slaves do not represent people in whom great authority was placed in Jesus' time. On the contrary, under the prescriptions of Roman law at the time, they would not even be considered persons. Yet Jesus appeals to their examples repeatedly to indicate how the disciples should conduct themselves. McKenzie concludes:

> These sayings of Jesus are more than conventional exhortations to a vague humility. … The sayings of Jesus not only forbid self-assertion in general, but in particular that kind of self-assertion which is seen in the exercise of authority. Effectively his answer to the question of who is the greatest among the disciples is this: no one.[15]

Thus, the purpose of Jesus' explicit comparison of his followers with the existing secular authorities of the day seems to be aimed at proscribing the introduction of the authoritarian use of authority into the community of his disciples.

In rejecting the model of the secular authorities of his day, Jesus also had harsh words for the Jewish religious leadership. He cautions his disciples to do as the scribes and Pharisees say, but not as they do (Matthew 23ff.). And what is it that they do that is so wrong? They create heavy burdens for others which they themselves refuse to bear. They are attracted to ostentatious displays of their importance and power. They place formidable obstacles in the way of true believers and they are legalists, concerned with every jot and tittle of the law. They are, in Jesus' own evaluation, hypocrites.

If neither the secular leaders nor the religious leaders are good examples for the disciples, is Jesus proposing a model heretofore unseen for the governance of the church? Perhaps it would be more accurate to state that Jesus seems concerned with how the church is not to be governed. His instructions on how the community should function often come in stories and images. But it is clear that Jesus perceived the models of power in vogue during his time in both secular and religious institutions to be threats to and possible corrupting influences on his followers. This is not to say that Jesus espoused the complete lack of organization or some form of anarchy as a method to proceed. Rather it indicates what dangers he believed to lay ahead for his followers.

Jesus' example and admonitions present a model decidedly at odds with those who held power during his time. Even when tempted to display his power, whether it be by Satan in the desert or by the crowds as he hung on the cross, Jesus resisted the self-assertion of his will. When his ultimate, divine power was used, it was always at the service of others, to meet others' needs, to effect a healing, to usher in a moment of grace. In fact, Jesus refuses to act in his own legitimate self-defense, so complete is his aversion to the unbridled use of power. When challenged by what authority he acted and spoke as he did, Jesus appealed exclusively to the will of the Father. He did not argue from accepted religious or biblical traditions, nor did he spell out in any detail how his ideas could be developed in daily life. But he refused to characterize his own mission in terms of rule over others. Leading as Jesus led, therefore, necessarily involves a use of power that is oriented to service for others rather than responsibility over others. Those who aspire to leadership in Catholic education and who desire to teach as Jesus did are called in similar fashion to lead as Jesus led.

In its early days, the church attempted to follow Jesus' advice on the use of power and to model a different style of leadership. As we shall see, the earliest communities displayed a considerable degree of improvisation in their management and organization of the church.[16] One important example in this regard is the relationship between the disciples.

Using Power in a Christian Community: Relationships Between the Disciples

The nature of the relationships among the disciples of Jesus exhibits very strong tendencies to put into practice the model of leadership described above. History and Scripture both show evidence of the earliest disciples, even those called apostles,[17] exercising leadership as service rather than as power to command. Four examples from the apostolic period are striking in this regard: (1) the selection of Judas Iscariot's successor; (2) the Council of Jerusalem; (3) Paul's early disagreement with Peter; and (4) the early church's overriding concern for the poor.

The Book of Acts chronicles the choice of Judas Iscariot's successor in 1: 15–26. It should be noted that this is no small decision. Whoever is chosen is to be considered an apostle. Once he has told the story of Judas' tragic death, Simon Peter makes the case for selecting a new apostle:

> "Therefore, it is necessary that one of the men who accompanied us the whole time the Lord Jesus came and went among us ... become with us a witness to his resurrection." So they proposed two, Joseph called Barsabbas, who was also known as Justus, and Matthias. They prayed, "Lord you know the hearts of all, show which one of these two you have chosen to take the place in this apostolic ministry from which Judas turned away to go to his own place." Then, they gave lots to them, and the lot fell upon Matthias, and he was counted with the eleven apostles.

Note that the eleven apostles do not pick Judas' successor, nor even exercise any jurisdiction over the selection process. They are not in charge of the process. Furthermore, the designated process is the casting of lots, not an election. There were no votes taken, no ballots cast. The casting of lots suggests a total and complete dependence on what God does and wants. In essence, the gathered community surfaces the two names and presents the two candidates, but in the eyes of the Scriptures, it is God who makes the final selection. Even given the serious decision to find a replacement for one of their number, the eleven do not act on their own, nor do they attempt to control the selection process in any way. The entire community assembled the acceptable candidates, then left it to God to choose. Clearly, the eleven saw themselves as equal participants in this process and not as special individuals with knowledge or insight that no one else could claim to possess. This is a remarkable example of how the early church, even in the midst of a momentous decision like selecting an apostle, chose to rely more on God and God's will than on their own knowledge and experience.

The Council of Jerusalem, held in the summer of AD 49, provides another example of early apostolic leadership.[18] The principal question under consideration at the gathering was whether or not Gentiles, coming to

Christianity from paganism, had first to observe the Mosaic law by being circumcised. This is one of the earliest problems recorded in Scripture that faced the early church. In Acts 15: 2–12, it was decided that, as proposed by Paul and Barnabas, Christians coming from paganism need not undergo circumcision or observe the precepts of Mosaic law. But the decision comes as a result of a judgment given by James, not Peter. Acts 15: 13 begins:

> After they had fallen silent, James responded, "My brothers, listen to me. Simon has described how God first concerned himself with acquiring from among the Gentiles a people for his name. ... It is my judgement, therefore, that we ought to stop troubling the Gentiles who turn to God."

The apostolic decision, settling what was perhaps the first significant organizational dispute in Christianity, is proposed by the leader of the local church in Jerusalem, in this case James. Peter, for his part, far from asserting any type of domination over the council, is subjected to rebuke by Paul for being inconsistent on this very question. Indeed, in Galatians 2: 11–14, Paul seems to feel very free to openly criticize Peter:

> And when Cephas came to Antioch, I opposed him to his face because he was clearly wrong. For, until some people came from James, he used to eat with the Gentiles; but when they came, he began to draw back and separated himself, because he was afraid of the circumcised. And the rest of the Jews also acted like hypocrites along with him, with the result that even Barnabas was carried away with their hypocrisy. But when I saw that they were not on the right road in line with the truth of the Gospel, I said to Cephas in front of all, "If you, though a Jew, are living like a Gentile and not like a Jew, how can you compel the Gentiles to live like Jews?"

If there were precise distinctions of rank and importance among the disciples, it is not clear from texts such as these that they were always honored. On the contrary, it seems that the relationships among the disciples were focused on service to Jesus and, as Galatians states, "the truth of the Gospel." That Paul, not one of the original twelve, could openly challenge not only one of the twelve, but their acknowledged leader, suggests that fidelity to the truth of the gospel was a more important value in this time than personal loyalty and personal power.

Perhaps the most visible characteristic of this early apostolic community was its day-to-day communal life, especially as manifested in its attention to the poor. Yet the poor were not to be regarded as mere recipients of Christian charity. The church saw itself as one body in Christ, with the Holy Spirit operating not only in the apostles, but also in all the members.

Therefore, the designated leaders had to be sensitive and respectful to the action and voice of the Spirit whenever and wherever it showed itself, whether in the highest or the lowest. Of this early experience of church, McKenzie says:

> In a secular society authority is conceived as the central motive function which directs and moves subordinate functions. In the Church direction and motivation is from the Spirit to all the functions of the body; authority is not and cannot be absolute, for authority too has its inter-dependence.[19]

The Book of Acts presents what appears to be a picture of the ideal community. There was a positive insistence on the absence of status and sharing within the community. In describing what it was like to live in this earliest of Christian communities, Acts emphasizes the mutual concern that animated the believers:

> The community of believers was of one heart and mind, and no one claimed that any of his possessions was his own, but they had every-thing in common. With great power the apostles bore witness to the resurrection of the Lord Jesus, and great favor was accorded them all. There was no needy person among them, for those who owned property or houses would sell them, bring the proceeds of the sale, and put them at the feet of the apostles, and they were distributed to each according to need.[20]

This strong emphasis on the unity of the Christian community can also be found in the case of the first converts. "They devoted themselves to the apostles' teaching and fellowship, to the breaking of bread and the prayers" (Acts 2: 42). The converts learned very quickly the expectations of living as a believer: "All who believed were together and had all things in common and they sold their possessions and goods and distributed them to all, as any had need" (Acts 2: 44–45). There is no indication that any spiritual divisions were ever permitted to find their way into this ideal community, in which such great care was taken to remove all material divisions that might have led to the introduction of different social strata. The believers lived as equals.

We learn in Acts as well that it was at Antioch that the disciples were first called "Christian."[21] The term does not seem to have been popular as a way for the early communities to refer to themselves; the Scriptures prefer the designation "disciples" or "believers."[22] What is more striking and revealing is the early Christians' use of the term "saints" to describe themselves. Time and time again, both in Acts and the letters of Paul, believers in the community are called "saints." While this designation seems devoid of the modern concept of saintliness as holiness or piety, the entire assembly of believers is considered to be saintly. The community at Jerusalem was holy; there were also saints in Rome, Corinth, and the whole of Achaia.[23] This holiness, the result of being a believer, transformed the entire community and was passed on to the children, even if only one of the parents was a Christian.[24] There were no distinctions of class in this community; all the members were saints, all were called to holiness. Paul captured this insight when he wrote, "So then, you are no longer strangers and sojourners, but you are fellow citizens with the saints and members of the household of God" (Ephesians 2: 19).

In summary, the relationships between the disciples can be characterized by a strong focus on fidelity to the gospel and to the service model of authority espoused by Jesus. Even when facing crucial decisions that would have great bearing on the future, the earliest disciples persisted in following Jesus' example of being of service to one another. No one behaves in an authoritarian fashion or gives directives to others, even those thought to be empowered to. Rather, the good of the community of believers comes first. So radically committed to this ideal was the early church that material goods were held in common and shared as needed. This ideal community life, where all are equals and all needs are met, found its fullest expression in the community's self-understanding, declared repeatedly in Scripture, that believers are saints.

In following the example of Jesus, Catholic educators have a special responsibility to lead as Jesus led. The model of community life in the early church is a compelling example for contemporary Catholic educational communities. Leading as Jesus led not only entails leaders using their power as he did, it also means establishing communities that clearly reflect this common life in and under Christ. This is part of the challenge to Catholic school leaders in the third millennium of Christianity and to all who would dare to lead as Jesus did.

Notes

1 National Conference of Catholic Bishops, *To Teach As Jesus Did*, Washington, DC (1972).
2 John P. Kealy, CSSp, *Jesus the Teacher*, Denville, NJ: Dimension Books (1978).
3 Matthew 28: 18–20.
4 See Josef Blank, "The Concept of Power in the Church: New Testament Perspectives", in James Provost and Knut Walf (eds.) *Power in the Church*, Edinburgh: Clark (1988), pp. 3–12. A similar analysis of power in the New Testament can be found in "Power and Authority in Early Christian Centuries" by David N. Power, in *That They Might Live*, ed. Michael Downey, New York: Crossroad (1991), pp. 25–38.
5 Blank, op. cit., p. 5.
6 Mark 1: 27.
7 Mark 8: 11–13.
8 Mark 11: 27–33.
9 John 13: 12–15.

10 John J. McKenzie, SJ, *Authority in the Church*, New York: Sheed & Ward (1966), p. 32.

11 Blank, op. cit., p. 8. *Diakonia* is typically rendered in English by "ministry" or "service." *Diakanos*, the one who performs the *diakonia*, has given us the title "deacon." Blank argues that our familiarity with current ministerial office and church organizational patterns obscures the original intent of these terms. McKenzie (*Authority in the Church*, op. cit., p. 23) agrees. *Diadonos*, far from indicating an ecclesiastical title deserving of respect, means a lackey, a menial. It is almost a colloquial expression for one's runner or errand boy, what today's society calls a "gopher."

   Arche is a later, more complex philosophical term occurring in later New Testament writing, especially the Johannine texts. The opening phrase of the gospel of John, "In the beginning was the Word" (John 1: 1), uses the term *arche* to denote "beginning." The term was popular in philosophical circles during biblical times to indicate an original force or power that gave direction to all things.

   In stating that New Testament power is *diakonia* and not *arche*, Blank is drawing a logical conclusion from Jesus' example and from an analysis of these terms.

12 Alexandre Faivre makes this point in *The Emergence of the Laity in the Early Church*, Mahwah, NJ: Paulist Press (1984), pp. 3–14. Chapter One of Faivre is entitled, "The Wonderful Time When There Was Neither Clergy Nor Laity."

13 See Esther 1: 10; 2: 2; 6: 1–35; Proverbs 10: 4; I Maccabees 11: 58; 4 Maccabees 9: 17.

14 Blank, op. cit., p. 9.

15 McKenzie, op. cit., pp. 30–31.

16 McKenzie, op. cit., p. 32.

17 For an in-depth discussion of the nature of discipleship in New Testament writings, see Kenan B. Osborne, OFM, *Ministry: Lay Ministry in the Roman Catholic Church: Its History & Theology*, Mahwah, NJ: Paulist Press (1993), pp. 48–113.

18 For an explanation on the precise dating of this gathering, see F. Cocchini, "Jerusalem," in *Encyclopedia of the Early Church*, New York: Oxford University Press (1992), p. 432.

19 McKenzie, op. cit., p. 52.

20 Acts 4: 32–35.

21 Acts 11: 26.

22 See Acts 6: 1; 7: 7; 9: 1; 10: 9; 10: 45; Ephesians 1: 2; Colossians 1: 2.

23 Romans 1: 7; 16: 15; I Corinthians 1: 1.

24 Corinthians 7: 14.

Contributors

Father Michael Garanzini is a Jesuit priest. He is an associate professor of counseling at Saint Louis University and teaches regularly for the Institute of Catholic Educational Leadership at the University of San Francisco. He is presently a visiting professor of counseling at Fordham University in New York.

Brother Thomas F. Giardino is a Marianist brother presently serving in his second term as International Director of Education on the General Council in Rome, Italy. He has co-authored several books as well as served as an education and training consultant on several continents.

Michael J. Guerra has served as the National Catholic Educational Association's Executive Director for Secondary Schools since 1982. Prior to joining NCEA's staff, he was headmaster of Loyola School in New York City from 1968 to 1982.

Father James Heft is a priest in the Marianists. He is presently the Professor of Faith and Culture and the Chancellor of the University of Dayton. He has served as Department Chair of Religious Studies and Provost. Before coming to the University of Dayton, Father James worked as a religion teacher and also as Director of Youth Retreats.

Thomas C. Hunt currently holds the position of professor in the School of Education at the University of Dayton. Until recently he was Professor of Foundations of Education at Virginia Tech. He has authored or edited nine books on religion and education in the last seventeen years.

William F. Losito is Professor of Educational Philosophy in the Department of Teacher Education at the University of Dayton. He has served on the Education Committee of the US Catholic Conference, where he participated in the development of several educational documents and policies.

Louise Moore is the principal of Holy Angels Catholic Elementary School in Dayton, Ohio. In addition, she has eighteen years' experience as an elementary school teacher and is currently pursuing her doctoral degree at the University of Dayton in Catholic School Leadership.

Father Ronald Nuzzi is a center associate in the Center for Catholic Education at the University of Dayton. He is also the coeditor of *Catholic Education: A Journal of Inquiry and Practice*.

Father Joseph M. O'Keefe is a Jesuit priest who is currently associate professor at Boston College. A former high school teacher and administrator, along with his academic work he is a trustee of four Catholic schools and is actively involved in pastoral ministry.

Brother Thomas E. Oldenski is a member of the Society of Mary (Marianists). He is presently an assistant professor in the School of Education at the University of Dayton. He has been a teacher, counselor, and principal of Catholic secondary schools for twenty-one years.

William J. Raddell, Jr. earned his Master of Pastoral Studies from Loyola University of Chicago. He is currently the Religion Department Chairperson and teacher at Villa Angela–St. Joseph High School in Cleveland, Ohio.

Margaret Reif is an associate professor in the School of Education at the University of St. Thomas in St. Paul, Minnesota. She is the former Chair of Secondary Teacher Education at St. Thomas.

Karen Ristau has been the Vice President for Academic Affairs/Dean at Saint Joseph College in West Hartford, Connecticut, since the fall of 1997. She previously directed programs in Educational Leadership at the University of St. Thomas in Minnesota.

Joseph F. Rogus, recently deceased, was at the time of his death Kuntz Professor of Education in the School of Education at the University of Dayton and served as a faculty member since 1981. He also was the coeditor of the journal *Catholic Education: A Journal of Inquiry and Practice*.

Charles J. Russo is a professor in the Department of Educational Administration and Fellow in the Center for International Studies at the University of Dayton. He has written and spoken extensively on a wide array of topics in education law as it relates to both Catholic and public schools.

Gini Shimabukuro began her teaching career at the Catholic elementary level. She is currently an assistant professor and associate director of the Institute for Catholic Educational Leadership at the University of San Francisco.

Sister Mary Peter Traviss is a Dominican sister. She has been actively involved in Catholic schooling for fifty years as a teacher, principal, supervisor, and director of community-staffed schools. She is currently Director of the Institute for Catholic Educational Leadership at the University of San Francisco.

Theodore J. Wallace is director of the Dare to Dream Foundation and of the PACE Scholarship Program in Dayton, Ohio. He has served as director of the Center for Catholic Education at the University of Dayton and as president and principal of Catholic high schools in Sandusky and Dayton, Ohio.

Colleen A. Wildenhaus is Managing Editor of *Catholic Education: A Journal of Inquiry and Practice*. She has worked as an administrative assistant at the University of Dayton for more than twenty-five years.

Sister Angela Ann Zukowski is Mission Helper of the Sacred Heart Sister. She is an associate professor in the Department of Religious Studies and the Director of the Institute for Pastoral Initiatives at the University of Dayton. She is the World President for the Catholic Association for Radio and Television.

Index